Contents

Report summary and conclusions

This review analyses the results of 128 studies of workplace counselling that were published between 1980 and 2005. The key findings are:

- more than 55% of workers in private sector companies in the USA, and 10% of the UK employed population, have access to workplace counselling services;

- within the organisations that make workplace counselling available, around 6.5% of employees make direct personal use of the service each year;

- the vast majority (more than 90%) of employees who make use of workplace counselling are highly satisfied with the service they have received, would use it again if necessary and would recommend it to colleagues;

- people who make use of workplace counselling typically report high levels of psychological distress;

- counselling interventions are generally effective in alleviating symptoms of anxiety, stress and depression in the majority of workplace clients;

- counselling interventions have been found, in the majority of studies that have examined this factor, to reduce sickness absence rates in clients by up to 60%;

- counselling interventions have a lesser, but still significant, impact on job commitment, work functioning, job satisfaction and substance misuse;

- there is no evidence that any one approach to counselling is more effective than any other in this field; positive results have been found using a variety of models of counselling: cognitive-behavioural, psychodynamic, person-centred, rational emotive and solution-focused;

- significant benefits for clients can be achieved in three to eight sessions of counselling; only the most severely disturbed clients appear to require long-term counselling help or referral to specialist services;

- placing a limit on the number of counselling sessions available to service users makes no difference to the cost of operating a service; the average number of sessions per client is the same in 'capped' and 'uncapped' services;

- research has not found any consistent association between the structure of a counselling/EAP service (internal vs external) and its overall effectiveness or utilisation rate;

- all published studies of the economic costs and benefits of workplace counselling have reported that counselling/ EAP provision at least covers its costs – some studies have found substantial positive benefit:cost ratios;

- studies of the uptake of counselling services have found no consistent trend for services to be used more or less frequently by different sub-groups of employees (age, seniority, status, type of work), except that in a number of studies women have been found to be higher users of services than their male colleagues, when compared with the gender composition of the specific workplace.

It is important to use caution when interpreting these findings, due to the methodological limitations of much of the research that has been carried out. More research needs to be done on all forms of workplace counselling. There are many significant sources of bias within the current knowledge base. Workplace counselling is difficult to research because of issues such as confidentiality, commercial secrecy, multi-site provision of services, the establishment of appropriate control or comparison groups, and the achievement of consensus over measurement instruments. Despite these difficulties, a substantial number of studies have been carried out, which provide plausible and convergent evidence of the significant contribution that counselling can make to the alleviation of psychological problems in work settings. However, the workplace counselling industry, and profession as a whole, needs to prioritise the conduct and publication of well-designed studies. The current review, for example, has not been able to identify any high-quality outcome studies that evaluate workplace counselling and employee assistance services currently being offered in the UK.

To ensure quality of service delivery, and to meet the challenges of changing work environments, practitioners and researchers urgently need to collaborate on the design and implementation of research that is academically rigorous and practically relevant.

Chapter 1. Introduction to the review: themes and issues in research on workplace counselling

Introduction

The relationship between the paid work, and the psychological wellbeing of the worker, is a topic that has received a huge amount of attention in recent years. Wainwright and Calnan (2002) characterise work stress as a 'modern epidemic', which has effects in terms of health, absence from work and costs to the national economy. Concepts such as 'work' or 'occupational' stress have been used to refer to a wide range of pressures experienced by workers, including work overload, perceived lack of control over work tasks, poor work environment, difficulties in relationships with colleagues and managers, frustration around career development and achievement, the effect of oppressive organisational culture and norms (eg around blame and bullying), and dilemmas in balancing the home-work interface (see Cooper, Sloan and William (1988), and Dewe and Cooper (2004) for further explanation of these factors).

Wainwright and Calnan (2002) have traced different positions around the issue of work stress adopted by workers, managers, trades unions, the government, the legal system, the medical profession, occupational health workers, researchers and counsellors. It is important to recognise that fundamental debates still exist concerning the nature and significance of occupational stress. For example, Wainwright and Calnan (2002), and other commentators, have pointed out that uncertainty over security of employment, working conditions and working hours were much worse during the depression years of the 1930s, and at many earlier times in history, without any mention of a 'stress epidemic'. Why is it that the closing decades of the 20th century have marked an explosion of interest in the emotional and psychological pressures associated with working life?

There are possibly two main reasons why work stress, and the proliferation of interventions designed to deal with this problem, have emerged as critical issues in recent years. First, it can be argued that the economic system has evolved into what Sennett (1998) has termed 'the new capitalism'. Although many of the old industries remain, the dominant culture of contemporary working life is shaped by forces such as globalisation, increased competition, mechanisation/deskilling, short-term contracts, erosion of unionisation and fragmentation of career structures. Within the workplace, the consequences of the new capitalism are found in what Bunting (2004) calls 'the overwork culture', characterised by an increasing intensification of work and the growing intrusiveness of work into home life.

A further reason why the emotional, psychological and personal cost of working life may be more salient now in the early years of the 21st century than they ever were in previous times may be that, basically, people are no longer willing to put up with it. In a series of research studies spanning 25 years, Marmot (2004) has established that the health and wellbeing of individuals depends to a significant extent on their *status* within work hierarchies. Essentially, high-status workers are healthier and live longer than their low-status colleagues, even in situations where the lowest paid have incomes that allow them access to good-quality housing, education and healthcare. Status is important, according to Marmot (2004), because it gives the person more control over their life and greater opportunities for social engagement and participation.

It could be argued that, in general terms, we live in a culture in which personal autonomy and participation are accepted as unequivocal 'goods'. This means that members of a workforce perceive as psychologically damaging any actions or conditions laid down by their employers that don't properly acknowledge their autonomy and right to participate. Another word for this is *respect* (Sennett, 2003). In the workplace, people are not willing to be treated as potentially dispensable (Bauman, 2004) – they want to be respected, to be treated as valued colleagues. The convergence of these two factors – a work culture derived from the practices of supra-national corporations, and a citizenship that believes in the validity of its own human rights – has served to highlight the importance of the psychological contract between employer and worker.

In the context of an increasing sense on the part of many workers that work demands might be potentially psychologically damaging, the concept of 'stress' emerged as a means of making sense of this discomfort (Wainwright and Calnan, 2002). The desire of employers to maximise the commitment and productivity of employees (and reduce sickness absence) caused a great deal of thought and effort to be devoted to the question of finding practical ways of ameliorating the negative effects of work stress.

It is possible to identify five distinct strategies that have been adopted by workers and management to address this set of issues. First, some of the earliest workplace psychological interventions were quasi-disciplinary in nature, directed at employees with alcohol problems, and consisted of protocols for identifying such individuals, requiring them to attend treatment (provided externally) and then closely monitoring their work performance when they eventually returned to their duties. Second, there have been attempts to redesign jobs – for example, to allow workers more autonomy or to reduce task overload. Third, many organisations have introduced stress-management training programmes, which teach workers how to be aware of stressful situations, and help them to develop appropriate coping skills. Fourth, organisations have recognised the potential value of psychological interventions such as counselling and psychotherapy, and have made arrangements for these forms of help to be made available to employees. Fifth, and most recently, some organisations have acknowledged that a cultural shift is required, and have initiated integrated organisational wellbeing initiatives, that may include health, diet, exercise, flexible working and work-life balance policies, and which are aimed at having a preventative role in relation to psychological problems, as well as providing a comprehensive response to employee difficulties (Attridge, 2004; Csiernik, 2005a; Sharar and Hertenstein, 2004). There is evidence that all of these strategies for addressing work-related psychological problems can be effective (or not) in specific circumstances.

The historical evolution and development of counselling-based employee assistance and occupational stress programmes has been documented by Carroll (1996), Coles (2003), Csiernik (2005b) and many other authors. It can be demonstrated that the provision of counselling services for employees has been a part of organisational life since the 1930s (Dickson, 1945; Dickson and Roethlisberger, 1966; Vonachan et al, 1954), and can be viewed as having developed out of earlier traditions of welfare capitalism (Csciernik, 2005b) that emphasised the moral responsibility of employers to accept their duty of care in relation to their workforce. There has been a steady growth over the past 20 years in the number of organisations making use of in-house workplace counselling services, Employee Assistance Programmes (EAPs) and other methods of arranging psychological support for workers. A survey carried out by

Hartwell et al (1996) found that 33% of all private sector/ non-agricultural worksites in the USA with more than 50 employees offered EAP services to their employees. In companies with more than 1,000 employees, the proportion was 76%. Within these larger organisations, 9% were actively considering introducing an EAP. Hartwell (1996) calculated that more than 55% of workers in private sector companies in the USA had access to EAP provision. In Britain, research conducted by the EAP Association (2006) found that more than 1,000 organisations in the UK made use of EAPs, covering more than two million employees (around 10% of the UK working employee population). Compared to other stress amelioration strategies that can be used by employers, the key strength of counselling is that it is individualised and the methods applied by the counsellor are (or should be) tailored to the specific needs of the client.

In Britain, a recent policy initiative has highlighted a different aspect of the relationship between psychological therapies and the workplace – the cost to the state of providing sickness and incapacity benefit to those who are unable to work because of anxiety and depression. A commission chaired by the economist Lord Layard (Mental Health Policy Group, 2006) calculated that there are one million people in the UK receiving incapacity benefits for mental health problems, and there would be significant financial savings for the government (as well as positive outcomes for individuals, families and communities) if substantial investment were to be made in the provision of counselling and other psychological therapies for this group.

Implicit in the recommendations of the Layard Commission is the assumption that engagement in the workplace can have positive psychological effects. There is, in fact, considerable evidence that the loss of employment can have a significant negative impact on mental health and wellbeing, and for unemployed people, gaining employment can reduce symptoms of anxiety and depression (Allen, 1999; Fryer and Fagan, 2003; Murphy and Athanasou, 1999). Indeed, a review of research into the psychological effects of unemployment, carried out by Murphy and Athanasou (1999), suggests that, for someone who is unemployed, the effect of gaining a job is broadly equivalent to the effect of receiving therapy. The relationship between work on the one hand and stress, wellbeing and mental health on the other is therefore far from simple.

It can be seen, therefore, that there have been a range of social, economic, cultural and political factors that have contributed to the emergence of work-related counselling and psychotherapy services over recent decades. However, the provision of such services is only of value if the counselling that is delivered is effective in eliminating or improving the problems of those who make use of it. Research into workplace counselling consequently plays a key role in relation to the development of policy and practice. Over the years, despite the fact that many research studies have been carried out into the effectiveness of EAPs and work-related counselling, there have been few attempts to carry out comprehensive reviews of the findings of this body of research. The need for such a review at this time is highlighted by the increasing pressure on all types of counselling services to be accountable, and to ground their practice in a basis of the best possible evidence. The aims and scope of the current review are described in the following sections of this chapter.

Aims of the review

The primary aim of this work has been to produce a comprehensive review of all English-language studies of workplace counselling published between 1980 and 2005. In order to enable users to gain ready access to the primary sources, it has been restricted to items published in books and journals that are in the public domain. The review incorporates research into a wide range of aspects of workplace counselling: effectiveness, utilisation, attitudes to counselling provision, the costs of counselling, referral networks, the process of counselling and the characteristics of counsellors. A basic objective has been to map the *scope* of currently available research on this topic. As a result, the review has attempted to include as many studies as possible. The review has been intentionally pluralistic, incorporating qualitative as well as quantitative studies. A key priority has been to reflect the diversity and current status of research into workplace counselling, and to construct a narrative that links research findings to policy and practice.

An important goal of the review has been to produce a report that is relevant and accessible for counselling practitioners and administrators, and for purchasers and users of workplace counselling services. Each piece of research is summarised in a standard format, which offers a succinct account of the key points of the investigation being described, highlighting any methodological weaknesses.

Definition of workplace counselling: inclusion and exclusion criteria

In compiling a review that addresses the issues associated with the provision of *counselling* as a distinctive form of workplace stress/wellbeing intervention, it is necessary to be as explicit as possible about what is to be considered as a study of the subject. For the purpose of this review, counselling has been defined as:

(i) a form of intervention that is voluntarily chosen by the client. For example, studies in which employees are selected to participate in an intervention (eg Lindquist and Cooper, 1999) have not been included in the review, even though the intervention may involve the delivery of counselling. Where studies have involved referral of clients into counselling by managers or occupational health advisors, these studies have only been included in this review if there is a meaningful degree of choice incorporated within the referral process (eg a mix of self-referred and management-referred cases);

(ii) a form of help that is responsive to the individual needs of the client or group. Programmes in which individuals or groups receive a pre-determined schedule of exercises or classes have been defined as educational or training interventions rather than counselling. Counsellor *responsiveness* to the process and needs of individual clients is viewed, through this criterion, to be intrinsic to counselling. An example of a study that was excluded on this criterion is Bond and Bonce (2000) – although this study examined the effect of a psychotherapeutic intervention (emotional acceptance, as outlined in Acceptance and Commitment Therapy; Hayes et al, 2006), the intervention was delivered in a didactic, psycho-educational format, with no possibility for specific individualised facilitator-client interaction;

(iii) an activity that is primarily intended to bring about change in an area of psychological/behavioural functioning (eg emotional, relationships, self-esteem, symptoms of depression or anxiety, work functioning, substance misuse, absence from work etc). Interventions that are primarily focused on organisational (eg team functioning) or physical health outcomes (eg exercise, diet) have been excluded, even though these interventions may have important incidental effects on psychological wellbeing.

Studies of the effectiveness of stress management, critical incident response or debriefing interventions (eg structured group sessions following employee exposure to traumatic incidents), meditation and fitness/wellbeing are excluded by this definition, because they are either not voluntary (eg sets of workers are required to attend training) or not individualised (eg everyone receives the same intervention), or because they do not focus on psychological problems.

Interventions labelled as 'psychotherapy' have been included in the study, where they satisfy the criteria listed above. The counselling-psychotherapy distinction has been regarded as concerned for the most part with cultural and situational factors rather than reflecting any fundamental difference in the therapeutic process and relationship that is offered to clients. It will be seen in the review that there are many studies describing similar interventions that are labelled as 'counselling' or 'psychotherapy' depending on the organisational context in which they were conducted. The definition allows for the inclusion of some forms of executive or life coaching (ie individual consultation intended to enhance the work effectiveness of the employee), and the use of counselling skills embedded in management or HR roles. However, no studies of these interventions could be located.

In order to compile a review that is in itself accountable, and open to alternative and further analyses of its constituent studies, only research studies that have been published in publicly accessible sources have been included. All the studies reviewed in this report can be obtained through libraries. Internal organisational reports that would not be openly available (eg for commercial reasons) have not been included, since it is clear that such studies could not satisfy criteria for external review.

The term *workplace counselling* has been interpreted within this review to include any intervention in which the provision of counselling/psychotherapy is linked in some fashion to being an employee suffering from work-related psychological problems or where therapy has an impact on work functioning. There are two broad categories of workplace counselling intervention that can be identified. The first category, which describes the majority of studies discussed in this review, comprises situations where counselling is provided or paid for by the employer, either through in-house (internal) or externally contracted counselling services. Externally delivered services are typically described as Employee Assistance Programmes (EAPs). Also included in this category are services that consist of special projects in which therapy is made available for people with work stress difficulties (for example, within a University research clinic). From the point of view of the client or service user, all of these services are similar in that the workplace is the initial point of referral, and access to therapy is conditional on being an employee of a specific organisation.

A second category of workplace counselling comprises situations in which a person consults a counsellor or psychotherapist, independent of their work setting, for a problem that includes a work dimension, or where the outcome of the therapy has a primary impact on their work functioning. Within the current review, there are relatively few studies of this second type. However, the existence of such studies is important, because they provide valuable evidence of the extent to which counselling can have an impact on work outcomes, and may reflect populations that differ from those who utilise employee assistance programmes or in-house services. There have been many psychotherapy outcome studies that have included assessment of work

functioning as a secondary outcome factor, usually embedded within a broader scale of social functioning. There has been no attempt to discuss this wider set of studies within the current review, because they address work factors as secondary or incidental aspects of therapy, rather than as central to the aims and outcomes of the intervention that is being offered.

It is important to acknowledge that there are a number of factors that make it difficult to arrive at a satisfactory definition of the term 'workplace counselling'. Counselling is a form of helping that is flexibly oriented to the needs of the individual client. As a result, the person receiving counselling describes their problem in their own terms, and in the context of their life as a whole. Even when a counselling client focuses mainly on a work-related issue, it is likely that they will also touch on a range of other topics, such as their family, personal history, and so on. Moreover, most employee assistance counselling services advertise themselves as willing to work with any issues (personal, work-related, or a combination of both) that the person wishes to bring. It is relatively rare, therefore, to find counselling or psychotherapy cases that solely concentrate on work problems. Another factor that undermines any attempt to arrive at a firm definition of workplace counselling is that, increasingly, employee assistance programmes tend to incorporate other services, such as positive wellness projects and psycho-educational seminars and workshops on themes such as stress management and violence at work, that blur the boundaries between formal, contracted counselling for psychological difficulties, and receiving a similar type of help under the guise of 'lifestyle counselling' or 'wellness counselling'. A further difficulty, in relation to arriving at a definition of workplace counselling arises from the fact that in North America, EAP counselling is typically viewed as short-term intervention and when a serious issue arises (eg depression, addiction or childhood sexual abuse), the client is referred out of the EAP to a specialised programme or service – in more severe cases, counselling may not occur within the EAP, which is merely utilised as an assessment and referral system.

In the light of these uncertainties, this review has positioned itself within a broad conceptualisation of workplace counselling used by key figures in the UK such as Carroll (1996) and Coles (2003: Chapter 2). Carroll (1996), for example, reflects the diversity of workplace counselling provision in his statement that 'it would be wrong to think of employee counseling as a uniform concept' (p.12). For Carroll (1996) 'a general definition of employee counselling includes one major component: the organisation pays for counselling provision for its employees' (p. 16). The general aim and strategy adopted has been informed by an underlying intention to draw attention to any studies that provide knowledge about the relationship between the world of work and the processes and outcomes of counselling.

The review procedure

The literature search has encompassed articles published in journals that operate a process of peer review, and chapters in books that report original research. The search has considered articles from a range of disciplines: counselling, psychotherapy, psychology, social work, sociology, management studies and occupational health. Strategies have included the use of online search tools, physically examining relevant journals, writing to potential informants and enlisting contributions through presentations at conferences. The review is restricted to studies published between 1980 and 2005, because the field of workplace counselling has undergone significant change over time, with the result that studies published prior to 1980 are unlikely to be relevant to the current organisational and service delivery context. Specifically, the majority of studies carried out before this time refer to services that focused on alcohol and drug abuse interventions, whereas contemporary workplace counselling services adopt a wider 'broad brush' approach, which includes substance abuse but also offers counselling for a wide range of psychological, emotional and relationship problems (Csiernik, 2005). Summaries of early research into EAP outcomes and processes can be found in Cairo (1983) and Lubin, Shanklin and Sailors (1992).

The methodology of the review comprised the following stages:

1. Call for information about relevant published work made at conferences and by contacting known authors on workplace counselling.

2. A cumulative series of online searches were conducted between 1995 and 2006 using PsycInfo, Medline, OVID, Web of Science, Google Scholar and Business Source Elite, using combinations of the following keywords: counselling, psychotherapy, work, worker, workplace, employee, staff, management, employee assistance, EAP, stress, burnout, depression, stress management, coaching, mental health, sickness absence and work functioning. This search strategy identified more than 2,000 potential articles. Identification of additional studies was made through analysis of reference lists and bibliographies in published papers, books and dissertations.

3. Handsearching of key journals: American Journal of Health Promotion; British Journal of Guidance and Counselling; Counselling and Psychotherapy Research; Counselling at Work; Counselling Psychology Quarterly; Employee Assistance Quarterly (renamed in 2005: Journal of Workplace Behavioral Health); European Journal of Psychotherapy, Counselling and Health; Health Bulletin; Industrial Health; Journal of Advanced Nursing; Journal of Applied Psychology; Journal of Behavioral Health Services and Research; Journal of Counselling and Development; Journal of Counselling Psychology; Journal of Occupational and Environmental Medicine; Journal of Occupational and Organisational Psychology; Occupational and Environmental Medicine; Occupational Medicine; Personnel Psychology; Psychological Medicine; Psychosomatic Medicine; Psychotherapy Research; Work and Stress.

4. The articles identified were assessed by two independent judges for relevance to the review (ie whether they reported original research findings and whether they satisfied the inclusion criteria).

5. Each item was summarised and the information extracted was checked by an independent reader, who verified the summary against the text of the original article.

6. The methodological quality of studies that assessed the outcomes of counselling was determined by two independent raters, using a standardised rating scale.

7. Narrative summaries of key themes and findings within different areas of workplace counselling research were compiled.

8. A draft report was sent to expert external reviewers, along with material on the aims and scope of the project, and a set of review issues to be addressed.

9. The comments of external reviewers were incorporated into the final report.

This review strategy has resulted in the exclusion of a number of studies that have the potential to contribute to the evidence base for workplace counselling. Several interesting studies were identified that have been reported in professional magazines such as *EAP Digest* and the *EAPA Exchange*. However, these articles comprised no more than brief (one or two page) summaries of research studies that had not been subjected to a review process. Also excluded were Masters and Doctoral dissertations, on the grounds that they may not be of publishable quality and are not generally accessible. This has meant that excellent studies, such as those conducted by Cheeseman (1996) and Worrall (1999) in the UK, and other dissertations completed in the USA and Canada, have not been included. Reports published by companies and counselling agencies have similarly been excluded, on the grounds that they have not been submitted to a quality control or review process, and were not accessible in a form that comprised a permanent public record.

Assessment of methodological quality of studies

The issue of assessment of the methodological quality and rigour of research studies included in the review presented a number of challenges. In many research reviews, guidelines such as those produced by Deeks et al (2003), Downs and Black (1998) or Murphy (1996) have been employed in order to filter out studies that are of low quality, or to give added weight to evidence from studies that are considered to be particularly robust (such as well-conducted randomised, controlled trials). However, to use such criteria in a blanket fashion ran the risk of imposing a set of expectations and values derived from medicine and psychology on a field in which many researchers were based in disciplines such as social work, sociology and management studies, and who did not espouse these principles. Focusing only on studies that might be deemed to be of higher methodological quality would detract from the goal of assembling a comprehensive review of current knowledge in the area of workplace counselling, on the basis that even studies that have methodological weaknesses may nevertheless be capable of making a meaningful contribution to knowledge and understanding. In addition, it is clear that there are fundamental debates within the broader research community concerning the most appropriate methods and strategies for studying therapeutic interventions. In the UK, a government-funded agency, the Medical Research Council, has published consensus guidelines on the development and evaluation of complex interventions to improve health, which recommend that qualitative studies, case studies and descriptive research should be carried out alongside, and in preparation for, the conduct of large-scale randomised, clinical trials (MRC, 2001). Within the field of psychotherapy research, there has been sharp criticism of what has been perceived as an over-reliance on clinical trial methodologies that collect data in conditions that have little relevance for everyday practice (Westen and Morrison, 2001; Westen, Novotny and Thompson-Brenner, 2004).

It was decided to address the challenge of evaluation of methodological quality in two ways. First, relevant methodological issues are highlighted in the summaries of all studies included in the review (available in Appendices) making openness and reflexivity possible. This strategy also enabled a flexible approach to the identification and discussion of methodological issues, reflecting the aims and approach adopted by each individual study. Second, it seemed valuable to adopt a standardised set of criteria for evaluating the methodological quality of studies into the outcomes of workplace counselling. The topic of outcome evaluation has particular significance for researchers and policy-makers, and it was therefore both necessary and appropriate to base recommendations and conclusions around counselling effectiveness on a scrutiny of the best available evidence.

The process for evaluating the methodological quality of outcome studies adopted by Connell et al (2006) was utilised. The quality of each of the outcome studies reviewed in Chapter 2 (summaries of studies available in Appendix A) was assessed by two independent judges, using the checklist developed by Downs and Black (1998). This checklist requires judges to assess the rigour of a research study in terms of four key dimensions: quality of reporting, external validity (representativeness and ability to generalise), internal validity (procedures for addressing potential sources of bias) and statistical power. The range of possible scores yielded by the scale is 0–27. Following Connell et al (2006), a score of 11 was selected as a cut-off point. Studies that received a rating of 12 or above were classified as high methodological quality; studies receiving ratings of 11 or below were classified as low methodological quality. The two judges were counselling researchers trained to Masters level or above. Studies receiving ratings (from either judge) in the range 10–13 were re-analysed and, if necessary discussed further in order to arrive at an agreed classification. Appendix A also includes three qualitative studies, whose methodological quality was not amenable to rating using the Downs and Black (1998) scale. For these studies, the author evaluated methodological rigour in terms of the criteria set out by Elliott, Fischer and Rennie (1999).

Summary of previous reviews

A number of previous reviews of research into the effectiveness of EAPs and other forms of workplace counselling have been carried out in recent years. In order to place the present review in context, a brief summary is provided below of the aims and findings of those published since 2000.

Arthur (2000). The aim of this review was to develop a critical perspective on research into the effectiveness of workplace counselling schemes and EAPs. Rather than systematically analyse all of the studies that were available, Arthur concentrated on selected key studies and discussed their contribution to the evidence base for EAPs. He argues that the studies that have been carried out have largely been methodologically weak: 'the research is often too brief, with no longitudinal collection of data, rarely employs control groups and, because of confidentiality and limited access to company records, organisations are deterred from conducting proper evaluations…few evaluations are conducted and many of these suffer from serious methodological inadequacies' (pp. 552–553). Following a close analysis of studies into the effectiveness and cost-effectiveness of EAPs, Arthur concluded that, although counselling may have a positive impact on individual problems, such services have 'failed to deliver' in relation to organisational outcomes because they are 'superficial' and do not reflect the complex, interactive nature of work stress.

Reynolds (2000). This review examines the evidence for the effectiveness of three forms of occupational stress intervention: individual counselling/psychotherapy, stress management training and organisational level interventions. No information is provided on the search strategy employed to identify articles, although it is mentioned that evidence from randomised, controlled trials was used where possible. The conclusions of the review are that there is little evidence for the efficacy of organisational interventions. The studies that are discussed suggest that group-based stress management results in short-term, minimal improvements in employee wellbeing. In respect of counselling and psychotherapy, Reynolds (2000: 318) concludes that 'research evidence suggests that the optimal psychological treatment for mental health problems in employees is an established, formal method of psychotherapy, such as cognitive behaviour therapy…the evidence for the use of employee counselling services is not well established…however, counselling services…in the workplace appear to be very popular.'

Van der Klink et al (2001). This group carried out a systematic review of research into the effectiveness of interventions designed to reduce occupational stress. This review was limited to quantitative studies that used an experimental design comparing a treatment group with a no-treatment comparison condition. Van der Klink et al located 48 studies carried out between 1977 and 1986 that met these criteria. However, the majority comprised organisational interventions (eg changing work arrangements) or the use of relaxation and meditation techniques. None of the studies were based on populations of people who were actively seeking help. The relevance of this review to an understanding of the role of workplace counselling is therefore limited, because counselling is by definition voluntarily initiated by the client, and most workplace counselling services deal with personal/family issues as well as occupational stress problems. The conclusions of the Van der Klink et al review were that individual-orientated interventions were more effective than organisational-level stress reduction programmes, and that interventions that used cognitive-behavioural therapy (CBT) principles were more successful than those based on other models. However, within the studies that applied CBT methods, there was a wide variation in effectiveness, with some interventions associated with low success rates.

Kirk and Brown (2003). This paper comprises a narrative review of research into the characteristics of EAP counsellors and interventions, and evaluation studies. There is a particular focus on the development of EAPs in Australia. For example, they report on research demonstrating that EAP counsellors in Australia are more highly qualified and trained than those practising in the UK. In relation to the effectiveness of EAPs, Kirk and Brown concluded that:

> 'EAP evaluations have not yet produced the quality of evidence that would enable an unqualified endorsement of EAP interventions in the management of stress and other personal and organisational issues in the workplace… it seems that the best that can be said in relation to EAPs is that employees in general report perceptions of improved mental and physical wellbeing, but that there is little evidence of an impact on organisational-level data such as improved job satisfaction or productivity' (p. 141).

Kirk and Brown conclude their review by discussing the emerging trend for EAPs to become part of wider positive wellness programmes within organisations.

Giga et al (2003). The review conducted by Giga et al focuses specifically on research carried out in the UK. These authors organise research in stress interventions into three categories: individual, individual/organisational and organisational. The search was limited to articles published since 1990, which were studies of evaluations of interventions. Within the category of individual interventions (which encompasses counselling), 13 studies were located. Several of these were concerned with non-counselling methods, such as time management, exercise and relaxation. In their conclusion, Giga et al noted the methodological limitations of the studies that had been published, particularly the relatively short post-intervention follow-up periods that were used in many studies.

However, they suggested that methodological quality had improved, with more recent studies being of higher quality than those that had been published earlier. In relation to the effects of counselling interventions, they found that there was more impact on individual symptoms of stress and depression than on organisational outcomes, and that effects appeared to be relatively short-lived.

DeGroot and Kiker (2003). This paper argues that the development of EAPs has passed through three distinct phases: occupational alcoholism programmes (1939–1962), broad-brush employee assistance programmes (1962–present) and, more recently, occupational health promotion (1980s to present). In this review, the role of EAPs within organisational health promotion is analysed. The review strategy included only studies that were long-term orientated and intended to promote positive wellness, and identified 22 relevant studies. These covered a range of different types of intervention, such as fitness and smoking cessation programmes as well as counselling. In the analysis provided by DeGroot and Kiker (2000), it is not possible to separate the distinct effects of counselling programmes, as opposed to other types of intervention. Nevertheless, the findings of the review do have important implications for the provision of counselling and other EAP services. There were four main conclusions arising from this review. First, it was found that wellness programmes only had a positive impact on job performance when participation in the programme was required and not voluntary. Second, programmes that were more focused on specific outcomes had more impact on job performance than those where the intervention is comprehensive and wide-ranging. Third, voluntary participation in a wide-ranging, varied wellness programme has a significant impact on reducing sickness absence. Finally, wellness programmes appeared to have no effect on levels of turnover or job satisfaction.

Csiernik (2004). This review considers 39 published EAP evaluations published during the 1990s. A broad conception of 'evaluation' is employed, with studies being classified and discussed in terms of five evaluation categories: needs assessment studies; case studies; input evaluations; outcome evaluations and process evaluations. Of particular interest is the section on outcome evaluations, which analyses nine cost-effectiveness case studies. The cost-benefit ratio reported in these studies ranges from cost neutral to 7:1. There is also a review of studies that examine managers' perceptions of the impact of counselling on employee performance, with one study showing that the majority of managers perceived no improvement in employee work performance, and two other studies reporting 43% and 73% of managers perceiving performance improvements. Overall, this review paper aims to provide an overview or flavour of the research that has been carried out, rather than seeking to carry out any kind of systematic analysis. In his conclusion, Csiernik (2004: 32) reflects:

> 'is the glass half full or is it half empty? Thirty-nine studies in ten years, less than four per year, a third of which were primarily descriptive in nature and several others that would not withstand the scrutiny of an undergraduate research methodology course. The 1990s did not provide an extensive EAP evaluation legacy.'

From the point of view of the present review, one of the most useful aspects of the Csiernik paper is that it reports, even if briefly, on several articles that were published as company reports or in professional trade journals in the USA, and were therefore not available for review in this report. However, none of these 'grey literature' studies present findings that are in conflict with the outcomes of the present review.

British Occupational Health Research Foundation (2005). The aim of this review was to evaluate the evidence around workplace interventions for people with mental health problems. Studies relating to a wide range of interventions were identified: stress management, counselling/ psychotherapy, organisational change, exercise and other approaches. The review considered three key questions: (i) how can mental health problems at work be prevented? (ii) for employees identified as at risk, what interventions most effectively enable them to stay at work? (iii) for employees who have had periods of mental health-related sickness, what interventions best support their rehabilitation and return to work? A systematic and thorough search strategy was employed, and the studies that were located were screened in terms of methodological rigour. The findings and recommendations of this review are wide-ranging and detailed, and provide a rich and valuable analysis of the relationship between workplace support and the management of mental health problems. In relation to the value of counselling interventions, the review concludes that there is no evidence that counselling prevents mental health problems, but that it is effective in helping people with mental health problems to stay at work, and those absent from work to make a return. The review recommends that cognitive-behavioural approaches to counselling and psychotherapy are more effective than other approaches, and that the evidence available suggests that individual therapeutic interventions are more effective with employees in high-control (ie management and professional) jobs. The review calls for further research on all aspects of the topic of mental health and work, and in particular for studies into the experiences and needs of disadvantaged workers.

In addition to the reviews summarised above, an earlier version of the current review was published in 2001 (McLeod, 2001).

What are the themes that emerge from these reviews? The most immediately salient issue, identified by several reviewers, is that the amount of research that has been published is not commensurate with the size and scope of what is an international, professionalised industry. Further, the research is often of marginal quality. Reviewers comment on the reasons for the absence of research, and its poor quality, and make suggestions for how this state of affairs can be improved. Another theme that emerges from these reviews is that the evidence suggests that counselling and EAP provision can claim a reasonable level of effectiveness in relation to assisting clients to deal with symptoms of stress, anxiety and depression, but has less of an impact on organisational outcomes such as reducing sickness absence, staff turnover and accidents, and enhancing work performance and organisational commitment. Some reviewers have suggested that the evidence supports the effectiveness of cognitive-behavioural therapy (CBT) interventions rather than general counselling approaches. There is little evidence in these reviews that counselling could claim to serve a preventative function, in terms of ameliorating future emotional crises of clients. Finally, each of these reviews comments, in different ways, on the complexity of the organisational and cultural milieu in which EAPs and other workplace counselling services need to operate, for example in relation to the mutation of problem-orientated services into wellness programmes.

All the specific research studies cited in these reviews that meet the inclusion criteria for the present review are incorporated into this report. It also includes a substantial number of studies not included in the reviews discussed here.

A comprehensive model of workplace counselling

In order to understand the strengths and weaknesses of the studies that are reviewed in later sections of this report, it is necessary to appreciate the complexity of the context within which workplace counselling takes place. Figure 1 provides an outline of the multiple factors that are potentially involved in determining the effectiveness of counselling in relation to workplace issues. It seems probable that workplace counselling is more contextually sensitive than other forms of counselling and psychotherapy. For example, when counselling is carried out in a healthcare setting, or within a university or college counselling service, there can be a high degree of congruence between the overall purpose of the organisation and the aims of counselling carried out within it.

This is not the case with workplace counselling. On the whole, the primary goal of organisations, such as finance, retail or manufacturing companies that make use of EAPs or other forms of workplace counselling is not the enhancement of the wellbeing of employees. What this means is that there are significant tensions associated with the provision of workplace counselling, that in turn may influence the levels of up-take of counselling and the effectiveness of the therapy offered. The existence of such tension is reflected in the observation, reported by many studies, that confidentiality is a crucial factor for users of workplace counselling services (see, for example, the studies by Butterworth, 2001; Gyllensten et al, 2005; Hall et al, 1991; Harlow, 1998; Milne et al, 1994; Muhset and Donaldson, 2000; West and Reynolds, 1995). By contrast, while undoubtedly important, confidentiality appears less of an issue for users of other types of counselling services (McGuire et al, 1985). For the most part, counsellors can do relatively little to influence employee perceptions of the confidentiality of their service – this is a factor that largely depends on other aspects of organisational life, such as the culture of the organisation. The range of factors that may have an influence on workplace counselling, and their relationship with outcome, are briefly explored in the following paragraphs.

The social context of workplace counselling

It is important to recognise that the effectiveness of workplace counselling may be influenced by social factors that are beyond the direct control of the counsellor, employee or organisation. It is clear that workplace counselling has evolved within advanced industrial economies in North America, Europe and Australia, but has not developed to any extent in developing countries in Africa and Asia, in the post-Soviet states or (until very recently) in Japan. Although it is beyond the scope of the present analysis to interpret this cultural pattern, it seems inarguable that the choice of counselling as a remedy for employee difficulties is a strategy that fits well with the way that some societies construct the relationship between worker, employer and State, and not with others. Levels of economic growth also influence the uptake of employee assistance services – counselling costs money and is always a likely candidate for cutting at times of economic downturn.

There are major differences between societies, and sub-groups within societies, concerning knowledge, beliefs and attitudes in relation to counselling, and in basic assumptions about healthcare. Finally, there can be major differences within sectors of society regarding the availability of different forms of psychotherapeutic intervention. It seems probable that individuals who have ready access to counselling or psychotherapy through their health insurance, or through private practice, will prefer to take that route rather than risk being perceived within their organisation as 'unable to cope'.

The utilisation and effectiveness of workplace counselling schemes may therefore depend, in part, on what other services are available and how these alternatives are perceived; high utilisation rates in some employee counselling services may simply reflect the fact that stressed employees have nowhere else to go. It is clear, therefore, that there are many cultural and social factors that may influence the uptake and outcomes of workplace counselling, and that a comprehensive analysis of research in this field needs to take account of the social context within which services are delivered.

The organisational context

There are many dimensions of organisational structure and culture that may impact upon workplace counselling services. For example, the size of an organisation is likely to influence the type of counselling provision that is available to employees. Larger organisations generate enough demand for counselling to be able to establish in-house services, and have the occupational health and Human Resources infrastructure to manage such a provision. By contrast, smaller organisations may be more likely to buy into an external EAP service. The geographical spread of organisations may similarly influence the type of counselling provision that is developed. The cultures of organisations vary a great deal – the meaning of counselling in a uniformed, discipline-orientated organisation such as a police force differs from its meaning within an organisation such as a university. Public sector, private/commercial sector and voluntary/not-for-profit organisations also differ around cultural values such as the profit motive vs. service orientation and collectivism vs. individualism. The culture of an organisation is symbolised and transmitted through stories that are told, and through the behaviour and attitudes of chief executives or legendary founding figures. These narratives may convey subtle attitudes towards the value of therapy, or the acceptability of vulnerability and emotional 'weakness'. The activities that organisations carry out are another source of influence on the type of counselling that is required. Organisations where employees are exposed to traumatic events have different therapeutic needs to organisations where employees need to spend extended periods of time away from home. Finally, organisations may evolve a range of systems for managing counselling services. Some schemes are administered by groups that include trade union/labour representatives, occupational health representatives and managers; while other schemes are solely controlled by management. In some services, employees themselves are involved in volunteer or peer support roles; elsewhere, there may be wholly professional-delivered services.

Employee factors

The characteristics of staff within an organisation represent another source of influence on the uptake and effectiveness of counselling services. Age, gender, ethnicity, religion or belief systems, cultural attitudes and educational level are all factors that may be associated with the decision to use counselling, and to the presence (or otherwise) of positive attitudes towards it. The type of employment contract held by a worker may also be relevant. Part-time employees may experience less work stress, and may have other, external sources of support that they have cultivated, in contrast to permanent employees whose identification with, and embeddedness in, the organisation may make them more vulnerable to organisational sources of stress, and more likely to look to the organisation for help and support in times of crisis. The attitudes and beliefs about counselling held by employees may influence their willingness to use a counselling

Figure 1. A model of factors involved in determining the effectiveness of workplace counselling

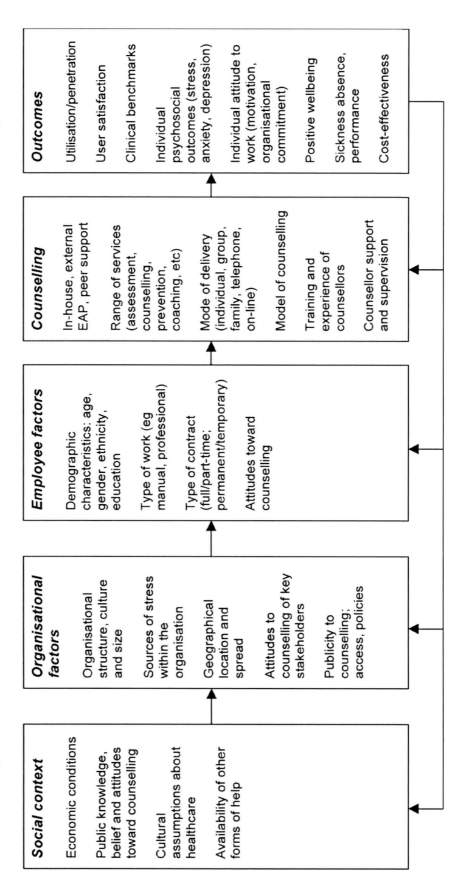

Social context

Economic conditions

Public knowledge, belief and attitudes toward counselling

Cultural assumptions about healthcare

Availability of other forms of help

Organisational factors

Organisational structure, culture and size

Sources of stress within the organisation

Geographical location and spread

Attitudes to counselling of key stakeholders

Publicity to counselling; access, policies

Employee factors

Demographic characteristics: age, gender, ethnicity, education

Type of work (eg manual, professional)

Type of contract (full/part-time; permanent/temporary)

Attitudes toward counselling

Counselling

In-house, external EAP, peer support

Range of services (assessment, counselling, prevention, coaching, etc)

Mode of delivery (individual, group, family, telephone, on-line)

Model of counselling

Training and experience of counsellors

Counsellor support and supervision

Outcomes

Utilisation/penetration

User satisfaction

Clinical benchmarks

Individual psychosocial outcomes (stress, anxiety, depression)

Individual attitude to work (motivation, organisational commitment)

Positive wellbeing

Sickness absence, performance

Cost-effectiveness

service – these attitudes may be reinforced by 'word of mouth' networks.

Counselling – service delivery factors

It is clear that 'workplace counselling' is not in any straightforward sense a single entity. Employment-linked services may be organised on the basis of a team of counsellors directly employed within an organisation (an 'in-house' model) or delivered by external counsellors (the EAP model). Some organisations have developed hybrid models of service delivery, featuring a combination of internal and external provision. There are many successful services that make use of peer support networks. The therapeutic services that are available may be significantly different across schemes, and may incorporate any, or all of the following list of modalities: face-to-face counselling, assessment, couples counselling, family work, group therapy, telephone counselling, online counselling, consultation, mediation, referral to external therapy providers, training and prevention work. The counsellors that deliver a service may be highly qualified psychologists or counsellors, with Masters or PhD credentials, or minimally trained counsellors, or may have a background in drug, alcohol, social work or nursing interventions. Some employee counselling services also make use of peer volunteers. Cutting across these modalities and practitioner differences are a wide range of theoretical models that counsellors in workplace settings might apply: cognitive-behavioural, person-centred, psychodynamic, solution-focused or integrative.

Workplace counselling outcome: a multi-dimensional construct

The intended outcomes of workplace counselling encompass a multiplicity of potential effects. In most cases, a person will seek help from a workplace counsellor because he or she is experiencing distress, which is manifest in symptoms of anxiety, depression and low self-esteem or difficulties in relationships at work or home. At the most basic level, workplace counselling seeks to eliminate or ameliorate these symptoms. However, there are many other dimensions of outcome that have been identified within the workplace counselling literature. There are specific forms of psychological distress that may be relevant in some counselling situations, for example drug/alcohol abuse, burnout and post-traumatic stress disorder. Beyond this, there are several aspects of work functioning and work behaviour that have been claimed to be amenable to counselling intervention: job satisfaction, organisational commitment, work performance/productivity, relationships with co-workers, sickness absence, employee retention and reduction of accidents. A further dimension of the effect of workplace counselling is reflected in utilisation rates: what proportion of a workforce makes use of the service? The relevance of utilisation rate is that it represents an estimate of the acceptability and perceived credibility of a counselling service, in the eyes of potential users. From the point of view of an organisation that invests in workplace counselling for its staff, an additional outcome is cost: to what extent does a counselling service cover its costs by reductions in sickness absence, accidents, staff recruitment and other items, and enhancement of productivity? These outcomes or effects of workplace counselling can be described or measured in a variety of ways, for example through information gleaned from questionnaires, interviews, case records and personnel files. Perceptions of outcome can be based on the perspectives of various stakeholders, such as counselling clients, counsellors, other employees in an organisation, the client's supervisor or line manager, or the senior management of an organisation. Research into any outcome variable may produce contrastingly different results depending on how the variable is measured and from what perspective.

The importance of context in making sense of research findings

The central question that has driven research into workplace counselling is the issue of outcome: does it work? A central aim of the present review, and of previous reviews of the workplace counselling research literature, has been to establish a reliable evidence base for the effectiveness of this type of intervention. The brief outline of a model of factors involved in determining the effectiveness of workplace counselling, offered above, is intended to underscore the point that this is an area in which valid and practical knowledge relies on an appreciation of contextual factors. On the whole, outcome research in counselling and psychotherapy has tended to focus on the impact of a specific approach to therapy (eg CBT) with a specific client group (eg depressed people), and has largely ignored contextual factors such as the culture of the organisation in which counselling is offered, the model of service delivery or the attitudes and beliefs of clients. By contrast, contextual factors are hugely important in understanding workplace counselling. This is because employee counselling takes place in a closed system. The counselling that is available to an employee is only partly constructed in response to that individual person's needs and is also shaped by the needs and goals of various parts of the organisation within which the person is employed. The effectiveness of counselling feeds back into the organisational system in a variety of ways – for example when someone tells a colleague that counselling is helpful and encourages him or her to try it out. In many services, counsellors utilise various means of reporting back to the organisation about stressful work practices and policies. The significance of context, in the field of workplace counselling, has two main implications for this review. First, in reading the many studies that are summarised and discussed in the following pages, it is necessary to look beyond the information given and to visualise the different concrete circumstances in which counselling was provided and how the information about its effectiveness was collected. Second, in order to capture as much as possible of the contextual complexity of counselling, the review has not focused solely on outcome studies, but has also included research into all such aspects in this area.

Conclusions

This introductory chapter has highlighted key themes within theory and research into workplace counselling, and has provided an outline of the review process that was followed. The report is divided into a series of chapters, each of which addresses a different area of research. Chapter 2 reviews studies of the effectiveness of workplace counselling. Chapter 3 looks at research into the economic costs and benefits of this type of staff support. Chapter 4 brings together studies that have considered the degree to which counselling services are utilised by employees, their attitudes toward such services and research into other organisational factors. In Chapter 5, studies of the process of workplace counselling are considered. Chapter 6 discusses the difficult methodological issues associated with research into workplace counselling and suggests directions for further research. The series of Appendices that close the report seek to summarise each of the research studies that have been identified in this review in a succinct and accessible fashion.

Chapter 2. Research into the outcomes of workplace counselling

Introduction

Research into the outcomes of EAP/workplace counselling provision has largely focused on the impact of this type of intervention on three distinct areas of psycho-social functioning: (i) psychological functioning, for example symptoms of stress, depression, anxiety and low self-esteem, (ii) the meaning of work, for example job commitment and satisfaction; and (iii) work behaviour, for example sickness absence, job performance and accidents. In addition, several studies have used client satisfaction as an indicator of the effectiveness of EAP/counselling programmes. The findings of research into these three specific areas of outcome, and into client satisfaction as a global reflection of outcome, are summarised below.

It is important to acknowledge that there are significant methodological problems associated with research into the outcomes of EAP/counselling services. These methodological issues are discussed more fully in a later section of this report. The key issue concerns a trade-off between scientific rigour on the one hand and relevance to everyday practice (or realism) on the other. It is extremely difficult to carry out a rigorous, controlled study of workplace counselling that reflects the conditions of everyday service provisions. It is also extremely difficult to carry out a study of workplace counselling under normal circumstances that meets the criteria for best scientific practice, since typically there is little control over the quality or amount of counselling that is delivered, only a limited set of measures can be administered and many clients choose not to complete questionnaires.

The effectiveness of workplace counselling

The analysis of the effectiveness of workplace counselling is organised around four key areas: client satisfaction; psychological functioning; the meaning of work; and work behaviour. A review of research findings within each of these areas is provided, followed by discussion of a number of key issues and questions associated with research in this topic area. Summaries of each of the research studies that are mentioned in this section are available in Appendices A and B.

Client satisfaction

The extent to which users of counselling are satisfied with the service they receive is an important outcome for any agency or organisation that provides counselling. Client satisfaction represents a fundamental benchmark for good practice. Also, allowing clients to record their dissatisfaction, and make suggestions for improvement of services, is part of an ethical approach. Despite the value of using client satisfaction measures, however, there are also significant limitations to the concept of satisfaction as a measure of service quality. Clients who have felt that their counsellor has taken their problem seriously, and treated them with care and respect, are likely to give high satisfaction ratings, regardless of whether their problem has changed. Satisfaction should be regarded as more of an assessment of whether a service has been delivered professionally, rather than as a measure of the actual benefit or outcome that may have accrued to the client. In addition, the method of administration of client satisfaction scales needs to be taken into account when interpreting findings. In most counselling organisations, client satisfaction scales are distributed at the final session

only. Given that many clients have unplanned endings, this means that there is a tendency for satisfaction scales to be completed by more satisfied clients (those who return for a formal ending) than by less satisfied ones (who may have quit therapy because it had not been helping them). For these reasons, it is conventional to look for a satisfaction rate of at least 85% or 90% of clients being highly satisfied with the service they have received, as an indication of an adequate service. This kind of level of overall satisfaction has been reported in a substantial number of studies of workplace counselling, reflecting a wide range of organisational settings (Chandler et al, 1988; Csiernik, Atkison et al, 2001; Gam et al, 1983; Goss and Mearns, 1997; Highley-Marchington and Cooper, 1998; Iwi et al, 1998; Macdonald, Lothian and Wells, 1997; Masi and Jacobson, 2003; McAllister, 1993; Millar, 2000; Mitchie, 1996; Philips, 2004; Reynolds, 1997; Rogers et al, 1995; Sloboda et al, 1993; Whelan, Robson and Cook, 2002). No studies have been published that have reported low levels of client satisfaction with workplace counselling. In many of the studies that have been carried out, clients have identified specific aspects of the service with which they are less than wholly satisfied, while at the same time giving a service a high overall satisfaction rating. This finding suggests that clients are able to discriminate in their use of satisfaction ratings and that high ratings deserve to be taken at face value. It can be concluded, therefore, that users of workplace counselling services and agencies are generally satisfied with the interventions they receive, reflecting overall high standards within the workplace counselling profession.

Four studies have used qualitative methods to explore levels of client satisfaction. Denzin (1995) carried out an observational study into the views of employees when their organisation changed its EAP provider, with resulting reduced benefits for staff. There were substantial protests by employees, indicating the importance of the EAP provision for this group of staff. This study provides rich naturalistic data regarding the meaning of workplace counselling for employees. In a particularly well-designed and thorough study carried out with a regional ambulance service in Australia, Shakespeare-Finch and Scully (2004) used focus group interviews to elicit information about staff views of a workplace counselling service. Elliott and Williams (2002) and Millar (2002) conducted individual interviews with staff who had received counselling. These studies demonstrate how qualitative methods can be used not only to analyse levels of employee satisfaction, but in addition to generate detailed accounts of employee views regarding specific aspects of a counselling service and their suggestions for improving it. Overall, the findings of these qualitative studies have yielded high estimates of satisfaction, similar to those obtained in quantitative studies.

An underlying issue, in relation to research in client satisfaction with EAPs and other workplace counselling services, concerns the validity of the questionnaire instruments that have been used to assess satisfaction. For the most part, these scales are developed by individual researchers for the purposes of their own particular study, thus issues of validity and reliability are suspect. There would be advantages if researchers used a standard scale, which would allow results from different studies to be compared. Dersch, Shumway, Harris and Arredondo (2002; see also Shumway et al, 2001) have developed a new EAP satisfaction scale, which may provide a basis for widespread adoption. These researchers have published promising initial validation data for a 17-item scale, which assesses five dimensions of satisfaction: impact on relationships and family functioning; satisfaction with the counsellor and counselling process; adequacy of administrative processes; impact of counselling on work; and global satisfaction.

The impact of workplace counselling on psychological functioning

The most widely used strategy for studying the impact of workplace counselling on psychological functioning involves the administration of a standardised scale for measuring some aspect of functioning before counselling, at the end of counselling and, if possible, also at follow-up. Change in psychological functioning can be estimated by comparing scores pre- and post-counselling. The extent to which the level of change is observed across a course of counselling can be estimated in two different ways. First, the average (mean) scores of a group of clients can be compared pre- and post-counselling, using a test of statistical significance. This method makes it possible to determine whether the change that has been observed is so small as to have been due to chance factors, or is in fact statistically significant (ie the differences found would be very unlikely to be the result of chance variations). This approach to analysing change is used in almost all studies, but if the sample of cases is large enough, a statistically significant result can be produced even when the actual amount of change in each case is slight. There is, therefore, a limitation in merely reporting whether a statistically significant change has occurred. In order to provide a way of indicating the degree of change that has been produced by an intervention, an *Effect Size* (ES) calculation can be made. *Effect Size* is a technique for conveying magnitude of change across a group of subjects or research participants, as a standardised metric (eg *small*, *medium* or *large* effects), and is widely employed in counselling and psychotherapy research (Fidler et al, 2005; Trusty, Thompson and Petrocelli, 2004). All outcome studies that use standardised scales to evaluate change in psychological functioning should be able to report their findings in terms of Effect Sizes and proportions of clients who have exhibited clinically significant change. However, as can be seen from the research summaries presented in Appendix A, relatively few studies have adopted this rigorous standard.

An alternative approach to reporting on the effectiveness of a counselling or psychotherapeutic intervention is to estimate the proportion of individual cases that have improved or recovered (Jacobson, Follette and Revenstorf, 1984; Jacobson and Revenstorf, 1988). The concept of *clinical significance*, in relation to change resulting from therapy, was introduced by Jacobson, Follette and Revenstorf (1984: 340) in the following terms: 'a change in therapy is clinically significant when the client moves from the dysfunctional to the functional range during the course of therapy.' To decide whether the changes recorded by clients are meaningful in practical terms (ie clinically significant), two criteria need to be met. First, the client needs to have shifted by a certain number of points on the measurement scale (*reliable change* has occurred). Second, the client needs to have moved out of the problem or 'caseness' range of scores and into the 'normal' or 'non-clinical' range (*clinical change* has occurred). The cut-off points for 'clinical' and 'non-clinical' scores can be established by administering a scale, in its development phase, to groups of people known to represent clinical and non-clinical populations. The advantage of analysing effectiveness research data in terms of clinically significant change is that it yields information on the proportions of clients who have achieved practice-relevant outcomes: *recovered* (reliable and clinical change recorded for that client), *improved* (reliable change, but not sufficient to move the client into the 'normal'

range), *unchanged* and *deteriorated* (reliable level of increase in symptoms). Although the principles for defining clinically significant change, first stated by Jacobson in the 1980s, are widely accepted within the counselling and psychotherapy research field, with authors being encouraged to use clinical change indicators in their reports wherever possible (Fidler et al, 2005), there remains some debate within the research community concerning the most appropriate techniques for determining cut-off points, and estimating reliable and clinical change levels (see Atkins et al, 2005; Wise, 2004).

In relation to research reporting practices that address issues of clinical and practical relevance, it may also be that indicators of clinical significance could be further enhanced if these change rates were presented in the context of attrition rates (ie the proportion of clients seen for assessment and then taken into therapy).

A further approach to studying the impact of counselling or psychotherapy on psychological functioning is to interview clients once they have completed counselling, to elicit their personal account of how the intervention has had an effect on their psychological problems. While this approach can yield rich descriptions of the ways in which counselling may or may not have affected individuals, it may be difficult for the informant to recall exactly how they felt at the start of counselling, or to be precise about how much they may have changed. Because of the uncertainties associated with qualitative, interview-based research into outcomes, the findings from these studies are discussed separately from the analysis of quantitative studies.

The findings of research into the outcomes of workplace counselling, in relation to its effect on psychological functioning, are summarised below.

General levels of stress or psychological symptoms

Several studies have examined the effect of workplace counselling on employee levels of stress and wellbeing. Typically, this factor is assessed by administering a symptom checklist or screening instrument for mental health difficulties, such as the General Health Questionnaire (GHQ; Goldberg and Williams, 1998). The studies that have identified work-related counselling that can have a positive impact in terms of reducing psychological symptoms and stress are:

Studies with high methodological quality: Cooper and Sadri (1991); Gardner, Rose, Mason, Tyler and Cushway (2005); Gersons, Carlier, Lamberts and van der Kolk (2000); Guppy and Marsden (1997); Reynolds (1997); Shapiro and Firth (1987; Sheffield Psychotherapy Project I); Shapiro, Barkham, Hardy and Morrison (1990; Sheffield Psychotherapy Project II); Barkham, Shapiro, Hardy and Rees (1999; Sheffield Psychotherapy Project III); and Van der Klink, Blonk, Schene and van Djik (2003).

Studies with low methodological quality: Gray-Toft (1980); Harris et al (2002); Highley-Marchington and Cooper (1998); Masi and Jacobson (2003); Mitchie (1997); Selvik, Stephenson, Plaza and Sugden (2004).

One study found that, compared to employees in a control condition, counselling had no effect on stress symptoms (Iwi et al, 1998; high quality study). A further study (Doctor, Curtis and Isaacs, 1994; low quality study) reported a slight worsening of symptoms, measured by the GHQ, following a group counselling intervention.

Taken as a whole, these studies into the impact of workplace counselling on stress/psychological symptoms encompass a wide range of research designs, including naturalistic, practice-based studies as well as controlled trials, and also a wide range of client populations and therapeutic approaches. It is perhaps worth noting that each of the studies that reported neutral or negative findings was problematic or atypical in relation to the type of intervention that was delivered. Iwi et al (1998) offered only four sessions of Cognitive-Analytic Therapy, a therapy model that is usually delivered in longer-term work; Doctor et al (1994) study used a form of group analysis that did not specifically focus on stress symptoms and would also have normally been provided on a more long-term basis. Only one of the studies listed above (Shapiro and Firth, 1987) included a long-term follow-up. The balance of evidence, therefore, appears to support the position that participation in workplace counselling is generally effective in ameliorating current symptoms of stress and low wellbeing.

Depression

Depression is a particularly significant area of psychological difficulty in relation to work functioning. While general psychological symptoms, or signs of stress, may reflect current situational crises, depression is a more specific difficulty that may possibly reflect a continuing area of difficulty for the person. Moreover, depression is associated with patterns of low motivation, withdrawal from others, fatigue and hopelessness, that are likely to result in problems around work performance and attendance. A number of studies have reported positive outcomes in relation to the impact of workplace counselling on depression:

Studies with high methodological quality: Grime (2004); Reynolds (1997); Shapiro, Barkham, Hardy and Morrison (1990); Barkham, Shapiro, Hardy and Rees (1999); and Sprang (1992).

Studies with low methodological quality: Harris et al (2002); Preece et al (2005).

In these studies, levels of depression have been assessed through questionnaires such as the Beck Depression Inventory (BDI). In a further study, Rost, Fortney and Coyne (2005) examined the sickness absence patterns of patients who had been diagnosed by their physician as depressed, and who had been prescribed with either psychological therapy or antidepressant medication. Rost et al (2005) found significantly greater decreases in sickness absence in the psychotherapy group than in the patients who had received antidepressants.

The balance of evidence, therefore, supports the position that participation in workplace counselling is generally effective in bringing about a reduction in symptoms of depression.

Other psychological outcome variables

Two studies with high methodological quality have found that workplace counselling can be beneficial in relation to anxiety in clients: Cooper and Sadri (1991); and Grime (2004). Cooper and Sadri (1991) and Goss and Mearns (1997; low methodological quality) reported evidence for the impact of workplace counselling in respect of self-esteem. Other high-quality studies have found beneficial impacts of counselling in relation to burnout (Salmela-Aro, Naatanen and Nurmi, 2004; Van Dierendonck, Schaufeli and Buunk, 1998) and occupational post-traumatic stress disorder (Gersons, Carlier, Lamberts and van der Kolk, 2000). A number of studies (including studies published earlier than the cut-off date for the present review) have yielded positive results for the effectiveness of workplace counselling for employees

with drug and alcohol problems (Finke, Williams and Stanley, 1996; Guppy and Marsden, 1997; Schneider, Casey and Kohn, 2000).

There is therefore evidence from a limited number of studies that workplace counselling can be beneficial for a range of specific work-related psychological and behavioural problems, such as anxiety, low self-esteem, emotional burnout, occupational PTSD and substance abuse.

Qualitative research into psychological functioning

Qualitative outcome studies, in which users of workplace counselling have been interviewed about their perceptions of the effect that counselling has had on their problems, and their life as a whole, have been carried out by Elliott and Williams (2002) and Millar (2002). Elliott and Williams found that clients reported that counselling had helped in relation both to psychological problems and work performance. Millar discovered that police personnel described themselves as having much higher levels of wellbeing, when interviewed several months following the end of counselling, alongside improvements to physical and psychological health, social functioning and work performance. Most of the participants in the Millar study believed that, for them counselling had yielded an 'added value', because it impacted on them in ways that went beyond their presenting problem.

Conclusion: the impact of workplace counselling on psychological functioning

The findings of the studies reported in the previous section suggest that workplace counselling has consistent and significant short-term benefits, in terms of effects on psychological functioning, when comparisons are made between levels of symptoms reported by clients pre- and post-counselling. The research that has been carried out embraces a range of methodologies, including randomised, trials, naturalistic practice-based studies and qualitative studies. The research also reflects a wide range of client populations and models of therapy. While each of the studies that have been included in this review can be regarded as having methodological limitations, which are discussed in the summaries of the studies provided in the Appendix, the evidence as a whole is compelling, and no significant counter-evidence was identified in the process of the review. However, it is not clear, on the basis of the current research evidence, whether workplace counselling has an enduring impact on psychological difficulties, or merely serves to assist clients to deal more effectively with a current episode of stress or depression – further research that included long-term follow-ups would be valuable.

The level of impact of workplace counselling, in relation to overall Effect Size (ES) (the magnitude of change resulting from an intervention), is illustrated in Table 1. Here, Effect Size calculations are presented for all of the good-quality outcome studies that have been reviewed, and for which sufficient information was provided to allow ES to be calculated (ES estimates could not be derived for the following studies: Guppy and Marsden, 1997; Iwi et al, 1998; Reynolds, 1997; Salmela-Aro et al, 2004). The average ES of 0.90 that is reported for pre-counselling to post-counselling comparisons, and 1.17 for pre-counselling to follow-up, is similar to the ES figures reflected in meta-analyses of other fields of psychological therapy (see Lambert and Ogles, 2004). Within the domain of psychological and behavioural research as a whole, an ES of 0.8 or higher is considered 'high'. It can be concluded, therefore, that the effects of workplace counselling

Table 1. Effect Sizes of good-quality studies on the impact of workplace counselling on psychological functioning

Author(s)	Date	Occupational group	Therapy approach	Outcome variable	Effect Size – end of counselling	Effect Size – follow-up
Barkham, Shapiro, Hardy and Rees	1999	Professional and managerial	Psychodynamic	Depression	1.63	1.32
			CBT	Depression	1.74	1.89
Cooper and Sadri	1991	Post office workers	Client-centred	Anxiety Somatic anxiety Depression Self-esteem	0.77 0.93 0.79 0.42	Not available
Gardner, Rose, Mason, Tyler and Cushway	2005	Health workers (all grades)	Cognitive	Symptoms	0.94	2.55
			Behavioural	Symptoms	0.73	0.89
Gersons, Carlier, Lamberts and van der Kolk	2000	Police officers	Brief eclectic	Phobic anxiety Depression	1.18 1.22	1.20 1.13
Grime	2004	Health workers	CBT	Anxiety Depression	0.38 0.70	0.70 0.71
Guppy and Marsden	1997	Transport workers	Counselling	Symptoms	0.63	N/A
Shapiro and Firth	1987	Professional and managerial	CBT/psychodynamic	Depression Symptoms Self-esteem	1.92 1.68 1.25	1.76 1.94 1.24
Shapiro, Barkham, Hardy and Morrison	1990	Professional and managerial	CBT/psychodynamic	Depression Symptoms Self-esteem	1.77 1.64 1.11	1.63 1.74 1.03
Van der Klink, Blonk, Schene and van Djik	2003	Postal workers	CBT	Symptoms Depression	1.11 0.62	1.26 0.63
Van Dierendonck, Schaufeli and Buunk	1998	Health workers	CBT	Emotional exhaustion Depersonalisation Personal accomplishment	0.27 0.08 0.19	0.27 0.36 0.03
Mean Effect Size (all studies)					0.90	1.17

interventions are in the 'high' range, compared to other behavioural interventions. The range of occupational groups represented in Table 1 suggests that these results are applicable to a wide range of employees, in comparison to the review by BOHRF (2005), which found that benefits were more likely to be reported by white-collar employees, rather than lower status employees.

An important limitation of pre- to post-counselling analyses (known as 'effectiveness' studies) is that they do not take into account the possibility that those who received counselling may have improved in the absence of any intervention. In some of the studies reported in this review, researchers collected information from comparison groups. The ES data from these studies is summarised in Table 2. It can be seen that the outcomes for employees who do not receive counselling vary substantially. In interpreting the data in Table 2, it is necessary to take into account the different forms of non-counselling comparison groups that were utilised. The studies by Cooper and Sadri (1999) and Van Dierendonck et al (1998) collected information from employees who were not actively seeking help for psychological difficulties. These samples report limited change over time in employee levels of symptoms. By contrast, the other studies listed in Table 2 utilised comparison groups of help seekers (ie people who had applied for counselling and were placed on a waiting list, or who were receiving support from occupational health). In these studies, some quite substantial ES figures can be found, suggesting that people who are in work may have a range of potential sources of support and assistance available to them at the point when they experience stress or other psychological problems. The existence of significant levels of change in employees who do not receive counselling underscores the need for further randomised trials to be carried out, in which the differential impact of counselling (over and above the effect of other sources of support) can be determined.

Further discussion of the methodological issues involved in outcome studies of this kind is provided in Chapter 6.

The assessment of change in psychological functioning in workplace counselling research: issues and recommendations

This review of research into the effect of workplace counselling on psychological difficulties reveals a number of methodological

Table 2. Effect Sizes in comparison groups of employees not receiving counselling

Author(s)	Date	Outcome variable	Effect Size
Cooper and Sadri	1999	Anxiety Somatic anxiety Depression Self-esteem	-0.18 (4 months) 0.10 (4 months) -0.02 (4 months) -0.23 (4 months)
Gardner et al	2005	Symptoms	1.43 (3 weeks) -0.16 (3 months)
Gersons et al	2000	Phobic anxiety Depression	0.46 (4 months) 0.10 (7 months) 0.56 (4 months) 0.37 (7 months)
Van der Klink et al	2003	Symptoms Depression	0.94 (3 months) 1.29 (12 months) 0.61 (3 months) 0.95 (12 months)
Van Dierendonck et al	1998	Emotional exhaustion Depersonalisation Personal accomplishment	-0.22 (6 months) -0.21 (12 months) -0.11 (6 months) 0.03 (12 months) -0.13 (6 months) -0.09 (12 months)

issues. The research reviewed above has utilised a range of different measurement tools, most of which were developed for research in clinical/psychiatric settings rather than for use within the field of occupational health, and which may not be sufficiently sensitive to work-related manifestations of psychological problems. It is important that future research into the psychological outcomes of workplace counselling should make more extensive use of recently developed assessment tools that may better reflect the types of psychological difficulties reported by employee clients. The Clinical Outcome Routine Evaluation Outcome Measure (CORE-OM; Evans, Mellor-Clark et al, 2000) is a 34-item scale that measures four factors: wellbeing, symptoms, functioning and risk, and has been designed around a model of psychological dysfunction that is highly relevant to work settings. The CORE-OM has already been adopted by many workplace counselling services in the UK and elsewhere. The Outcome Questionnaire (OQ-45; Lambert, Burlingame et al, 1996; Lambert and Finch, 1999) is a 45-item scale that has been designed to assess client progress in therapy, and is being extensively used by EAPs in the USA. In future years, analysis of practice-based data generated by practitioners and EAPs using each of the questionnaires has the potential to create a much more substantial evidence base for the effectiveness of workplace counselling in relation to psychological problems. Another scale that may play a valuable role in future workplace counselling research is the Four-dimensional Symptom Questionnaire (4DSQ; Terluin, van Rhenen, Schaufeli and de Haan, 2004). This questionnaire has been designed on the basis of a model that makes an important distinction between work-related stress and clinical levels of mental health difficulties. Finally, the Outcome Rating Scale (ORS; Miller, Duncan, Brown, Sparks and Claud, 2003) is an ultra-brief measure that utilises analogue(visual) scaling and is readily integrated into routine practice.

A further methodological issue arises from the strategy of seeking to assess change in broad-based factors such as wellbeing, anxiety or depression. Given that most workplace counselling is short-term in nature, comprising eight (or fewer) sessions of counselling, it may not be realistic to expect change to occur across a whole area of functioning. Instead, the client may be looking for (and be satisfied with) change that is targeted on a specific problem area. The Personal Questionnaire (Phillips, 1986) and the Target Complaint Rating method (Deane, Spicer and Todd, 1997) invite clients to describe their problems and goals for therapy, and rate their severity. This approach therefore tracks change in a way that is maximally sensitive to the therapeutic agenda of each client.

The majority of outcome studies identified in the current review have evaluated change in terms of statistically significant differences between pre-counselling and post-counselling scores. Very few studies have attempted to analyse and report the proportion of clients who have demonstrated clinically significant change (ie have recovered). This means that, although several studies have found that workplace counselling has a significant impact on wellbeing, stress and depression, most of the clients in these studies remain relatively unwell (ie with scores higher than those in the 'normal' population) at the end of counselling. It is important to keep this point in perspective. Statistically significant change is undoubtedly a welcome result, because it indicates that people have been helped. However, if studies were routinely to report on all three indices (statistically significant change, reliable change and clinically significant change), it would be easier for consumers and policy-makers to understand just what was being delivered by workplace counselling, and what was not. For example, analysis along these lines has shown in other areas of psychotherapy (Lambert and Ogles, 2004) that while brief (less than eight sessions) psychotherapy or counselling is beneficial to people, it generally requires 12 or more sessions for at least half of the client group to achieve 'recovery'.

A final methodological point that can be made is that, on the whole, the studies reviewed in this chapter (and, indeed, in the current report as a whole) have not addressed hypotheses that are derived from specific theories of work stress. Most of the studies have looked only at the effect of counselling on generic factors, ie 'psychological distress' factors such as symptoms, anxiety, low self-esteem and depression.

Three studies demonstrate the value of basing research on more fine-grained theoretical formulations: Shapiro and Firth (1987; Sheffield I Study) explored a model of the relationship between emotional change and work functioning; Salmela-Aro, Naatanen and Nurmi (2004) evaluated the effectiveness of a group therapy intervention for burnout in professional workers; Van der Klink, Blonk, Schene and van Djik (2003) evaluated a therapy package specifically designed to meet the needs of a group of workers suffering from occupational post-traumatic stress disorder. What these theoretically informed studies make possible, in ways that are beyond the scope of this review to discuss in detail, is an exploration of the ways in which specific therapeutic strategies, techniques and methods interact with specific kinds of emotional, cognitive and behavioural problems. These studies have the potential, therefore, not only to yield information about effectiveness, but to provide pointers as to how workplace counselling can best be tailored to the needs of specific groups of clients.

The impact of counselling on the meaning of work

It seems reasonable to assume that workplace counselling might have a positive impact on the meaning of work, in terms of variables such as job satisfaction, motivation, relationships with colleagues, perceptions of the organisation as a source of stress and organisational commitment. Some people who seek counselling clearly do so because they have difficulties with co-workers, managers or organisational demands. Other people, who seek counselling primarily for reasons allied to family and personal issues, may nevertheless experience themselves as detached and alienated from their work, and may as a result feel more positive about their jobs if counselling is successful. Three studies have found a positive impact of counselling on attitudes to work: Gray-Toft (1980; low-quality study); Shapiro and Firth (1987; Sheffield Psychotherapy Project I; high-quality study); Shapiro, Barkham, Hardy and Morrison (1990; Sheffield Psychotherapy Project II; high-quality study). However, six studies have reported no effect of counselling on attitudes to work: high-quality studies are Cooper and Sadri (1991); Guppy and Marsden (1997; Iwi et al (1998); and Reynolds (1997); low-quality studies are Highley-Marchington and Cooper (1998); Mitchie (1997). It is important to note that all of the studies that reported no relationship between counselling and change in work attitudes but did report positive outcomes in respect of client satisfaction, and (with the exception of Iwi et al, 1998) positive shifts in psychological symptoms. It was definitely not the case that these studies represented situations where clients felt that counselling was ineffective across the board. How, then, can the discrepancy between studies that found an effect of counselling on work attitudes, and those that did not, be explained? To answer this question, it is necessary to look more closely at the three positive outcome studies. The Gray-Toft (1980) study was a small-scale investigation that was not typical, in terms of the type of counselling that was provided, and there is reason to believe that data was collected in a way that may have influenced participants to bias their answers in the direction of positive results (see entry in Appendix A). The two Sheffield studies, by contrast, were carried out with a high degree of scientific rigour. However, these were based in a university unit that specialised in research on work behaviour. The clients in these studies were screened and selected to include only those whose problems had an impact on their work. This inclusion criterion tended to skew the sample of clients in the direction of those who were more likely to have work-related problems (rather than personal and family problems), and therefore to create a sample in which there was more opportunity to demonstrate change in work attitudes. By contrast, in some of the studies that failed to show a link

between counselling and work attitudes, only a minority of clients deemed their problems to have a substantial work component.

Overall, therefore, it would appear that workplace counselling has the potential to facilitate constructive change in work attitudes (as demonstrated in the two Sheffield studies), but that, in the majority of studies, clients do not report a sufficient severity of work attitude dysfunction for change in this factor to be a goal of counselling or a measurable outcome.

One of the difficulties within the domain of such research is that the instruments used to measure different aspects of the meaning of work have been lengthy questionnaires originally devised for organisational research, rather than as counselling outcome measures. These measures may be relatively insensitive to change, and also perhaps too detailed and time-consuming for inclusion in counselling studies. Two measures that have been recently developed for workplace counselling research may represent a way forward in this respect: the Satisfaction with Organisation Scale (SOS; Kimball et al, 2002) and the generic job satisfaction scale (Macdonald and MacIntyre, 1997).

The impact of counselling on work behaviour

From the perspective of organisational stakeholders, such as managers and Human Resource professionals, the capacity of workplace counselling to have a beneficial effect on work behaviour is a key criterion in establishing the value of this kind of service, because it opens up the possibility that the availability and utilisation of counselling may be associated with cost savings. One of the areas of work behaviour extensively studied is employee absence from work. There seems to be wide agreement that a substantial proportion of episodes of sickness absence can be attributed to work stress, and that the length of absences primarily attributable to physical illness may be extended if there are stress factors involved. Several studies have found that participation in counselling has resulted in reduced sickness absence: Blaze-Temple and Howat (1997); Bruhnsen (1989); Chandler, Kroeker, Fynn and MacDonald (1988); Cooper and Sadri (1991); Gam, Sauser, Evans and Lair (1986); Gersons, Carlier, Lamberts and van der Kolk (2000); Goss and Mearns (1997); Guppy and Marsden (1997); Highley-Marchington and Cooper (1998); Mitchie (1997); Nadolski and Sandonato (1987); Rost et al (2004); Rost et al (2005); Selvik, Stephenson, Plaza and Sugden (2004), Van Dierendonck, Schaufeli and Buunk (1998) and Van der Klink, Blonk, Schene and van Djik (2003). These studies have generally found that sickness absence rates in employees seeking counselling have been much higher than rates in comparison samples of employees in the months prior to entering counselling. Typically, counselling reduces sickness absence by 20% to 60%, with these gains being maintained over a one-year period. However, even after counselling, the sickness absence rates of the client population remain slightly higher than those of other employees.

One study reported mixed findings with respect to sickness absence. Saroja (1997) found a decrease in short-term absences (less than seven days), alongside an increase in long-term absences (seven or more days) in those who had received counselling. Three studies found that counselling made no difference to sickness absence rates: Macdonald, Lothian and Wells (1997); Macdonald, Wells, Lothian and Shain (2000); Reynolds (1997). These four studies were carefully conducted, and their findings raise questions for any claim that counselling has a straightforward effect on absence rates. The Saroja (1997) study was carried out in an industry with a pattern of seasonal differences in sickness absence, which made the findings of that investigation difficult to interpret. The Macdonald, Lothian and Wells (1997) study was based on an

EAP in a transportation company, in which it appeared that a significant proportion of absences might have been due to accidents (and therefore not readily affected by counselling interventions). The Reynolds (1997) study comprised a special project, set up for a limited period of time in an organisation undergoing high levels of change (and therefore stress). It may have been that the short-term and transient nature of this counselling intervention prevented the highly positive psychological outcomes reported by clients being followed through into sustained shifts in sickness absence.

It seems reasonable to conclude, taking all of the studies listed above into consideration, that workplace counselling does have a significant effect on sickness absence rates, but that a range of contextual factors may attenuate the magnitude of this effect. For example, there are important cultural and economic factors (eg the structure of sickness benefit arrangements) that influence the decision of an individual to take time off work. In addition, attendance at work may not necessarily be an indicator of personal wellbeing if the person is in fact unwell but remains at his or her job. It would be valuable if further research was carried out on this topic, in which sickness absence episodes were classified not only in terms of duration, but also in terms of the meaning of the absence for the employee (see Chadwick-Jones, Nicholson and Brown, 1982). Such a research strategy might make it possible to identify more of the contextual factors that mediate between counselling and absence from work, and clarify the precise role of counselling in relation to this aspect of work behaviour.

Research has been carried out into the effect of workplace counselling on other aspects of work behaviour, such as staff retention, productivity and frequency of accidents. A significant impact of counselling on staff retention has been reported by Blaze-Temple and Howat (1997), Gam, Sauser, Evans and Lair (1987), and Gray-Toft (1980). Reductions in accidents were found by Chandler, Kroeker, Fynn and MacDonald (1998), and Nadolski and Sandonato (1987) and in staff assaults by Flannery (2001). Reductions in the number of disciplinary cases were found by Gam, Sauser, Evans and Lair (1987) and Nadolski and Sandonato (1987). Improved self-rating of work performance have been reported by Macdonald, Lothian and Wells (1997), Park (1992), Philips (2004), Rost, Smith and Dickinson (2004) and Selvik, Stephenson, Plaza and Sugden (2004). However, no change in self-rated work performance, following counselling, was found in a study by Mitchie (1997). Improvements in supervisor-rated work performance have been reported by Guppy and Marsden (1997), Hiatt, Hargrave and Palmertree (1999), and Nadolski and Sandonato (1987). Improvement in counsellor-rated work performance was reported by Preece et al (2005).

The importance of research into the relationship between engagement in counselling and work behaviour lies in the fact that work behaviour represents an outcome that is objectively measurable through third-party ratings and personnel records, and that has direct economic benefits to both the employee and the organisation. The research that has been reviewed shows that counselling has a consistent and significant impact on important dimensions of work behaviour.

The relationship between the type of counselling and outcome

The outcome studies reviewed in this report provide evidence for the effectiveness of the use of a variety of different approaches to counselling in work settings:

■ cognitive therapy: Gardner, Rose, Mason, Tyler and Cushway (2005);

■ cognitive-behavioural therapy (CBT): Grime (2004); Mitchie (1997); Reynolds (1997); Shapiro and Firth (1987), Shapiro, Barkham, Hardy and Morrison (1990); Barkham, Shapiro, Hardy and Rees (1999); Van Dierendonck, Schaufeli and Buunk (1998); Van der Klink, Blonk, Schene and van Djik (2003);

■ integrative: Gersons, Carlier, Lamberts and van der Kolk (2000);

■ person-centred/experiential: Cooper and Sadri (1991); Goss and Mearns (1997); Salmela-Aro, Naatanen and Nurmi (2004);

■ psychodynamic: Barkham, Shapiro, Hardy and Rees (1999); Shapiro and Firth (1987); Shapiro, Barkham, Hardy and Morrison (1990); Salmela-Aro, Naatanen and Nurmi (2004);

■ rational-emotive therapy: Klarreich, DiGiuseppe and DiMattia (1987);

■ solution-focused: Reese, Conoley and Brossart (2002); Sprang (1992).

However, it needs to be noted that the majority of outcome studies, particularly those that were based in naturalistic practice-based research on EAPs, did not specify the approach to counselling that was used, presumably because several counsellors were involved, each of whom espoused different theoretical models, or employed their own unique integrative/eclectic approaches. The small number of studies that reported the use of specific theoretical approaches, combined with the diversity of client populations included in these studies, means that it is not possible at this time to estimate the relative effectiveness of competing theoretical approaches within the field of workplace counselling. It is of some interest, however, that the study that reported by far the highest rate of effectiveness (Gersons, Carlier, Lamberts and van der Kolk, 2000) developed a treatment package that was designed to meet the needs of a specific group of clients, and which drew upon several theoretical traditions.

The impact of the length of counselling on outcome

One of the distinctive features of workplace counselling, in contrast to some other fields of counselling and psychotherapy, is the limited number of sessions that are offered to clients. The research reviewed in the current report indicates that successful outcomes have been achieved across a wide spectrum of number of sessions:

■ three sessions: Barkham, Shapiro, Hardy and Rees (1999); Mitchie (1997); Reese, Conoley and Brossart (2002); Reynolds (1997); Shakespeare-Finch and Scully (2004);

■ four sessions: Cooper and Sadri (1991); Klarreich, DiGiuseppe and DiMattia (1987);

■ five sessions: Macdonald, Lothian and Wells (1997); Van der Klink, Blonk, Schene and van Djik (2003); Vermeersch, Lambert and Burlingame (2000);

■ six sessions: Rogers, McLeod and Sloboda (1995); Sloboda et al (1993);

■ seven sessions: Rost, Fortney and Coyne (2005);

■ eight-10 sessions: Gardner et al (2005; hours of group therapy); Gray-Toft (1980); Grime (2004); Selvik, Stephenson, Plaza and Sugden (2004); Shapiro, Barkham, Hardy and Morrison (1990);

- 16 sessions: Gersons et al (2000); Shapiro and Firth (1987); Shapiro, Barkham Hardy and Morrison (1990); Van Dierendonck, Schaufeli and Buunk (1998: hours of group therapy);

- long-term: Salmela-Aro, Naatanen and Nurmi (2004).

These findings reinforce a general trend found in health and educational settings, that there is an expectation that effective counselling should take place within a relatively brief number of sessions. This pattern has potentially significant practical implications, in terms of client wellbeing. In a large-scale study by Lambert, Hansen and Finch (2001), it was found that, while some improvement was visible in clients who had received seven sessions of EAP counselling, clinically significant change was only apparent in those who had received 14 sessions or more. The question of duration of treatment reflects an underlying debate around the purpose of workplace counselling. If the aim is to enable some level of problem resolution, commensurate with an acceptable level of work functioning and attendance, then around six to eight sessions may be sufficient, particularly if employees are able to make use of the service on future occasions if a problem should reoccur. If, on the other hand, the aim is to provide employees with an opportunity to deal with deep-rooted difficulties, then at least 12 sessions will be necessary. In this context, it is of some interest to consider the policies on session limits imposed by EAPs and other workplace counselling providers. In a survey of EAPs in Canada, Csiernik (2002) found that the average number of sessions taken up by employee clients was five, regardless of whether the organisation placed a cap on the number of sessions or not.

Quality of service delivery

An important strategy for evaluating the effectiveness of workplace counselling provision is to use standardised quality-assurance benchmarks, agreed within the profession, as a tool for estimating the performance of specific EAP or in-house counselling services. The advantages of this method are that it takes a holistic approach to evaluation rather than relying on a narrow range of outcome measures, and that it can be carried out using routine data that is collected by a counselling service rather than requiring additional information to be obtained, stored and analysed. Within the current literature, different approaches to quality assessment have been described. Courtois et al (2004) have reported on the establishment of a set of performance indicators developed through a broad-based consensus exercise carried out within a leading EAP professional body in the USA. These indicators cover a broad set of domains, ranging from the length of time it should take to answer a phone call to the proportion of substance abuse cases that would normally be expected within a service. At this time, however, no studies have been published that reflect the use of these indicators in practice. Masi et al (2000) have published an overview of a set of evaluation procedures that involves an eight-step clinical review process, carried out by independent expert clinicians on a random selection of case files, using a standard protocol. Masi et al provide an analysis of the use of this system with a large sample of external EAP providers, in which it was found that the level of overall documentation in clinical files was generally poor, and that client assessment protocols were systematically under-detecting or under-recording alcohol and drug problems, and psychiatric symptomatology. Finally, in the UK, the *Clinical Outcomes in Routine Evaluation* (CORE) information management system (Evans et al, 2000; www.coreims.co.uk) has been widely adopted by workplace counselling services in recent years, although no studies utilising this quality-assessment system have been reported

yet. In future, it is likely that benchmarking and performance indicator methodologies will become more widely used, and will generate research knowledge that will make a significant contribution within the field of workplace counselling (see Barkham et al, 2006; Mellor-Clark et al, 2006).

The nature and severity of presenting problems reported by users of workplace counselling

An understanding of the research findings on the outcomes of workplace counselling needs to take into account the context of this type of intervention, in relation to the type and severity of problems presented by clients. A number of UK studies have analysed the intake characteristics of workplace counselling clients, in the area of severity and chronicity of mental health difficulties, in comparison with population norms (Arthur, 2002; Cooper and Sadri, 1991; Gardner et al, 2005; Shapiro and Firth, 1987). Vermeersch, Lambert and Burlingame (2000) carried out a similar study in the USA. These studies have found that 70–80% of clients report mental health problems as severe as those who make use of psychiatric and clinical psychology services in contrast to a 25–30% rate of psychiatric 'caseness' within the general employed population. In addition, more than half of clients report their problems as having lasted for six months or longer. Problems are mainly personal or family-based in nature, with no more than 30% of clients reporting problems that are primarily work-based. The majority of clients believe that their problems affect their capacity to carry out their work duties. In addition, users of workplace counselling services are more likely to be absent from work on health grounds than their colleagues who do not seek counselling (see separate section of this chapter for a review of studies of sickness absence). It is essential to acknowledge that the evidence on this topic is limited in important respects – the studies by Gardner et al (2005) and Shapiro and Firth (1987) reflect special counselling services set up for the purposes of research, and therefore may not wholly reflect the client mix of routine services. Also, interpretation of the studies by Arthur (2002) and Cooper and Sadri (1991) is complicated by the fact that many clients chose not to complete start-of-counselling questionnaires. (The Vermeesch et al (2000) study is based on a somewhat more robust data-set in terms of levels of client compliance with research requirements.) It is clear that further research into the issue of client severity is urgently required. Nevertheless, the evidence that is currently available implies that many of those who seek workplace counselling tend to have moderate to severe problems that encompass complex personal issues of some duration. Research into the effectiveness of counselling and psychotherapy as a whole tends to suggest that, in contrast to the average six to eight (or fewer) sessions of counselling available to users of workplace counselling, a figure in the region of 12–20 sessions is necessary in order to address more severe problems in a way that produces enduring benefits (Lambert and Ogles, 2004). The apparent discrepancy between the 'dose' of therapy that seems to be necessary for clients seen in workplace agencies and the length of therapy that is required in other clinical settings, may be due to a number of factors, all of which require further research. It may be that the ready availability of workplace services allows clients to be seen earlier. Alternatively, it may be that those using workplace counselling may be helped in the short term, but this leads to early relapse and recurrence of problems at a future date.

The issue of negative outcomes

The general impression that is gained from research into the outcomes of workplace counselling is that this form of help is largely beneficial for those who make use of it. Within the broader field of counselling and psychotherapy research, however, it has been established that 5–10% of those who receive therapy report deteriorations in their condition over the course of treatment (Lambert and Ogles, 2004). In response to these findings, a number of projects have been established to develop ways of detecting potential therapy 'casualties', and implementing enhanced interventions that might prevent deterioration – for example, by changing the focus of treatment, or referral to in-patient services (Lambert, 2005). In the context of these concerns, it is notable that none of the studies of the outcomes of workplace counselling included in this review have provided an estimate of the proportion of negative outcomes in their samples of cases. It seems likely that deterioration effects do occur in workplace counselling settings – for example, one study not included in this review (an unpublished study by Worrall, 2005) found a negative outcome rate of 8% in a large sample of clients receiving counselling from a UK employee counselling service. The absence of greater attention to negative outcomes represents a serious gap in the workplace counselling literature. Given the substantial proportion of workplace counselling clients who have high levels of mental health difficulties (Arthur, 2000), it is not credible that all of these individuals will be appropriate for the type of short-term focused counselling on offer in the majority of workplace counselling services. Even if counselling services are effective in making referrals on to other agencies, for these clients, it seems very likely that at least some of them will get worse (ie during counselling) before they get better. It may be that negative outcome is an issue that is particularly sensitive within the workplace counselling arena, a field that has been heavily influenced by concerns about confidentiality (on the part of users), commercial competition (on the part of providers) and the desire of organisations to underplay the levels of stress experienced by their staff. More consistent reporting of negative outcomes, and of the effectiveness of interventions designed to minimise this category of outcome, should be a priority for future research in this area.

Conclusions

It is essential to examine the possibility that more methodologically rigorous studies may produce less favourable results, compared with less rigorous naturalistic studies, which could be seen as providing a biased and over-optimistic estimate of outcome. In this chapter, wherever possible, a distinction has been made between evidence that is based on studies of higher methodological quality and those of lower quality. However, there is no evidence that the level of benefit to clients reported in studies is associated with degree of rigour. For example, among the group of studies that employed the scientifically highly rigorous method of randomised comparison across groups receiving different types of counselling, Shapiro et al (1992) reported the largest positive outcome for counselling, while Iwi et al (1998) reported the lowest. There have been only two studies that have randomly assigned clients seeking help to either counselling or to an alternative non-counselling control condition. This kind of study provides the most rigorous test of the efficacy of workplace counselling, since it enables researchers to conclude with confidence that differences between clients at follow-up could only be due to counselling, and not to any other factor. Iwi et al (1998) randomised clients into counselling or a waiting list condition, while Reynolds (1997) allocated groups of staff to counselling, an organisational intervention or no intervention. In the Iwi et al (1998) study, the randomisation broke down. In Reynolds (1997), the counselling intervention was shown to be much more beneficial than the alternative stress-management

condition. Clearly, there is a need for more studies of this kind. However, as will be discussed in Chapter 6, there are major practical and ethical difficulties associated with this type of research design.

All of the outcome studies reviewed in this chapter have been methodologically flawed in some way. The studies that have used randomised, controlled designs have employed counselling interventions that are not typical of everyday practice, and have tended to recruit highly selected samples of clients. While logically robust, the results of these studies may not generalise to routine practice. By contrast, while naturalistic or practice-based studies may closely mirror the conditions of routine practice, the fact that a high proportion of clients in these studies do not complete questionnaires, and the difficulties in specifying the type(s) of intervention that were provided, and in what circumstances, makes interpretation of findings problematic. The particular methodological questions raised by specific studies are outlined in the summaries available in the Appendix to this report.

Despite these methodological issues, which have been identified in all reviews of research into workplace counselling (see Chapter 1 for an analysis of previous reviews), it seems reasonable to conclude that there is convincing evidence to support the claim that workplace counselling represents an effective means of assisting employees to cope with psychological, emotional and behavioural problems, and that the successful resolution of these issues can have a constructive impact on work behaviour, in terms of reduced sickness absence and enhanced work functioning. The evidence suggests that, for the most part, these gains are most apparent in the short term, and may not persist over time periods of longer than one year. There is ambiguous evidence in respect of the effect of counselling on job satisfaction and organisational commitment. It appears that while workplace counselling may have an impact on these factors for some clients, there are many (perhaps the majority) of clients who do not initially present with deficits or issues in these areas. The workplace counselling outcome research suggests that a range of therapy approaches and treatment lengths may be effective. However, the research base is not sufficiently extensive to determine whether different approaches, numbers of sessions or models of service delivery (eg external EAP vs. in-house service) are associated with differential levels of effectiveness. Finally, it seems clear that most of the people who seek help from workplace counsellors present with problems of substantial severity and duration – there is a significant overlap between the problem profiles of workplace counselling services and those who attend clinical psychology or community mental health services.

The conclusions reached in the present chapter reinforce the findings and recommendations of previous reviews of research into the effectiveness of workplace counselling (see Chapter 1), in supporting the value of counselling interventions for a range of psychological, behavioural and mental health difficulties in employees. However, the current review differs from Reynolds (2000), Van der Klink et al (2001) and BOHRF (2005) in finding no differential effectiveness for interventions based on cognitive-behaviour therapy (CBT) principles. While the current review identified a number of studies that provided good evidence for the effectiveness of CBT, it also found studies that reported equivalent effectiveness for a number of other therapy approaches. The current review also differs from BOHRF (2005) in finding that counselling is effective not only for employees with high levels of job control, but also for employees engaged in manual and clerical roles. This difference can be attributed to the larger number of studies included in the present review.

Chapter 3. The economic costs and benefits of workplace counselling

The provision of workplace counselling and EAP services is not part of the core business of employers and companies. The availability of these services to employees is a *cost* to an employer, to be set against income and profits. The cost of an EAP needs to be balanced against other Human Resource costs, such as occupational health, personnel, training and so on. The question of EAP/counselling costs is made even more acute by the competition that exists to provide counselling programmes and the alternative models of service delivery (internal, external, mixed) that are on offer. The economic dimension of offering EAP/counselling to employees has therefore been a major issue within the research literature. There are different kinds of economic analysis that can be carried out in relation to the provision of counselling (Tolley and Rowland, 1995), for example cost-effectiveness, cost-benefit, cost-utility and a large array of complex issues associated with the collection of reliable and valid economic data. One of the central themes in economic research into workplace counselling, as in other forms of counselling and psychotherapy, therefore concerns the construction of appropriate methods for arriving at acceptable economic estimates of the costs and benefits of therapy.

The recognition given by management to the economic valuation of EAPs is reflected in a survey of EAP directors in the USA conducted by Houts (1991). The majority (83%) of these respondents believed that cost saving represented an important criterion on which to evaluate EAP performance, with 98% believing that the cost-savings potential of their EAP was 'moderate' or 'high'. However, only 40% actually collected cost-savings data, most commonly referring to absenteeism, accidents, costs of medical and insurance services, sick leave, disciplinary action, training costs, lost productivity and grievance costs.

The workplace counselling literature is replete with articles claiming substantial cost-effectiveness of EAPs. The majority of articles are in professional journals and company reports, provide little information regarding the methodologies that have been applied in determining cost-effectiveness, and have not been subjected to a process of peer review. These articles are not included in the present review. A study by Hargrave and Hiatt (2004) is included in the review, but cannot be regarded as providing a reliable economic analysis, because it extrapolates from changes in wellbeing/symptom ratings, using a number of assumptions about the putative relationship between symptom levels and work productivity rather than being based on any kind of direct economic evidence.

There have been six published studies that are based on analysis of economic data. The key findings of these studies are briefly summarised below:

Blaze-Temple and Howat (1997) reported that an EAP produced significant costs savings in absenteeism and turnover – the cost-benefit ratio for counselling compared with no counselling was 1:1 (ie the EAP paid for itself). However, this study also included data on employees who arranged their own counselling/psychotherapy, independent of the organisation. It was found that self-arranged counselling produced a higher cost-benefit ratio for this company than EAP counselling.

Bray, French, Bowland and Dunlap (1996) reviewed economic data relating to EAPs across a range of organisations. Higher utilisation rates were consistently associated with higher costs per employee. They found that EAPs have different cost mixes while arriving at the same overall cost (eg in one site, 70% of costs were spent on personnel; in another site, personnel accounted for 36% of costs). In this study, internal EAPs were more costly than external provision (but had higher utilisation rates).

Bruhnsen (1989) collected economic data on employees for six months pre-EAP consultation and six months post-consultation. A cost:benefit saving ratio was calculated at 1.5:1.

Dainas and Marks (2000) compared costs in employees/family members who had used an EAP and those who had not. Those who had used the EAP were associated with higher mental health costs, but lower general medical costs and lower overall healthcare costs. An overall 2:1 cost saving was reported in favour of EAP availability.

Klarreich, DiGiuseppe and DiMattia (1997) carried out an economic analysis based on absenteeism and cost of supervisor time saved in dealing with troubled employees. A cost-benefit ratio calculated at 2.74:1.

McClellan (1989) in a careful study of the costs and benefits associated with an EAP, these researchers concluded that it was cost-effective as an *employee* benefit: therapeutic services are delivered, which employees regard highly, at a reasonable cost. However, the EAP did not produce a financial benefit to the *employer*: no plausible cost offsets could be identified in such areas as health insurance costs, paid sick leave, productivity improvements or employee turnover.

Findings of economic studies: issues and conclusions

Only a limited amount of research into the economic costs and benefits of workplace counselling has been carried out. This kind of study is technically time-consuming and complex, requiring high levels of co-operation from the organisations being studied. While there is not enough evidence to draw firm conclusions, it is nevertheless possible to make some tentative suggestions about the main trends that appear to emerge from this body of work:

- there appears to be the basis for a robust methodology for carrying out economic analyses, exemplified in the work of Blaze-Temple and Howat (1997) and McClellan (1989);

- even the most rigorous economic analyses show that workplace counselling schemes and EAPs cover their costs in terms of economic savings that are generated for employers.

There is also some preliminary evidence from Bray et al (1996) to suggest that:

- there are wide variations in costs of EAP/counselling services;

- external EAPs appear to be less costly than internal providers;

- higher cost EAPs are associated with higher utilisation rates.

A central theme in the workplace counselling literature, which certainly requires further research, concerns the issue of whether an EAP or counselling service becomes *more* cost-effective over time – for example, as utilisation and self-referral rates increase, and employees develop greater trust in the confidentiality and effectiveness of the counselling that is on offer. It is also worth noting that there have been no studies of the costs of closing down an EAP or reducing the level of services that are provided – when an EAP has closed down, are immediate increased costs apparent within an organisation, in respect of sickness absence, staff turnover and decreased productivity?

The main underlying issue, in relation to studies of the economic costs and benefits of workplace counselling, is the question of why it is that so little research on this key topic has been published? Within the broader field of counselling and psychotherapy research, there exists a growing appreciation of the necessity for economic analyses, and a well-established body of knowledge regarding methods of undertaking this kind of research (see, for example, Miller and Magruder, 1999; Tolley and Rowland, 1995). The absence of published studies of the cost-effectiveness of workplace counselling may be due to the fact that such studies are highly commercially sensitive, within the competitive environment of EAP provision. If this is the case, then it is to be hoped that, at some point, organisations involved in purchasing counselling services will realise that it is in their interest to sponsor rigorous economic research, suitable for publication through a peer review process of quality control, rather than relying solely on the marketing claims of EAP provider organisations.

Chapter 4. Organisational factors in workplace counselling

Traditionally, counselling and psychotherapy have been regarded as activities that can be understood in terms of a two-way contract between client and therapist. In most forms of workplace counselling, however, there is a three-way contract, between client, therapist and the client's employer, or even a four-way contract involving client, therapist, client's employer and therapist's employer (eg an EAP provider). The introduction of these additional stakeholders into the counselling process raises important ethical issues, for example around confidentiality, responsibility and choice (Carroll, 1996; Coles, 2003; Sugarman, 1992). Beyond these issues, the organisational context of workplace counselling may influence service delivery in a variety of different ways, for instance through facilitating or impeding access to counselling, control over the number of sessions that clients may have and creating positive or negative expectations regarding the potential value of counselling. The aim of this chapter is to provide an overview of the research that has been carried out into these issues.

Counselling as a means of managerial control

There has been considerable debate around the role that employee assistance programmes and workplace counselling services play within organisations. On the one hand, those who support the provision of counselling argue that it represents a form of employee benefit, alongside other benefits such as pensions, sick pay, or access to leisure and fitness facilities. On the other hand, some sociological writers have portrayed EAPs and counselling services as part of management surveillance and control of employees. Two recent theoretical papers have developed this latter perspective (Hansen, 2004; Weiss, 2005). It remains to be seen whether conceptualising workplace counselling as a form of managerial control leads to further research and/or to the development of different types of employee support services. Current evidence regarding the meaning of counselling services for employees in organisations is far from straightforward. Surveys of employees tend to show that those working in organisations, but who have not made use of a workplace counselling service, tend to be ambivalent about the value of counselling (Butterworth, 2001; Gyllensten, Palmer and Farrants, 2005; Muscroft and Hicks, 1998; West and Reynolds, 1995). By contrast, the majority of those who have made use of such a service place a positive value on work-based counselling services (see review of client satisfaction studies in Chapter 2, above). Indeed, Basso (1989) described the existence in one organisation of a 'consumer's grapevine', through which recommendations to attend counselling were passed on from former clients to their colleagues. Research into patterns of EAP provision has found that higher utilisation rates are associated with more democratically run organisations, in which counselling services are actively supported by trade unions (Csiernik et al, 2005). Clearly, further research is required on this topic. It may be that, up to now, the voices of those who perceive counselling as an aspect of managerial control have been silenced within research, and that there is more to be known on this topic. For example, the huge sensitivity to confidentiality within workplace counselling systems could be interpreted as an index of concern over management control. An additional factor, concerning the use of counselling as a form of managerial control, related to the degree to which managers are in reality able to exert influence over counselling referrals, outcomes and data; Steele and Hubbard (1985)

found that the EAPs taking part in their survey tended to be poorly integrated with the administrative hierarchy of the organisation.

Studies of employee attitudes and utilisation

Ultimately, the most important measures of the effectiveness of workplace counselling services and EAPs concern the extent to which the programme produces direct benefits to employees and employers, around such factors as the alleviation of stress and anxiety, the development of coping strategies, reduction in sickness absence and enhanced job commitment. However, as evident in earlier chapters of this report, the collection of reliable and valid evidence of effectiveness is not an easy matter. In the absence of effectiveness data, one of the ways in which the impact of workplace counselling and EAPs can be evaluated is through collection of information on the number of eligible employees and family members who use a service each year (utilisation) and the attitudes of employees toward the service. Utilisation rates can operate as a valuable proxy indicator of effectiveness, since it seems reasonable to assume that employees will make use of a well-run and trustworthy counselling service, and avoid poorly run and unsafe services. Similarly, the quality of a service will be reflected in the attitudes employees hold toward it, for instance around their perceptions of confidentiality and competence, willingness to use the service and awareness of its existence and location. All EAPs and workplace counselling providers should routinely collect utilisation data, and workforce attitude surveys are not difficult or costly to carry out. Research into utilisation and attitudes therefore makes a valuable contribution to understanding the issue of EAP/counselling effectiveness.

A summary of published utilisation rates taken from studies reviewed in this report is presented in Table 3. One of the most striking aspects of the data lies in the diversity of utilisation rates found in the literature, which range from 0.27% to 50% of employees making use of a counselling service per annum. Including only those studies in which it was possible to unequivocally categorise the EAP/counselling as external or internal (ie omitting cases of mixed EAPs or where EAP type was not specified), it was found that the average utilisation rate for internal programmes was 6.7% and for external programmes it was 6.4%. Although the sample of programmes included is relatively small, it seems clear that there is no clear trend in the direction of higher utilisation in either external or internal programmes.

Factors influencing utilisation rates

Several studies have examined the factors associated with differences in levels of utilisation of workplace counselling. It can be concluded, on the basis of current research evidence, that women are relatively more likely to use an EAP/counselling than their male co-workers (Asen and Colon, 1995; Blum and Roman, 1992; Braun and Novak, 1986; French, Dunlap, Roman and Steele,1997; Grosch, Duffy and Hessink, 1996; Harlow, 1998; Poverny and Dodd, 2000; Whelan, Robson and Cook, 2002). Although some studies have reported gender equality in EAP/counselling use, no studies have found higher male than female utilisation. The finding that women are more likely to use counselling is unsurprising, since it reflects the broader pattern of counselling use in society as a whole. Two studies have reported higher rates of EAP utilisation in ethnic minority employees (Blum and Roman, 1992; Poverny and Dodd, 2000). There is no evidence of consistent trends regarding associations between differential EAP/counselling utilisation and other demographic characteristics, such as age,

Table 3. Workplace counselling/EAP annual utilisation rates

Author(s) of study	Type of provision	Utilisation rate
Bennett and Lehman (2001)	External	6.0%
*Bruhnsen (1989)	Internal	4.0%
*Blaze-Temple and Howat (1987)	External	4.5%
Burke (1994)	Internal	6.0%
Csiernik (1999)	Internal	7.0%
	External	5.4%
Csiernik (2003)	Both internal and external	9.2%
*Elliott and Williams (2002)	External	1.2%
*Every and Leong (1994)	Internal	7.5%
*Goss and Mearns (1997)	Internal	1.4%
French et al (1997)	Internal – Company 1	2.0%
	External – Company 2	8.0%
	Internal – Company 3	20.0%
	Internal – Company 4	6.0%
	Internal – Company 5	7.0%
	Internal – Company 6	17.0%
Gammie (1997)	External – Company B	7.8%
	External – Company C	10.0%
	External – Company D	12.4%
	External – Company E	7.2%
Grosch, Duffy and Hessink (1996)	Both internal and external	7.0%
Harlow (1987)	Internal	2.8%
	External	2.1%
Hiatt et al (1999)	External	8.0%
Keaton (1990)	Internal	3.8%
*Klarreich et al (1987)	Internal	8.0%
*Macdonald et al (1997)	Internal	5.7%
Maddocks (2000)	Internal	4.0%
*McClellan (1989)	External	6.0%
*Michie (1996)	Internal	2.5%
**Muto et al (2004)	External	0.27%
*Philips (2004)	External	4.0%
*Shakespeare-Finch and Scully (2004)	Mixed	50.0%
Whelan et al (2002)	External	6.0%
**Total: all EAP/counselling services		8.1%
Internal services		6.6%
**External services		6.4%

Notes:

(i) Studies marked * are summarised in other sections of the report. In these studies, annual utilisation data has been provided as a background to other analyses.

(ii) ** The rate reported in a Japanese study by Muto et al (2004) has not been included in the calculation of overall utilisation rates, because it represents a significantly different cultural context. The average utilisation rate for all workplace counselling services is higher than the rates for internal and external services, because the latter do not include data from the Shakespeare-Finch and Scully (2004) study, which was based on a hybrid service in which high levels of peer support and contact were incorporated into the utilisation estimate.

seniority/status, length of years in employment, marital status, level of family commitments and type of job (manual/managerial/professional). Although single studies have reported higher rates of one or another of these sub-groups, no patterns emerge across studies. This finding suggests that EAPs and workplace counselling programmes are acceptable to a broad spectrum of employees.

There is substantial evidence that EAP utilisation is influenced by organisational culture and practices. Weiss (2003) found that higher utilisation rates were associated with: written procedures, training of first-line supervisors and dissemination of information to employees. The relationship between provision of information and utilisation rate was confirmed in a study by Bennett and Lehman (2001). Delaney, Grube and Ames (1998) found that employees were more likely to use an EAP if they believed in its efficacy, and were supported and encouraged by co-workers and by supervisors to use it. In a large-scale survey of EAPs in Canada, Csiernik (2003) reported that higher utilisation rates were found in organisations that were: private sector; unionised; placed no restriction on number of sessions; published a company EAP policy; operated an annual promotion/awareness campaign; where unions had been involved in setting up the service; where the service involved the use of volunteers from within the workforce in addition to paid counsellors; where the service was staffed by social workers rather than counsellors. A study by Zarkin et al (2001) demonstrated that an active outreach leads to increased global levels of utilisation, but that it was not possible to effectively target specific employee groups that had previously under-used a service. Supervisor attitudes to counselling, and competence/confidence in handling the referral process, can also influence utilisation rates. In a review of 18 studies of supervisor referral skills, Willbanks (1999) found consistent evidence for a positive association between likelihood to refer and the following factors: familiarity with the EAP; positive attitude toward the EAP; social distance between supervisor and employee (never worked as a peer with the subordinate); existence of a supervisor network; have personally been in previous receipt of help; and training in making referrals.

The themes running through the studies on organisational factors are that higher levels of utilisation are linked to awareness of a service, trust in the service (eg around confidentiality) and active endorsement of the service by managers, supervisors and co-workers.

There are many further research questions that can be asked about utilisation rates. Not enough is known about the factors, which are associated with utilisation. For example, it would seem sensible to imagine that rates would vary over time. When a programme is initiated in an organisation, it would be reasonable to expect a slow build-up of use as employees learn about the service. Alternatively, there may be a high initial use, as unmet demand for counselling is soaked up, followed by a decline. There have been no published studies on this issue. There are many other important questions for future research to address: does utilisation vary depending on the size of the organisation? Do utilisation rates differ between urban organisations (where there might be alternative sources of mental health care) and rural firms (where alternative services are difficult to access)? Is there a link between utilisation and organisational culture? What kinds of publicity or policies are most effective in increasing utilisation? At what point does high utilisation become an indicator of an 'organisation in crisis'?

Methodological issues in research on employee utilisation of EAPs

Although a substantial number of research studies have been carried out into various aspects of employee utilisation rates,

it is essential to acknowledge that there are serious issues associated with the validity of the utilisation indices that are reported (see Amaral, 1999). A survey of EAP utilisation in 154 organisations in Canada was conducted by Csiernik (2003). The survey questionnaire included questions about not only the utilisation rate, but how it was calculated within each organisation. Analysis of survey responses revealed that 19 different formulae for calculating EAP utilisation were reported by organisations:

> '…at the present time, for research purposes, the calculation and use of utilisation rates has restricted value and may even be a futile exercise; for how this statistic is examined, it appears as if we are comparing apples with kumquats' (Csiernik, 2003, p. 54).

The main areas of divergence in estimations of utilisation concerned: (a) whether family members were counted as users, and then whether each family member or the family as a whole was treated as an individual case; and (b) the question of what counted as a recordable case – a referral, a new case, a face-to-face meeting, a telephone contact, a return visit or only a situation where an actual treatment plan had been agreed. For example, to overcome service caps (ie contractual limits of the number of counselling sessions that could be received by a client within any one calendar year), one EAP would treat a client who returned within a year with two different problems as two cases; another EAP stated that after every 12 hours of counselling, it considered the situation as a new case. These issues are discussed in detail by Csiernik (2003), who makes a carefully argued proposal for a standardised approach to assessing two key variables: *utilisation rate* and *penetration rate*. The concept of penetration rate is defined as 'the depth of EAP involvement in the organisation', and incorporates data on number of referrals, telephone inquiries, participants in educational workshops/seminars, mediation sessions, debriefing, group sessions, and family members, retirees and employees using counselling. A framework is provided for a standard 'EAP utilisation scorecard', that encompasses these factors. Adopting the protocols published by Csiernik (2003) for estimating annual utilisation and penetration rates would make it possible to analyse the effect of demographic and organisational factors on utilisation with greater precision. It would also open up new possibilities for modelling the interactions between these variables across large data sets.

Employee attitudes to counselling

Research into employee attitudes to workplace counselling provides an estimate of the extent to which employees value a counselling service. This information complements data on utilisation rates, because while the former may be affected by practical considerations such as the staffing levels of a counselling service (it may not be worth even trying to make an appointment if it is known that there are long waiting lists), attitudes may be taken as reflecting an underlying positive or negative stance in relation to a service.

Research into employee attitudes has encompassed the following areas:

- awareness of EAP/counselling provision;
- likelihood to use services in the future;
- perceptions of those who use counselling;
- likelihood to refer or recommend service to co-workers;
- attitudes to counselling in general;
- perceptions of management attitudes to counselling;
- images of counsellors;

- perceptions of counsellor effectiveness, confidentiality and potential job threat;
- attitudes to EAP/counselling location.

The key study in this area was carried out by West and Reynolds (1995) in a hospital trust in the UK. They found that although attitudes to counselling were generally positive, attitudes to workplace counselling were somewhat less positive. Attitudes to those seeking counselling were neutral or negative. Counsellors were perceived as trustworthy but low in competence. There were low levels of awareness of the counselling service in this employee sample, and concerns about confidentiality. The questionnaire developed by West and Reynolds (1995) represents an invaluable tool for future researchers in this area. In other studies of attitudes to counselling, Butterworth (2001) and Gyllensten, Palmer and Farrants (2005) found a significant degree of stigma associated with going to a counsellor, and doubts over the effectiveness of counselling. Harlow (1998) found that women were more likely than men to believe that the EAP was useful. A unique study by Trubshaw and Dollard (2001) analysed the ways in which negative stereotypes of counselling were conveyed in the annual reports of an Australian public hospital.

Research into organisational factors in workplace counselling: issues and conclusions

Research into the role of organisational factors in workplace counselling has the potential to yield insights that could allow for a better fit between different forms of counselling service delivery and organisational structure and culture. At present, however, despite the existence of some valuable research studies, the methods for assessing key variables, such as attitudes to counselling, utilisation and penetration, have not been sufficiently developed to enable findings to be accumulated across a series of studies in a manner that would support generalisation. Moreover, there is an absence of relevant theoretical frameworks that might be used to guide further work in this area.

Chapter 5. The process of workplace counselling

In the field of counselling and psychotherapy research as a whole, the single most important research question has been: 'does it work?' The issue of effectiveness has dominated the research agenda for over 50 years. More recently, however, the counselling and psychotherapy research community has started to devote more attention to the question of process: 'how does it work?' A wide range of 'process' factors have been examined in research studies, including the use of specific therapeutic interventions such as empathic reflection, challenging, interpretation and homework assignments, the structuring of therapy through the use of time limits or contracting, and the impact of a variety of therapist and client factors (eg gender, age, and training). Despite the general importance of process research, in providing deeper understandings of what happens in effective therapy, very little process research has been carried out within the employee counselling domain. The aim of this chapter is to provide illustrative examples of the type of process research that has been published and make some suggestions for future work.

A landmark employee counselling process study was carried out by Butterfield and Borgen (2005), who interviewed clients about their experiences of outplacement counselling. In open-ended qualitative interviews, participants were asked to describe critical incidents relating to their satisfaction with outplacement counselling they had received, and their 'wish list' for how the service might have been improved. Categories derived from these data were analysed using a systematic method of qualitative analysis. The key themes emerging from participants' accounts were: the quality of their relationship with the outplacement counsellor; the need for counselling to be more tailored to their individual needs; space to deal with emotion/transition issues; and the poor clinical skills of some counsellors. Informants also made a large number of suggestions about ways in which the service they had received might have been improved. This study provides an example of the way in which process research can be used to generate knowledge that can directly enhance the effectiveness and responsiveness of services.

In recent years, increasing recognition has been given to the role of systematic case study research as a means of exploring complex, interconnected processes that occur within therapy. In the field of workplace counselling, systematic case studies have been published by Anderson (2003), Bayer (1998), Burwell and Chen (2002), Firth-Cozens (1992), Jenkins and Palmer (2003), Parry, Shapiro and Firth (1986), Potter (2002) and Sperry (1996). These cases encompass a wide range of presenting problems and therapeutic intervention strategies. Two common themes are apparent across all the cases. First, it is clear that work stress issues and personal/domestic/life history issues are inextricably interwoven in each case. Second, no matter which therapeutic orientation has been utilised, the therapist in each case has worked with the client to identify and work through an agreed central focus. The publication of more systematic case studies in workplace counselling would represent an invaluable resource for practitioners and trainers, and would also allow cross-case analyses to be carried out that addressed process questions.

Another process research topic that has been explored in some detail in the mainstream counselling and psychotherapy research literature concerns the characteristics of counsellors (eg their training, experience level and supervision) that may be associated with effectiveness. Research studies have shown, for example, that there can be marked differences between individual counsellors, but that neither experience level nor training appear to be significant factors in determining counsellor effectiveness (Christensen and Jacobson, 1994). There has also been research into the question of whether adherence to a fixed protocol or 'manual' contributes to effective outcomes, in contrast to adopting a more eclectic approach to working with clients. To date, the evidence around the utility of protocol/manualised approaches is inconclusive, with some studies suggesting that the use of manuals enables counsellors to be consistent in their use of best practice, with other studies indicating that manuals can stifle counsellor responsiveness and creativity (McLeod, 2003: 136–7). It is surprising, given the investment that both EAPs and in-house workplace counselling services make in recruiting and retaining good quality counselling staff, that there has been so little research into the role of counsellor characteristics in workplace counselling. Studies by Csiernik (2002), Highley-Marchington and Cooper (1998) and Kirk-Brown and Wallace (2004) have found that the majority of counselling providers will only employ counsellors who possess advanced qualifications and experience, but that these practitioners are drawn from a variety of professional backgrounds (counselling, psychology, social work, drug and alcohol work) rather than reflecting a unified or coherent professional cohort. Other studies, such as those by Finke et al (1996) and Shakespeare-Finch and Scully (2004) suggest that, in some circumstances, minimally trained peer counsellors can play an effective role within workplace counselling schemes. Another important question in this area concerns counsellors' previous experience and knowledge of their clients' work environments. For instance, it could be argued that a true appreciation of the work demands of police officers could only be acquired by having worked within the criminal justice system, and that counsellors who possessed such prior work experience would be more effective with police officer clients. However, again, there is an absence of research into this kind of issue.

A set of studies has explored aspects of the role pressures experienced by workplace counsellors. Using qualitative interview methods, Carroll (1997) found that such counsellors employed in in-house services in private sector commercial companies reported that a central challenge of their jobs was coping with competing roles and demands, and Fisher (1997) found that in-house counsellors within the UK National Health Service experienced significant challenges around understanding the organisational culture, networking and forming appropriate relationships with management. A survey by Highley-Marchington and Cooper (1998) found that workplace counsellors in the UK believed there were insufficient training opportunities available to enable them to develop essential competencies in relation to their role. A study by Cunningham (1992) found good levels of job satisfaction in workplace counsellors. This finding was reinforced by the results of a large-scale survey by Sweeney, Hohenshil and Fortune (2002), which additionally found that counsellors working for external EAPs were more satisfied with their jobs than those working for in-house services. Kirk-Brown and Wallace (2004) analysed factors that were associated with lack of job satisfaction and burnout in workplace counsellors. Their results indicated that overall levels of burnout were similar to those reported in other professions, such as social work and medicine, and that burnout in workplace counsellors was particularly associated with role ambiguity. However, counsellors who experienced their work as challenging, and who reported confidence in their knowledge of organisational procedures, had higher levels of job satisfaction.

How do users of workplace counselling decide to consult a counsellor? What are the processes and influences that lead to some employees taking up the offer of counselling, while others do not? These questions are directly relevant to the concerns of counselling providers, who may be evaluated by purchasers in terms of levels of utilisation or be faced with the problem of how best to advertise their services among groups of employees. A study by Sprang and Secret (1999) examined the ways in which employees respond to acute life events that threatened their performance at work – 61% of participants reported at least one personal crisis during their tenure with their current employer, with 30% reporting that the crisis had resulted in significant job disruption. Although 80% of these participants worked for organisations in which EAP services were available, only 7.5% utilised these services. Shortcomings in the organisational response to crisis were identified: taking time off without using sick or vacation time, and lack of emotional support from the employee's supervisor. Distinctive patterns of difficulty in dealing with crisis were found in employees of non-profit health and social care organisations. This study is of limited value in itself, because further research will need to be carried out to assess the ability to generalise its findings. Nevertheless, it illustrates the potential value of in-depth studies of help-seeking processes, as a means of developing a more detailed understanding of the decision-making context within which employees decide to seek counselling (or decide not to).

An important feature of the counselling process literature is that it encourages research into variants of routine counselling practice. Two recent studies have explored the use in counselling of different modes of contact with clients. Kurioka, Muto and Tarumi (2001) examined the acceptability and use of email counselling for employees in a Japanese manufacturing company. Employees were offered health counselling by email, telephone, ordinary mail or face-to-face contact. Email counselling was particularly popular with younger employees, and with those who had mental health issues. E-mail consultations were proportionally more likely to relate to prevention issues, compared to other methods, and more likely to refer to third parties (eg family members). Reese, Conoley and Brossart (2002) investigated client experiences around receiving telephone counselling from an EAP. Telephone counsellors were perceived as expert and trustworthy, and clients reported developing a strong bond with their counsellor.

In conclusion, it can be seen that process research plays an invaluable role in contributing to a comprehensive understanding of how workplace counselling operates in practice, and how its effectiveness might be enhanced. Unfortunately, very few process studies have been published in this area, and so it is impossible to arrive at any general conclusions. Greater attention to the possibilities of process research represents a significant priority for future research in the workplace counselling arena.

Chapter 6. Methodological issues in research into workplace counselling

The aim of this section of the report is to discuss methodological issues raised by the review of research literature. One of the objectives of the review has been to use the process of building a picture of the current knowledge base to stimulate reflection on what can be learned about how to improve and enhance the quality of research in this area.

The epistemological context of this review

The background to this review is the increasing pressure on counselling and psychotherapy providers to meet criteria for 'evidence-based practice' that have been defined and applied by the medical and health professions, for example in the UK through the National Institute for Health and Clinical Excellence (NICE). Within the world of health care, ever-expanding health costs and proliferation of new treatments have resulted in a range of measures that are intended to restrict available treatments to interventions that are supported by credible research evidence. Within the domain of medicine (eg drug treatments), a hierarchy of evidence has been developed, with randomised clinical trials (RCTs) being defined as offering the most reliable and valid form of evidence. However, there have been considerable tensions around the capacity and appropriateness of RCTs in relation to evidence concerning the effects of counselling and psychotherapy (see Rowland, 2007, for a succinct review of these tensions, and Rowland and Goss, 2000, for wider discussion). The present review has therefore been conducted in a context in which some readers may define valid knowledge primarily in terms of RCT evidence, while others may adopt a broader concept of epistemological quality. It is therefore necessary to supply a brief summary of the key issues.

The argument in favour of the special status of RCT evidence is made forcibly by Wessely (2006), who emphasises the central point that it is only through randomisation that bias can be controlled, and eliminated or minimised. Wessely (2006) argues that, in non-randomised studies, it is possible for unconscious sources of bias to lead to the over-estimation of the effectiveness of an intervention. He provides a vivid example of the development of knowledge around the success of post-trauma psychological debriefing – an intervention that was widely regarded as efficacious until shown otherwise through well-designed RCT studies. The implication is that practitioners have an ethical responsibility to their clients to take part in RCTs, and to base their work on interventions that have been validated through such trials.

Some of the issues in relation to the use of RCT-based evidence in counselling and psychotherapy are:

(i) *over-estimation of effectiveness of interventions*. The majority of medical researchers (see, for example, Schulz et al, 1995) support the view of Wessely (2006) that non-randomised studies yield estimates of effectiveness that are higher than those produced by RCTs (and as a result lead to the adoption of treatments that are falsely deemed to be useful). However, other medical researchers (Concato et al, 2000; Kunz and Oxman, 1998) have found equivalence in effects reported by randomised, and non-randomised, studies of the same interventions. In research into counselling and psychotherapy, however, a review by Shadish et al (2000) concluded that RCTs yielded *higher* estimates of effectiveness than non-randomised, studies, because RCTs tend to filter out more complex and hard-to-treat clients, who are more likely to be included in naturalistic studies;

(ii) *elimination of bias*. Recent analyses of patterns of outcome produced in RCTs of psychotherapy have concluded that researcher allegiance (ie the expectations and beliefs of the researcher regarding which therapy is best), along with other sources of bias, remain significant within this type of research design (Ablon and Jones, 2002; Luborsky et al, 1999);

(iii) *the ethics of research and practice*. The ethical argument in favour of RCTs is not clear-cut. Edwards, Lilford et al (1998) have identified a range of ethical dilemmas arising from both client/patient and practitioner involvement in RCTs – for example, does the clinician genuinely believe in the equivalent efficacy of alternative treatments that are being compared (equipoise), and does the patient trust the information that he/she is given?

(iv) *the relevance of RCT evidence to practice*. Because well-designed RCTs require therapists to adhere to treatment manuals, and recruit only clients who conform to narrowly defined inclusion criteria, it can be argued that the knowledge these studies generate is not readily applicable to everyday practice, where counsellors adapt interventions to client needs, use integrative approaches and work with clients who have multiple problems.

These are complex issues, which can be further debated from all sides (Black, 1996). Wessely (2006), certainly acknowledges the methodological challenges involved in devising RCTs of psychological interventions, while believing that these difficulties can be resolved by 'more trials, bigger trials and better trials' (p. 97).

In the light of these issues, it is important to be clear that the present review has not espoused a 'hierarchy of evidence' strategy that prioritises evidence from RCTs above other sources. Instead, an inclusive, non-hierarchical approach has been adopted, that seeks to acknowledge the strengths and weaknesses of all forms of available evidence. The position taken corresponds to that advanced by Slade and Priebe (2001):

'Randomised controlled trials in medicine have been used for evaluating well-defined and standardised treatments. The importing of this approach into mental health service research strengthens the position of pharmacotherapy (which tends to be a standardised and well-defined intervention) compared with psychological and social interventions… Regarding RCTs as the gold standard in mental health care research results in evidence-based recommendations that are skewed, both in the available evidence and the weight assigned to evidence. Mental health research needs to span both the natural and social sciences. Evidence from RCTs has an important place, but to adopt concepts from only one body of knowledge is to neglect the contribution that other, well-established methodologies can make' (p. 287).

Barriers to research

It is important to recognise the distinctive multiple and serious methodological difficulties associated with conducting research into EAP/workplace counselling services. In comparison with other research into the effectiveness of counselling and psychotherapy, studies of workplace counselling are faced with the following challenges:

■ *workplace counselling as an emergent profession*. The disciplines that have dominated the field of counselling and psychotherapy research – clinical psychology and psychiatry – achieved formal status as professions several decades ago. The consolidation of these applied disciplines within universities has provided a secure infrastructure for research. By contrast, the field of workplace counselling is still currently engaged in a struggle to establish itself as a distinctive professional area. As a result, the energies of leaders within this field have been understandably devoted to engagement in debates around training and standards rather than in pursuing the furtherance of an evidence base;

- *significant commercial pressures.* Most research into counselling and psychotherapy is conducted in the public health/social care arena, where it is accepted that public accountability and open exchange of information is desirable and taken for granted. In the EAP/counselling domain, however, there exist both providers of services in commercial competition with each other, and purchasers (employers and corporations) who fear commercial disadvantage or union reaction if they publish information about the proportion of stressed or 'mentally ill' staff in their organisation. There are two effects of this degree of commercial pressure. First, there are a large number of unpublished outcome/satisfaction/utilisation studies and stress audits, carried out by EAP providers and purchasers and which, if published, would make a significant contribution to the research knowledge base in this area. Second, there is a general avoidance of critical research. To gain access to clients and service users, researchers adopt measures and methods (for example, satisfaction studies) that will produce findings supporting the value of counselling rather than lead to conclusions that might challenge prevailing assumptions and clinical wisdom;

- *acute sensitivity around confidentiality.* Probably the single most important factor in the acceptability of workplace counselling to employees concerns the guarantee of confidentiality. Service users may tell their co-workers that they have used a counselling service, but they do not want their manager to know or for their visit to be recorded in their personal file. There are real anxieties around job security, promotion prospects and reputation as someone who can 'take the pressure'. As a result, it is very hard for researchers to collect organisational data on counselling clients around factors such as work performance, absence, disciplinary proceedings, accidents, promotion, retirement and so on. This situation can be contrasted with other areas of counselling/psychotherapy research. In the majority of therapy outcome studies, objective 'life' data has not been seen as particularly relevant. In areas where such data has been relevant, for example the health utilisation costs of patients receiving psychotherapy within the NHS, service users are generally comfortable about the confidentiality boundary being extended to include other health professionals. In research into workplace counselling, by contrast, absolute confidentiality is a central concern, and leads to practical barriers around obtaining follow-up data of any kind from clients;

- *missing data.* It will be apparent from close reading of the studies reviewed in this document that researchers have experienced extreme difficulty in getting both counsellors and clients to complete and return questionnaires. The problem of missing data (or attrition from the study, for example when clients do not turn up for a final counselling session and there is no way to deliver or administer the post-counselling measures) undermines the value of many studies. The more data that is missing, the more open the findings are to alternative interpretation. For instance, is it the case that dissatisfied clients are less likely to attend their final scheduled session and therefore do not complete end-of-counselling questionnaires? Or could it be that many people get what they need from two or three sessions, do not come back and therefore represent missing but 'good outcome'

cases? The issue of missing data could be addressed by (a) using a 'tracking' approach, in which clients completed a questionnaire on each occasion when they attended counselling, and (b) training and supporting counsellors to integrate research into routine practice;

- *multi-site research.* The issue of missing data (and how to interpret it) is closely linked to the realities of carrying out multi-site research. Typically, large EAPs and workplace counselling services respond to client needs by offering counselling on different work sites, or in a variety of counselling offices provided by affiliate practitioners. Ensuring that clients and counsellors at all these sites receive questionnaires, and know what to do with them, is a complex and expensive task. In 'controlled' studies of psychotherapy, it is usual for clients or patients to attend a single clinic, where a research assistant can be on hand to carry out interviews and administer questionnaires. There are few naturalistic, real-world studies of workplace counselling that can approach this level of consistency of data collection. In the absence of very substantial funding, multi-site research inevitably leads to missing data;

- *working across disciplinary boundaries.* EAPs and workplace counselling schemes have generally been studied and evaluated as forms of psychological intervention. While this strategy certainly reflects the realities of disciplinary boundaries in universities, it could be argued that it does not do justice to the realities of the world of work. EAP/counselling provision is embedded in the world of work. For an employee, the meaning of using the EAP is bound up with their work identity and role, and attitude to their employer. For a manager authorising EAP/counselling services, the decision is bound up with a multiplicity of political, legal and pragmatic issues. Developing an understanding of workplace counselling requires contributions from the sociology of work, organisation theory, labour relations, social history, workplace law, occupational health and other knowledge disciplines, not just psychology. The need for interdisciplinary collaboration can be seen even in very practical issues such as the use of sickness absence data to evaluate the effectiveness of counselling (following counselling, employees seem to take fewer days off sick each year). Many workplaces have developed an informal or even semi-formal culture that regards taking occasional sick days as an acceptable and desirable way of staying healthy and avoiding burnout. Is reducing the absence level of an individual to below that level *necessarily* a good outcome? Alternatively, presumably a good outcome in some counselling situations would be the decision of an employee to seek early retirement on health grounds, which might result in a significant *increase* in their sickness absence following counselling. Is this necessarily a poor outcome? These are fairly trivial examples of the value of developing a more interdisciplinary approach to research into counselling in the workplace. There are many other areas in which the sometimes contradictory results of studies of workplace counselling could be clarified by adopting a broader interdisciplinary perspective. In general, this is not a strategy that other therapy researchers have needed to follow. It represents one of the specific challenges of research in this setting.

These are some of the general underlying issues associated with research into the effectiveness of counselling in the workplace. The tensions arising from these issues can be seen in the body of work reviewed in this report, largely in the form of compromises made by researchers in order to be in a position to do any kind of meaningful research at all. It is of interest that, in compiling this review, it was possible to locate more papers around the theme of 'how to do research on EAPs' than papers that reported actual investigations. This finding is consistent with the existence of significant methodological *barriers* to carrying out substantive research on workplace counselling, and the parallel existence of significant barriers to publishing work completed under conditions of commercial secrecy.

Suggestions for improving the quality of research into workplace counselling

There are a number of practical ways in which the quality of research efforts in the area of workplace counselling might be enhanced. These are discussed below:

■ *moving beyond client satisfaction.* A great many studies of workplace counselling have relied on brief client satisfaction questionnaires administered at the end of counselling. These scales can be completed anonymously, are not time-consuming and are easy to analyse. Typically, the data from client satisfaction surveys show that around 90% of clients are highly satisfied, would return again, would recommend the service to a friend, perceived the counsellor as competent and so on. It is clearly essential, from the perspective of audit, democracy and accountability that all clients and service users should be given an opportunity to express their views on the treatment they have received. However, satisfaction data can make only a very minor contribution to the evidence base around the effectiveness of counselling. Satisfaction ratings are dominated by the client's appreciation of the efforts of the counsellor, and the willingness of the counsellor to listen to them with acceptance. Satisfaction ratings bear little or no relationship to the question of whether counselling has actually helped the person to deal with their problems. The uniformity of satisfaction ratings (virtually everyone is highly satisfied) means that it is impossible to differentiate between client groups who may be helped to a greater or lesser degree by the counselling that is provided. To develop an informed understanding of the helpfulness of workplace counselling, it is necessary to move beyond satisfaction research, and find ways of both tracking actual change over time (for example, through measures administered before and after counselling, and at follow-up) and of allowing clients/users to explore openly, and with depth, the meaning to them of the counselling they received;

■ *addressing the issue of publication bias.* Publication bias refers to any situation in which research is carried out on a topic, but not published. Failure to publish may be due to a variety of reasons – lack of interest in the topic on the part of journal editors and reviewers, and conscious or unconscious suppression of results by researchers and/or their sponsors. The issue of publication bias creates a major problem for reviewers, who can only work with the studies that are published, and can have no way of knowing how many unpublished studies are sitting in desk drawers and what these studies have found. If a large number of unpublished studies have been carried out, in comparison to the available number of published ones, there is a danger that the conclusions of reviews may be biased – the unpublished material may tell quite a different story. The issue of publication bias is potentially of great significance within the field of workplace counselling, because it seems unlikely that a well-established multi-million dollar international industry should only generate an average of five or six research studies each year. The implication must be that many research studies have been carried out and not published. In this area, the most credible rationale for non-publication is that a study has found counselling to be ineffective, since there are many incentives for researchers in gaining as much publicity as possible for 'good news' results. In order

to address the issue of publication bias, it is necessary for organisations that commission and undertake workplace counselling research to agree to create a register of research in progress, so that reviewers can determine whether a study has ultimately led to publication or not. Refusal to address the issue of publication bias will, in the longer term, have the effect of undermining the credibility of the research that is published;

■ *greater attention to theory.* It is apparent that the evidence base reviewed in the present report is largely based on studies that are informed by broad-brush common-sense empirical questions – is counselling effective? How satisfied are clients? What proportion of employees use a service? Woven through the research literature, however, are some studies that are based on more fine-grained theoretical analyses, for example of specific client presenting problems or types of intervention strategy. These theoretically informed studies are much more likely to lead to significant advances in knowledge than are broad-brush studies, because they narrow down the focus of inquiry to questions that can be answered with a higher degree of precision and confidence. It is perhaps surprising, given the rich theoretical literature in organisational and occupational psychology and sociology, and indeed within psychotherapy, that research into workplace counselling is so theoretically barren. Nevertheless, a greater attention to theoretical meaning-making has the potential to enable this research field to move to another level;

■ *greater appreciation of context and better definition of terms of the research.* In Chapter 1, a model of workplace counselling effectiveness was introduced, which highlighted the multi-layered context within which this type of counselling takes place. It is evident that very few of the studies discussed in this review give sufficient emphasis to describing the context within which the counselling being investigated actually took place. As a consequence, it is extremely difficult to make meaningful comparisons across studies, because it is impossible to know whether even basic terms such as 'counselling' or a 'case' have the same meaning in different settings;

■ *addressing the problem of control groups.* In medical research, it is widely accepted that 'randomised controlled trials' (RCTs) are the best means of establishing, beyond reasonable doubt, the efficacy of a treatment intervention. In an RCT, a series of patients are randomly assigned to competing treatments (or to an active treatment and a placebo condition), with the effectiveness of the treatment being assessed through measures or tests administered before and after treatment, and at follow-up. Any difference in effectiveness between the two treatments (for example in percentage of patients cured) can only be attributed to the treatment, since the assumption is implied in this type of research that all other factors have remained constant. Although RCTs have been used in research into psychotherapy, it is very difficult to set up this kind of study in the area of workplace counselling, since to exert this degree of manipulation or control over normal counselling practice is both ethically and practically highly problematic. The only outcome studies reviewed in this report that use an RCT research design are those of Barkham, Shapiro and their colleagues, Reynolds (1997) and Iwi et al (1998). These studies, in fact, illustrate very well the problematic nature of controlled trials in this area. The 'Sheffield' studies (Barkham, Shapiro, Firth et al) are tightly controlled and elegant, but are far from reflecting the everyday realities of counselling at work. The Iwi et al (1998) study set out as an RCT, but ran into ethical difficulties around the acceptability of withholding care to people in need, and was forced to change tack. Most of the studies reviewed in Chapter 2 of this report use a 'naturalistic' research design, in which EAP/counselling clients receiving therapy under normal conditions (ie 'practice-based' research) are assessed before and after intervention and perhaps also at follow-up. Typically, these studies show that, on average, counselling clients tend to improve significantly in terms of their levels of anxiety, stress, self-esteem and so on. However, this kind of research design does not allow us to conclude that these changes can be attributed to counselling. Perhaps these clients would have improved even if they had not received counselling. There is, in fact, substantial evidence that emotional and relationship problems are 'self-limiting', in that many people are able to mobilise their own resources and support networks to overcome crises and difficulties, without recourse to professional assistance. The key question is therefore: 'does counselling lead to higher rates of improvement than might have been reported without the use of formal therapy?' Naturalistic studies cannot, alone, answer this question. Some researchers have argued that it is possible to supplement naturalistic data with estimates of improvement rates for 'untreated' individuals. This is possible if tests or measures are used that have been validated not only on the general population but also in relevant workforce samples, and in previous controlled studies of counselling or psychotherapy. For example, in a study of stress counselling with police officers, if a test or questionnaire is used for which data is available on (a) the normal range of stress in serving officers, (b) the stability of stress scores in police officers, and (c) the extent to which these scores have changed in previous controlled studies of therapy, then it is possible to estimate whether the proportion of police offers in the study who have demonstrated clinically significant change (eg have moved into the normal range of scores) is similar to that achieved in previous (optimal) studies of therapy. (A guide to information about the technical details on how these 'benchmarking' calculations are made can be found in Lambert, 2004, and McLeod, 1994, 2003.) The key point here is that it is possible to overcome the absence of control groups by using assessment measures that have been appropriately validated and developed for use in counselling/psychotherapy research;

- *developing agreed methods for measuring utilisation and attitudes.* There is a wide range of interesting and important questions about workplace counselling that can be explored through analysis of routine service and audit data collected by organisations providing counselling services. In addition, it is a relatively straightforward matter to administer and analyse employee attitude surveys. However, at the moment, no one reading research into these topics can have any confidence that the figures produced by different organisations, for example relating to utilisation, are comparable. The discussion in Chapter 4 makes some suggestions for achieving consistency around utilisation and other benchmarking statistics.

Priorities for workplace counselling research

It is not easy to identify, with any confidence, the most fruitful directions for future research. Compared with other areas of counselling and psychotherapy, there has been so little systematic published research into EAPs and workplace counselling that one rational way forward would be to call for 'much more of the same', in terms of a mix of naturalistic and controlled outcome studies. Apart from the issue of client satisfaction, which has been explored in many studies, the primary areas of research focus covered in this review (psychosocial and economic effectiveness, and utilisation rates) can each be described as under-developed. Although there are

some interesting and valuable studies in each of these areas, they tend to be methodologically relatively unsophisticated, have not been replicated and are often specific to organisational, national or cultural patterns of workplace counselling provision. There is certainly a need for further studies of outcome, including well-designed randomised clinical trials.

On the basis of studies discussed in this review, it is possible to point in the direction of apparent gaps in the research literature on workplace counselling, and areas in which previous research has opened out questions that may repay further investigation. These include:

- *organisational effects of counselling.* Existing research has not been able to find any consistent link between EAP/counselling provision and organisational outcomes such as job satisfaction, commitment and productivity. Either this link does not exist (ie counselling operates largely at the level of the individual 'troubled worker') or the methods that have been used to study the issue have not been sensitive enough to detect the organisational impact of counselling. There is good reason to believe that the latter position is valid. Existing measures of organisational variables such as satisfaction, productivity and commitment have not been designed, or sufficiently adapted, for the purpose of evaluating counselling. Also, it seems likely that there could be a significant time lag between counselling and change in work performance. Research has shown that, when a person receives counselling, there is a tendency for beneficial changes to emerge first in the areas of symptom relief and sense of wellbeing, and only subsequently in social and life functioning (including work performance). It seems probable that carefully designed studies with longer follow-up times are necessary if organisational effects are to be appropriately investigated. In addition, research designs will need to consider ways of looking at group-level, rather than merely individual-level outcomes. For example, a person who has benefited from counselling may become a better colleague, and have a resulting impact on co-workers in his or her department or team. The study by Reynolds (1997) provides an example of this type of investigation;

- *patterns of client uptake of services.* It is clear in some studies that there are employees who make use of EAP/counselling services on a regular but intermittent basis. To date, outcome studies have looked only at the effects of specific counselling episodes (usually two to six sessions). It may be that there exists a sub-group of clients who regularly return for further brief episodes, perhaps annually. Does this kind of pattern represent a uniquely beneficial aspect of workplace provision (in enabling employees to draw on a trusted counselling resource at moments of crisis) or could it signify a misuse of workplace counselling (should such clients be referred elsewhere for long-term work)?

- *the effect of gender.* In several studies of EAP/counselling utilisation it appeared that women are more likely to use counselling and to believe that it will be effective. There is an array of further research questions that flow from this observation. Do women use counselling differently from men, for example in seeking more co-worker support when they decide to see a counsellor or presenting different issues in counselling? To what extent are women's attitudes to counselling connected to other aspects of gender relations in the workplace, such as differential rewards, sexual harassment, the 'glass ceiling' effect and the existence of dual carer/worker roles? Do gender differences in employee attitudes to counselling have anything to do with the fact that most counsellors are women? What are the factors involved in male resistance to counselling? How can male resistance be overcome, so that men may more appropriately make use of EAP/counselling services? Are there gender-informed approaches to counselling that may lead to more effective EAP/counselling services?

■ *access to services*. There has been very little systematic research into equity of access to workplace counselling for clients according to ethnicity, age and disability. On the whole, EAP provision appears to be associated with organisations that are unionised, and already highlight employee wellbeing. The experience of economically marginalised clients is largely absent from the workplace counselling literature;

■ *how do clients/users experience EAP/counselling services?* Although the various papers cited in this review are based on data collected from thousands of employees who have used EAP/counselling services, in *none* of these articles can the 'voice' of the client/user be heard. There are many studies that assess client satisfaction, and some studies that offer brief quotes from clients, but in all of these cases the experience of the client is heavily filtered through the questions, categories and purposes of the researcher. There has been no sustained research into the client's perspective on workplace counselling. An important direction for future research may be, therefore, to use qualitative methods to explore the experiences of clients (and, for that matter, counsellors and other stakeholders) regarding their use of EAPs and other forms of workplace counselling. Such research is likely to have considerable heuristic value, in generating new understandings, grounded in everyday experience, that can inform both practice and research;

■ *what are the relationships between counselling and health status?* One of the key 'objective' indicators that have been used in the evaluation of workplace counselling has been sickness absence, with considerable evidence that counselling interventions can reduce the number of absence episodes. There are a number of issues here that might repay further research. For example, what is the process through which workers define themselves as sick, and then, through counselling, re-define themselves as well enough to return to work? To what extent is 'illness' an attribution that can be employed to protect a person from the demands or pressures of work? To what extent does the success of counselling in reducing sickness absence mean that counsellors are working effectively with psychosomatic difficulties? What are counsellors doing, in typically brief treatment episodes, to make a difference to psychosomatic complaints that are widely regarded as being difficult to work with? How many supervisor referrals (as opposed to self-referrals) are persons who deny emotional and interpersonal difficulties and, as a result, channel their problems in living through bodily ailments that disrupt work efficiency?

■ *what are the differential and distinctive impacts of different modes of delivery of counselling?* The majority of studies reported in this review reflect a model of workplace counselling in which clients receive around six to eight sessions of face-to-face therapy at approximately weekly intervals. However, the research by Barkham et al (1999) suggests that a model of two sessions with a follow-up three months later can be effective in some circumstances. There are also many EAPs and counselling providers offering employment counselling by telephone, but there is a dearth of published research studies of the acceptability or effectiveness of this type of approach. In addition, although there is a rich literature on the effectiveness of the use of self-help books, leaflets and videos in psychotherapy, there are no studies at all of the value of this form of intervention in the workplace counselling arena. Over the next few years there are also likely to be further innovations around email counselling in the workplace, which will require documentation and evaluation. Although the practice of *executive coaching* has emerged within many organisations as an alternative to counselling, this approach has, as yet, generated no research base (Feldman and Lankau, 2005). There are important research questions to be pursued around the outcomes of executive coaching, and its role in relation to established counselling services.

The underlying priorities for workplace counselling research lie in the domains of co-ordination and resources. One of the central problems in this research field, that permeates the discussion within all the chapters of this report, is that not enough money has been invested in it. The companies that operate commercially successful EAPs, the large organisations that run in-house counselling services, and the government departments responsible for workplace health and industrial competitiveness have failed to make sufficient investment in research and development in this important, and growing, area of activity. The consequence of the lack of sustained investment in workplace counselling research has meant that there has been a lack of co-ordination of research, with good ideas and practices not being picked up by other researchers, an absence of programmes of research that address key issues in a systematic manner, and a lack of opportunities for key figures within the research community to devote time to the essential activities of critical thinking and theory building. A small levy per client, contributed by all workplace counselling services, would allow the establishment of a university-based centre for research in workplace counselling, and could act as leverage to release matching government funding, permitting strategically important research to be carried out. There is no reason why such a policy cannot be implemented by existing EAP professional associations in North America and the UK as a key priority goal.

Additional technical information

In order to write this report in a style that will be accessible to practitioners and clients of workplace counselling, we have included as few technical references and jargon as possible. Many of the summarised studies have used standardised tests or questionnaires administered before and after counselling. Reference details of these tests have not been included, to avoid unnecessary complexity in the report. Further information on the tests can be found in Bowling (2001; 2004) or McLeod (1999). Other technical information on aspects of research design and analysis can be found in Lambert (2004) and McLeod (2003).

Acknowledgements

This report could not have been completed without the efforts of a team of people. I would like to acknowledge the advice and assistance that was provided by Robert Elliott, Stephen Goss, Rick Hughes, Barry Macinnes and John Mellor-Clark, the highly efficient service of the staff in the inter-library loans section of the University of Abertay, the tireless efforts of Julia McLeod, who worked alongside me through this project, and the support, encouragement and patience of the research department of the British Association for Counselling and Psychotherapy: Angela Couchman, Sukhdeep Khele, Kaye Richards and Nancy Rowland.

Appendices

Appendix A. Studies of the outcomes of workplace counselling

Authors: Chandler, R.G., Kroeker, B.J., Fynn, M. and MacDonald, D.A.

Title: Establishing and evaluating an industrial social work programme; The Seagram, Amherstburg experience.

Date: 1988.

Type of publication: journal article.

Source: *Employee Assistance Quarterly*, 3(3/4): 243–254.

Aims of study: to examine the long-term effectiveness of a counselling programme.

Method: client questionnaires and personnel data were analysed between 1978 and 1984.

Sample: no details were given.

Type of counselling: 'broad-brush' internal EAP, delivered through a university social work department.

Organisational context: manufacturing, joint management-union project; Canada.

Results: 94% of users rated the service as helpful. 65% encouraged others to use the service. Absenteeism rates, for all employees, dropped from 11.9% in 1978 to 5.5% in 1983. Accidents and grievances also dropped significantly.

Methodological issues: the lack of detail around methods and findings made it difficult to evaluate the validity of this study.

Methodological quality rating: low.

Authors: Cooper, C.L. and Sadri, G. (The 'Post Office' study).

Title: The impact of stress counselling at work.

Date: 1991.

Type of publication: journal article.

Source: *Journal of Social Behavior and Personality*, 6(7): 411–423.

Aims of study: to examine the effectiveness of an in-house employee counselling service.

Method: counselling clients completed questionnaire measures of stress, anxiety and somatic symptoms (Crown-Crisp Experiential Index), Rosenberg self-esteem scale, and measures of job satisfaction, organisational commitment (Cooper and Sadri, 1991) and health behaviour before the first session and three months after the final counselling session. Similar measures were completed at four-month intervals by employees in a matched control group who had not sought counselling. Sickness absence data was collected from personnel records (six months pre-counselling; six months after ending).

Sample: from 250 clients using the service, 135 completed pre-counselling questionnaires and 113 post-counselling questionnaires. From a target group of 100 non-counselled employees matched for age and gender, 74 questionnaires were returned at time one and 37 at time two. Sickness absence data was available for 188 clients and 100 members of the control group. Age and gender of samples were not provided in this report (but in Cooper et al, 1990, it was given as 70% male). The majority of clients reported anxiety, depression or relationship difficulties. It included staff at all levels of the organisation.

Type of counselling: brief (three or four session) Rogerian (client-centred/person-centred) counselling provided by clinical psychologists.

Organisational context: Post Office. Regional office of government-owned, nationalised service industry; UK. New counselling service, although building on previous non-specialist counselling provided through welfare and occupational health departments.

Results: at intake, clients had anxiety, depression and somatic scores, which were significantly higher than those in a normative sample of UK workers. For counselling group, significant positive changes reported in anxiety, somatic symptoms, depression, positive health behaviours (eg less use of alcohol and coffee). No difference reported in organisational commitment or job satisfaction. For control group, no differences/gains were found on any of these variables. Around 60% of counselling clients showed significant improvement in mental health. Sickness absence for client group reduced from 27 days to 11. For controls, sickness absence remained constant at eight days per six months.

Methodological issues: the substantial amount of missing data (clients who did not complete questionnaires) made it necessary to interpret the findings of this study with caution. It was likely that at least some clients who dropped out of counselling because it was not helping them did not complete questionnaires, thus inflating the apparent effectiveness. In addition, the control group did not comprise people who were actually seeking help. A control group made up of those who were seeking help but who were offered either a waiting list, or some kind of comparison or placebo treatment, would have provided a better test of the effectiveness of counselling. The lack of follow-up data is a weakness of this study; it would be useful to know whether the gains reported lasted over time. Although shifts in depression, anxiety and somatic complaints were highly statistically significant, at the end of counselling the mean score for the client group was still markedly higher than the population norm. The lack of impact of counselling on organisational variables (job satisfaction and organisational commitment) is (as noted by the authors) not surprising given the nature of the scales used, which tended to include items referring to 'external' factors (eg work environment) that are unlikely to change as a result of counselling.

Methodological quality rating: high.

Notes: other reports from this study can be found in Allison, Cooper and Reynolds (1989) and in Cooper, Sadri, Allison and Reynolds (1990).

Authors: Doctor, R.S., Curtis, D. and Isaacs, G.

Title: Psychiatric morbidity in policemen and the effect of brief psychotherapeutic intervention – a pilot study.

Date: 1994.

Type of publication: journal article.

Source: *Stress Medicine*, 10: 151–157.

Aims of study: to explore the effect of group counselling on stress in police officers.

Method: the General Health Questionnaire (GHQ-30) and a police stress situations questionnaire (devised for this study) were sent to 171 male and female uniformed officers of constable and sergeant rank at two police stations. 61 questionnaires were returned (36%) – these respondents were invited to join a counselling or control group. Sickness absence records were then analysed for the 12 weeks before and after participation.

Sample: 61 police officers (the average age was 35; time in force 13 years; 59 male, two female).

Type of counselling: unstructured group led by a psychiatrist, who provided 12 one-hour sessions. The results of the stress situations questionnaire were used as a basis for initiating a discussion of key issues. Sessions took place within the police station.

Organisational context: police; UK.

Results: compared to scores for the control group, participation in the group had no impact on GHQ scores (stress and psychological problems) or on sickness absence. There was a slight tendency for those who had received counselling to report higher GHQ scores at the end.

Methodological issues: this study was avowedly exploratory in nature, and included a detailed discussion of implications for future research, and the design of more effective counselling services for police officers.

Methodological quality rating: low.

Authors: Elliott, M.S. and Williams, D.I.

Title: A qualitative evaluation of an employee counselling service from the perspective of client, counsellor and organisation.

Date: 2002.

Type of publication: journal article.

Source: *Counselling Psychology Quarterly*, 15: 201–208.

Aims of study: to evaluate the effectiveness of the employee counselling service of the Northern Ireland Fire Brigade.

Method: interviews with clients, counsellors, and organisational stakeholders. There was an analysis of sickness absence data for staff who had used the service. A survey questionnaire was distributed to 150 employees (47% return rate).

Sample: the key data source was interviews with 21 former clients.

Type of counselling: External service, counselling approach not specified.

Organisational context: local authority Fire Service; UK.

Results: the majority of clients reported issues arising from work-related trauma. All reported that counselling had been helpful and effective, and had enhanced their work performance. There was a description of organisational factors that inhibited use of counselling – for example, 40% of employees did not know that the service existed. There were substantial concerns around confidentiality. Senior members of the service were supportive of its value. Counsellors were unclear about organisational expectations. There was a 66% reduction in sickness absence for the six-month period following counselling. There was a low overall utilisation rate (1.2%).

Methodological quality rating: low.

Authors: Finke, L. Williams, J. and Stanley, R.

Title: Nurses referred to a peer assistance program for alcohol and drug problems.

Date: 1996.

Type of publication: journal article.

Source: *Archives of Psychiatric Nursing*, 10(5): 319–324.

Aims of study: to describe the characteristics of a group of registered nurses referred to a peer assistance programme for alcohol and drug problems, and to evaluate the outcomes of the programme.

Method: analysis of data collected from the files of nurses referred to a peer assistance programme.

Sample: all 221 nurses referred to the programme between 1984 and 1992. 82% female; 18% male (compared with only 4% males employed in the profession). The majority were between 26 and 45 years old. 72% used drugs; 53% used alcohol. 36% had diverted drugs from patients and/or institutional stock for their own use. 12% had legal records; 39% had received disciplinary action.

Type of counselling: peer support, including referral, education, support groups, re-entry monitoring and a telephone hotline. There were some paid staff, plus volunteers.

Organisational context: Indiana (USA) State Nurses' Association.

Results: 64% successfully completed the programme (54% good outcome; 10% showed partial recovery). The good outcome was associated with support from a marriage partner and referral by a healthcare provider (physician or counsellor).

Methodological issues: a lack of follow-up data and an absence of independent evaluation of outcomes were weaknesses of this study.

Methodological quality rating: low.

Notes: success rates reported are similar to those achieved by professional counselling/psychotherapy. Paper includes useful discussion of drug/alcohol abuse in nurses.

Authors: Gam, J., Sauser, W.I., Evans, K.L. and Lair, C.V.

Title: The evaluation of an Employee Assistance Program.

Date: 1983.

Type of publication: journal article.

Source: *Journal of Employment Counselling*, 20: 99–106.

Aims of study: to assess the benefits of an EAP 'as measured in terms of humanitarianism and productivity enhancement'.

Method: a brief (10-item) follow-up satisfaction questionnaire was sent to clients who had used the EAP in the first two years of its operation. There were therapist ratings of mental status. There was an analysis of absenteeism and disciplinary data from personnel records prior to and following the implementation of the EAP.

Sample: 60 clients (response rate 57%) completed questionnaires. There was an analysis of 95 case records.

Type of counselling: an external EAP, based at a mental health centre: emotional problems, substance abuse and child-rearing difficulties. Available to employees and family members.

Organisational context: manufacturing company; USA (clothing and sportswear).

Results: 90% of respondents believed that the EAP had helped them with their problem. Therapists rated 65% of clients as having improved. There was a non-significant correlation between client and therapist ratings of success. Users of the EAP were more likely to stay in employment with the company and to have lower rates of sickness absence and disciplinary problems.

Methodological issues: a lack of control/comparison group meant that alternative explanations for employee benefits could not be eliminated. There were some reliability and validity issues around methods used to assess client outcomes. The strength of the study was convergent evidence from different sources (clients, therapists and personnel records).

Methodological quality rating: low.

Authors: Gardner, B., Rose, J., Mason, O., Tyler, P. and Cushway, D.

Title: cognitive therapy and behavioural coping in the management of work-related stress: an intervention study.

Date: 2005.

Type of publication: journal article.

Source: *Work and Stress*, 19: 137–152.

Aims of study: to evaluate the effectiveness of cognitively orientated or behavioural group-based brief intervention for work stress, in comparison to a waiting list condition.

Method: National Health Service staff working in the areas of mental health and intellectual disability volunteered to participate in the programme and were randomly allocated into three groups. A set of questionnaires was administered before the start, at the end and at the three-month follow-up. The change measures used were: General Health Questionnaire (GHQ-12); Mental Health Professional Stress Scale; Support Questionnaire; Appraisal Questionnaire and Ways of Coping Questionnaire. Participants also completed a satisfaction questionnaire.

Sample: 138 NHS employees (the average age was 37; 82% female). Mainly clinical staff.

Type of counselling: group intervention (five to 12 participants; two facilitators) structured around three half-day (three and a half hours) sessions over three weeks. The cognitive therapy group emphasised negative thoughts, positive self-talk and imagery. The behavioural group emphasised time management, assertion, problem-solving and muscle relaxation.

Organisational context: large Health Trust; UK.

Results: the intervention groups improved significantly more than those allocated to the waiting list condition. The cognitive intervention was more effective than the behavioural: 90% of participants in the cognitive therapy group moved from 'case' status (measured by the GHQ-12) to 'non-case' status, compared to 50% in the behavioural group and 20% in the waiting list condition. A noticeable feature of the results was that the differential gains arising for the cognitive therapy group occurred largely in the period between the end of the group and the follow-up – participants reported that they needed time to practise the techniques.

Methodological quality rating: high.

Notes: this study is problematic in terms of the inclusion criteria for the review, since the intervention was largely organised around standardised didactic inputs, with limited time given to interactive work that was responsive to the needs of individuals. However, the intention of the researchers appeared to be to deliver a cognitive/behavioural therapeutic experience for participants, so on balance the study can be regarded as comprising a counselling intervention.

Authors: Gersons, B.P.R., Carlier, I.V.E., Lamberts, R.D. and van der Kolk, B.A.

Title: Randomised, clinic trial of brief eclectic psychotherapy for police officers with post-traumatic stress disorder.

Date: 2000.

Type of publication: journal article.

Source: *Journal of Traumatic Stress*, 13: 333–347.

Aims of study: to evaluate the effectiveness of a psychotherapeutic intervention, for police officers who had developed PTSD as a result of events experienced at work.

Method: participants were referred into the study by occupational health doctors and were required to meet diagnostic criteria for PTSD. They were randomly allocated to a treatment group (16 weekly sessions of psychotherapy) or a waiting list control condition. Assessments were made one week before the start of treatment, after four sessions, at the termination of treatment and at a four-month follow-up (or at equivalent times for those in the control group). The measures used were: structured psychiatric interview; an anxiety disorders interview and the SCL-90 symptom checklist.

Sample: 22 participants received therapy (20 in control condition); 96% male (the average age was 37; mean years in police force, 16; the average length of time since in-service trauma was four years).

Type of counselling: brief eclectic psychotherapy: integration of CBT and psychodynamic techniques and principles, including some involvement of spouse/partner, and completion through a farewell ritual. Therapy was conducted according to a manual, with adherence checks and regular supervision. Therapists were clinical psychologists.

Organisational context: police force; Holland.

Results: at follow-up, recovery from PTSD symptoms was found in 90% of those receiving treatment (35% of those in the control group). 86% of those who received treatment were able to resume work (60% of control group). At the termination of treatment, the SCL-90 symptom scores of participants who had received therapy were within the normal range.

Methodological issues: this was a carefully controlled and designed study. Its only limitations were that: (a) longer follow-up data was not available; and (b) the use of a waiting list control, rather than offering control clients another form of therapy, left open the possibility that other therapy approaches may have been equally effective with this client group.

Methodological quality rating: high.

Note: the paper includes a detailed description of the therapeutic intervention developed for this study, including discussion of how the specific needs of those who work in a police environment were taken into account.

Author: Gray-Toft, P.

Title: Effectiveness of a counselling support program for hospice nurses.

Date: 1980.

Type of publication: journal article.

Source: *Journal of Counselling Psychology*, 27: 346–354.

Aims of study: to evaluate the effect of a group counselling intervention for job-related stress in hospice nurses.

Method: a Nursing Stress Scale (developed for this study) and the Job Description Index (a standard measure of job satisfaction) were administered at the beginning and end of the group intervention. Staff turnover data was collected for the three-month period before the group and during the operation of the group.

Sample: 17 hospice nurses (age and qualifications not provided).

Type of counselling: insight-orientated, one-hour structured group sessions, facilitated by a counsellor and the hospital chaplain. Two groups were run, each for nine weeks.

Organisational context: hospice, located within a larger hospital; USA.

Results: modest but statistically significant changes were found in total stress, conflict with physicians, stress of dealing with death and dying, perception of workload and relationships with co-workers. Staff turnover was eliminated during the functioning of the group intervention.

Methodological issues: no follow-up data was collected, so it is impossible to determine whether the benefits reported were sustained over time. The counsellor was also the person responsible for designing the study and collecting data – it is possible that participants may have been influenced by this relationship, in the direction of producing 'positive' scores. The counsellor spent some time in the hospice to familiarise herself with the work setting – this may have contributed to the success of the group.

Methodological quality rating: low.

Author: Grime, P.R.

Title: Computerised cognitive behavioural therapy at work: a randomised, controlled trial in employees with recent stress-related absenteeism.

Date: 2004.

Type of publication: journal article.

Source: *Occupational Medicine*, 54: 353–359.

Aims of study: to compare the effectiveness of a computerised CBT therapy programme, 'Beating the Blues', against normal treatment for employees reporting stress-related absence from work.

Method: participants were recruited from occupational health patients who had reported 10 or more stress-related days off in the past six months. They were randomly allocated to the CBT package or treatment as usual/conventional care. Change was measured by the Hospital Anxiety and Depression Scale (HADS), and the Attributional Style Questionnaire (ASQ: a measure of optimism-pessimism), administered before entering treatment, at the end of treatment and at one-, three- and six-month follow-up.

Sample: 78 NHS and local government employees. The average age was 38. Treatment group: 46% female; conventional care group: 71%.

Type of counselling: an interactive computerised CBT programme, encompassing cognitive and behavioural exercises and homework tasks. Participants used the programme in a private room in the Occupational Health department for eight weekly sessions.

Organisational context: public service; UK.

Results: at the end of the treatment period, and at one-month follow-up, the CBT package clients were significantly less depressed and anxious, and more positive about life, than those in the conventional care condition. There were no statistically significant differences between the two groups at three- and six-month follow-up periods. Some participants in the CBT group withdrew from the study because they expressed a preference for face-to-face counselling. The author concludes that the 'Beating the Blues' package may facilitate faster recovery, particularly for clients with depressive symptoms.

Methodological issues: one of the interesting aspects of this study was reflected in the data collected on alternative treatments pursued by those allocated to the conventional care group. Only five of the 37 people in this group received no active care – the others engaged in counselling, CBT or antidepressant use. Also, within the CBT group, participants continued to be eligible for conventional care, and the majority of them sought counselling and other forms of intervention. The findings of the study, therefore, reflect the *additional* benefits of computerised CBT, in addition to other active interventions.

Methodological quality rating: high.

Authors: Goss, S. and Mearns, D.

Title: Applied pluralism in the evaluation of employee counselling.

Date: 1997.

Type of publication: journal article.

Source: British Journal of Guidance and Counselling, 25 (3): 327–344.

Aims of study: to evaluate the effectiveness of a local authority education department counselling service.

Method: clients completed questionnaires pre- and post-counselling and at follow-up. The questionnaires included satisfaction and expectation items, and Rosenberg self-esteem scale. Counsellors completed parallel questionnaires at the beginning and end of counselling. Qualitative interviews were carried out with clients. Sickness absence data was taken from personnel records (where clients gave permission).

Sample: 332 clients used the service in the period of the evaluation – 26% male, 74% female. Largest age group: 50–55 years. Questionnaire returns were received from 241 clients pre-counselling, 88 post-counselling and 40 clients at follow-up.

Type of counselling: person-centred, with six-session limit (average 3.73 sessions).

Organisational context: education; UK.

Results: 65% of clients reported that counselling had improved their problems. 86% of clients were highly satisfied with counselling. There were significant positive changes in self-esteem. Sickness absence for six-month period following counselling improved by 62%.

Methodological issues: the substantial number of clients who did not complete questionnaires led to difficulties in interpreting the results of this study.

Methodological quality rating: low.

Notes: this paper includes useful qualitative material from client interviews.

Authors: Guppy, A. and Marsden, J.

Title: Assisting employees with drinking problems: changes in mental health, job perceptions and work performance.

Date: 1997.

Type of publication: journal article.

Source: Work and Stress, 11(4): 341–350.

Aims of study: to evaluate the effectiveness of counselling provided for employees referred to a company alcohol misuse programme.

Method: structured interview using standardised questionnaires, carried out at time of referral and at six-month follow-up. Data collected on job satisfaction, job commitment, self-rating of work performance, work problems/stress and mental health (GHQ-12). Supervisor ratings of work performance were collected through telephone interviews. Absenteeism data was collected through personnel database.

Sample: 138 clients evaluated at assessment, 104 at follow-up (20 had been dismissed, eight had resigned, five had medically retired, one died). 96% male. The average age was 42; 18% white; 18% black or Asian.

Type of counselling: not specified. There was an average of eight sessions.

Organisational context: transportation; UK.

Results: there were significant improvements in mental health, client and supervisor ratings of work performance, and absenteeism. No difference in job commitment and job satisfaction. Around 35% of clients showed clinically significant levels of gain.

Methodological issues: it would have been useful to have included more information on the 28 employees who resigned or were dismissed, in relation to disciplinary procedures. Were these 'failure' cases or did they represent a small proportion of employees referred because of disciplinary action by the employer (indicating effective counselling)?

Methodological quality rating: high.

Authors: Harris, S.M., Adams, A., Hill, L., Morgan, M. and Solz, C. (2002)

Title: Beyond customer satisfaction: a randomized EAP outcome study.

Date: 2002.

Type of publication: journal article.

Source: Employee Assistance Quarterly, 17: 53–61.

Aims of study: to evaluate the effectiveness of counselling provided by an EAP.

Method: clients completed scales drawn from the Health Status Questionnaire before commencing counselling and three months following the end of counselling.

Sample: 150 clients completed the pre-counselling questionnaire; 83 at post-counselling (55%). Information on gender, age, ethnicity not collected to preserve confidentiality.

Type of counselling: not specified.

Organisational context: a large EAP; New York, USA – clients were from different types of organisation.

Results: statistically significant improvements were found in client perceptions of the impact of their emotional problems on social functioning and daily activities, and in levels of depression. Before counselling, 33 clients indicated that emotional problems affected the amount of time they spent on work activities; following counselling, 23 of these reported no such problems.

Methodological issues: the lack of demographic and other contextual information, and the substantial attrition of clients from the study, made it difficult to assess the ability to generalise these findings. The study used a questionnaire that had not previously been adopted in counselling/psychotherapy research, and was more widely used as a health-screening instrument. Some aspects of the data analysis were difficult to understand and lacked sufficient detail (for example, standard deviation statistics were not provided).

Methodological quality rating: low.

Authors: Highley-Marchington, J.C. and Cooper, C.L.

Title: An assessment of employee assistance and workplace counselling programmes in British organisations.

Date: 1998.

Type of publication: Government report (UK Health and Safety Executive).

Source: Her Majesty's Stationery Office (HMSO), Norwich.

Aims of study: to evaluate the benefits of counselling at the individual and organisational levels.

Method: clients completed questionnaires at their first counselling session, following their final session, and at follow-up three to six months after completion of counselling. Questionnaire scales included: mental health/symptoms (GHQ-12), and four sections of the Occupational Stress Inventory (OSI), (i) the job satisfaction (sub-scales: satisfaction with the job itself, organisational design and structure, organisational processes, personal relationships at work, value/growth); (ii) sources of pressure (sub-scales: home-work interface, relationships with others, organisational structure and climate, factors intrinsic to the job); (iii) mental health; and (iv) physical health. Questions on demographic information, attitudes to counselling, problem severity and satisfaction with counselling were also collected in the questionnaire. Similar data was collected from control groups of employees who had not sought counselling. Sickness absence data was taken from personnel records in four of the companies.

Sample: clients were from nine different EAP/workplace counselling schemes. 179 completed pre-counselling questionnaires, 103 completed post-counselling questionnaires and 28 at follow-up. The size of the control group (non-counselling) was 432 employees at time one and 251 at time two. Age, gender and other demographic information on clients was not given.

Type of counselling: not specified, but included both in-house (internal) and external provision. Clients had an average of seven sessions (range one to 40).

Organisational context: a range of UK organisations, which offered an employee counselling/EAP service to staff.

Results: presenting problems (in order of frequency): family/marital, work, health, legal, financial. Referral sources: self 36%; manager/supervisor 24%; Occupational Health, 21%; union, 3%. There were high levels of client satisfaction with the services. 15% believed that counselling had helped them to resolve their problem; 15% reported that counselling had 'not resolved the problem, but can handle it better'; 11% agreed that the problem was 'just as difficult as before'. Significant differences found pre- and post-counselling

on GHQ total score and mental health and physical health sub-scales of OSI. No differences found pre/post on any job satisfaction or 'sources of work stress/pressure' measures. This pattern was maintained at follow-up. No differences were found between the end of counselling and follow-up. Higher success rates were found in internal counselling schemes in comparison with external (pp. 127–8). For the whole sample, there was a significant improvement in sickness absence, comparing the six months pre-counselling and six months post-counselling. However, this pattern was not consistent across schemes, with two schemes showing minimal improvements in sickness absence. Levels of sickness absence in the control group sample remained stable.

Methodological issues: there were three important methodological problems associated with this study. First, it seemed clear that many more questionnaires were distributed than were completed, although precise details on response rates were not provided. From anecdotal information in the report, it seemed likely that there may have been a tendency for counsellors to distribute questionnaires to more compliant clients or those who were less distressed. Second, the attrition from the study (from 179 clients at outset to 28 at follow-up) was not addressed. It would appear that all those clients who dropped out of counselling were lost to the study (ie there was no way of sending questionnaires to clients who did not attend their final planned session). The effect of both of these sampling factors would lead in the direction of producing a more optimistic estimate of the benefit of counselling than would have occurred if a more representative sample had been included. Finally, no information was provided about the demographic characteristics of participants. Taken together, these methodological issues made it difficult to assess the reliability of the results reported by the study.

Methodological quality rating: low.

Notes:

1. The main effect of counselling was to improve clients' scores on the GHQ-12 mental health scale. However, it should be noted that even those clients who completed follow-up questionnaires (presumably the clients who benefited most from counselling) still had an average GHQ score of 23.86, substantially higher than the control group mean of around 11. These figures suggest that counselling clients were *much* worse off than their non-counselled colleagues before entering counselling, in terms of mental health problems, and even though they perceived counselling as being helpful, they still reported significant levels of psychological distress at the end.
2. Information on other aspects of this study can be found in Section 5.
3. This report gives details of the actual questionnaires used in the study.

Authors: Iwi, D., Watson, P., Barber, N., Kimber, N. and Sharman, G.

Title: The self-reported wellbeing of employees facing organisational change: effects of an intervention.

Date: 1998.

Type of publication: journal article.

Source: *Occupational Medicine*, 48(6), 361–368.

Aims of study: to investigate the effects of brief counselling on the self-reported wellbeing of employees facing organisational change.

Method: randomised trial in which groups of local authority housing staff were allocated to either a treatment group (offered counselling) or to a control condition (delayed counselling). Questionnaire measures of occupational stress (the Occupational Stress Indicator) and psychiatric symptomatology (12-item General Health Questionnaire) were administered before and after counselling (or after three months for control subjects and those who did not take up the offer of counselling). Clients' qualitative evaluations of counselling were collected by counsellors in review sessions. During the lifetime of the study, ethical concerns led to the abandonment of the control group design, so that later participants were not required to enter a waiting list condition.

Sample: 129 local authority housing employees (70 men, 59 women; the average age was 37; 49% educated to degree level) facing the imposition of compulsory competitive tendering.

Type of counselling: cognitive-analytic therapy. Four sessions followed by a review session.

Organisational context: local authority/municipal housing agency in UK. Counselling intervention introduced for purposes of the study only – no previous culture of EAP/workplace counselling utilisation.

Results: all participants reported significantly elevated levels of stress at outset. 37% of employees accepted the offer of counselling: 26 had four sessions, 14 had two or three sessions and 11 had a single session. Ten employees requested further counselling, and had between one and eight additional sessions. 98% of those who received counselling reported that it had been helpful. However, counselling had no effect on any of the occupational stress and job satisfaction factors measured by the OSI or the GHQ.

Methodological issues: this was an ambitious study, but one that exhibited a number of methodological problems. The disparity between the highly positive verbal appraisals of the value of counselling made by clients to counsellors and the lack of change on standardised stress measures was a striking feature of the study. It is necessary to be cautious in interpreting the qualitative data, since there might be good reason to believe that clients would have a tendency to wish to please their therapists. An additional factor that needs to be taken into consideration is the use of the GHQ as a change measure. Many researchers considered the GHQ to be best deployed as a screening tool, which is relatively insensitive to change. The failure to detect shifts in occupational stress (OSI) due to counselling reinforces the findings of the Post Office study (Cooper et al, 1990). It is also notable that OSI items refer largely to 'external' characteristics of organisational life, which may not be perceived as amenable to personal action. Finally, the use of cognitive-analytic therapy (CAT), as a stress intervention, was not adequately discussed by the authors. It is unusual to apply CAT in a four-session mode, and it is not a method of therapy that has been widely used in work settings. It is possible that the therapeutic goals of CAT were inappropriate to the needs of the clients in this study.

Methodological quality rating: high.

Authors: Macdonald, S., Lothian, S. and Wells, S.

Title: Evaluation of an employee assistance program at a transportation company.

Date: 1997.

Type of publication: journal article.

Source: *Evaluation and Program Planning*, 20(4): 495–505.

Aims of study: to determine the effectiveness of an EAP from client, counsellor and employer perspectives.

Method: all employees who had used the EAP in a three-year period were sent questionnaires, which asked them about their satisfaction with the service they had received and how helpful it had been. Counsellors were interviewed on their perception of the outcomes for each of their clients. Information on sickness absence and disciplinary actions was obtained from employee records. The sickness absence profiles of EAP users were compared with that of a matched group of non-user employees, matched for age, gender, occupational status and length of employment.

Sample: 101 clients completed questionnaires (response rate of 42%). Matched comparisons of sickness absence were made for groups of 259 EAP users and 259 non-user employees. 75% blue-collar workers (drivers, maintenance, guards). 90% male.

Type of counselling: 'Broad-brush' in-house EAP, located off-site, with professional counsellors employed by the company. Available to employees and family members. No limit on number of sessions. The average number of sessions was five (the highest was 40 sessions). 73% of clients received individual counselling; 14% couple counselling; 5% family counselling.

Organisational context: large unionised transportation company; Canada.

Results: utilisation rate of 5.7%. Women and younger employees were more likely to use the service. 63% voluntary referrals; 16% referred by supervisors. EAP users had lower levels of health than Canadian norms (eg smoking). More than 95% of employees were satisfied with the service they had received. 69% of EAP users believed that their quality of life had improved since using the service; 46% reported that their job performance had improved. Counsellors rated more than 70% of clients as having improved as a result of counselling. Compared to matched control employees, before counselling EAP users had significantly higher rates of sickness absence, work-related injuries and lateness. Following counselling, sickness absence rates of EAP users rose and remained significantly higher than those of the control group. When absence rates for users and non-users were compared before, during and after the treatment period (or for control employees, for three consecutive time periods of approximately six months), it was found that EAP clients reported 3.9 more days off before treatment, 37.4 more days off during the treatment period and 13.3 more days off following treatment.

Methodological issues: it is important to note that the matched control group were not actively seeking help, and would have had much lower levels of personal problems. A better test of the impact of the EAP on absence levels would have been to have compared users with non-user employees who had problems but chose not to take up the offer of EAP help.

Methodological quality rating: high.

Notes: this study is unusual in finding high levels of utilisation and satisfaction, but no decrease in sickness absence. The authors discuss this finding in detail and offer a number of different ways of analysing the absence data and its significance.

Authors: Macdonald, S., Wells, S., Lothian, S. and Shain, M.

Title: Absenteeism and other workplace indicators of employee assistance program clients and matched controls.

Date: 2000.

Type of publication: journal article.

Source: *Employee Assistance Quarterly*, 15: 41–57.

Aims of study: to evaluate the effect of EAP utilisation on sickness absence.

Method: analysis of company records 1989–1993.

Sample: 303 EAP clients, compared to other employees matched for age, gender, occupational status, and length of employment, who had not made use of the EAP. 31% male; the average age was 40.

Type of counselling: short-term counselling for a wide range of personal problems. Located off-site, 52% of clients received short-term counselling; 41% received telephone help; 7% referred to other agencies. 89% were self-referred. Most frequent problem area was mental health (47%). 85% of clients were satisfied with the service they received.

Organisational context: large company (2000 employees), sector not specified; Canada.

Results: compared to non-EAP users, clients reported significantly more sick days (mean 45 days over four-year study period; non-users 31 days) and incomplete work days (1.09 vs. 0.33 days). A time series analysis showed that, for EAP users, absenteeism rose substantially before and during their period of EAP treatment, and, following the EAP intervention, returned to their previous level. However, EAP user absenteeism rates were higher than those for non-users even after treatment. There were no differences between EAP users and non-users in time off or compensation claims for work-related injuries.

Methodological quality rating: high.

Authors: Masi, D.A. and Jacobson, J.M.

Title: Outcome measurements of an integrated employee assistance and work-life program.

Date: 2003.

Type of publication: journal article.

Source: *Research on Social Work Practice*, 13: 451–467.

Aims of study: to examine clients' view of the effectiveness of an EAP intervention.

Method: users of a major national EAP, whose cases had been closed, were contacted by telephone and invited to take part in a 15-minute phone interview. Questions included demographic information, initial concerns, types of EAP services received, current work status (level of work stress, attendance at work, performance and relationship with work colleagues), ability to manage work stress before and following the EAP consultation, current level of personal stress and satisfaction with service.

Sample: 1,300 clients were contacted; 201 agreed to be interviewed; useable interviews were achieved with 165. The age range was from 16 to 66 (the average was 39.1). Ethnic white: 75%. Gender – 70% female. The age and gender characteristics of the sample matched those in the client population served by the EAP.

Type of counselling: counsellors were qualified social workers; model not specified.

Organisational context: financial and insurance (46%); a wide range of other sectors was also represented.

Results: services received by participants were referral (55%), information (43%), consultation (38%) and education (16%) – most participants received more than one service. The majority of participants who received referrals followed them up and found them useful. Significant gains were reported in all work stress categories. 94% would recommend the EAP to another person.

Methodological issues: no information was provided on the reliability or validity of the outcome measure used in this study. The small proportion of service users who agreed to be interviewed suggested that there may have been some source of bias influencing willingness to comply.

Methodological quality: low.

Notes: the strategy of inviting counselling clients retrospectively to estimate their level of distress at the beginning of therapy is highly problematic – research by Safer and Keuler (2002) has found a significant tendency for clients systematically to overestimate pre-therapy levels of distress.

Author: McAllister, P.O.

Title: An evaluation of counselling for employer-referred problem drinkers.

Date: 1993.

Type of publication: journal article.

Source: *Health Bulletin*, 51 (5): 285–294.

Aims of study: to examine the impact of counselling for alcohol-related problems on a subsequent job tenure.

Method: a client profile was constructed by the counsellor at the initial session. Questionnaires were completed by clients (perception of service) and employers (satisfaction with service, referral process and whether the employee was still employed by the organisation).

Sample: profiles were obtained for 67 clients; follow-up data on employment status one year after counselling was collected for 104 clients.

Type of counselling: EAP focusing on alcohol-related problems. Brief counselling using an eclectic cognitive-behavioural approach. Number of sessions was not specified. Some clients were referred on to specialist services.

Organisational context: clients were drawn from a variety of organisations.

Results: for 70% of clients, the service was the first contact for their alcohol problem other than their GP. On average, clients had serious drink problems (average six years, 100 units/week). 51% voluntary referral; 49% disciplinary referral. They were mainly between 30 and 50 years old. Primarily manual workers. 17% female; 83% male. One-year follow-up: still in same employment (64%), redundancy (8%), retired (4%), resigned (11%), dismissal – not alcohol-related) (4%), deceased (2%), dismissal – alcohol-related (8%). >90% of clients were satisfied with the counselling service they had received.

Methodological issues: the lack of detail about procedures for collecting data meant that the findings of this study must be interpreted with caution.

Methodological quality rating: low.

Authors: Millar, A.

Title: Beyond resolution of presenting issues: experiences of an in-house police counselling service.

Date: 2002.

Type of publication: journal article.

Source: *Counselling and Psychotherapy Research*, 2: 159–166.

Aims of study: to explore the experience of clients who had received counselling through an in-house service in a UK police force.

Method: qualitative semi-structured interviews; grounded theory analysis.

Sample: 13 participants (male, seven; female, six; police officers, eight; civilian support staff, five); average length of service was 17 years; had completed counselling within previous two years. Employees were selected to reflect a cross-section.

Type of counselling: in-house; integrative theoretical orientation.

Organisational context: police; UK.

Results: all the participants reported that they had been significantly helped by attending counselling, with much lower levels of distress at follow-up, alongside improvements to physical and psychological health, social functioning and work performance. Most described 'added value' or ways in which the counselling had impacted on them beyond their presenting problem – for example, 'I am 100 per cent better now at listening to a person'. Participants described a stage of *initial engagement* with the counselling service, which involved learning about the counselling process, which then led into a stage of *deep self-examination*.

Methodological quality rating: low.

Author: Mitchie, S.

Title: Reducing absenteeism by stress management: valuation of a stress counselling service.

Date: 1996.

Type of publication: journal article.

Source: *Work and Stress*, 10: 367–372.

Aims of study: to assess whether absenteeism rates were lower following stress counselling for health service workers.

Method: employees attending the counselling unit completed an eight-item scale of mood and functioning, at the beginning of the first session and end of last session (only for clients seen more than once), and by mail at six-month follow-up. Sickness absence rate data obtained from personnel database.

Sample: 163 hospital staff attending the counselling unit over a two-year period. 92 completed pre- and post-counselling questionnaires; 41 (25%) completed follow-up questionnaire.

Type of counselling: clinical psychologist operating with Occupational Health Unit. Stress-focused cognitive-behavioural model. There was an average of three sessions.

Organisational context: large London hospital (3,200 employees).

Results: significant improvements in anxiety, depression and absenteeism. No change in job satisfaction or work functioning. Absenteeism data (available for all 92 clients) indicated 44% improvement in absenteeism.

Methodological issues: missing data made it difficult to interpret the findings from the questionnaire measures of anxiety, depression and work functioning. Quite possibly, satisfied clients would be more motivated to return the follow-up questionnaire.

Methodological quality rating: low.

Notes: low utilisation rate: approximately 2.5% per annum.

Authors: Nadolski, J.N. and Sandonato, C.E.

Title: Evaluation of an employee assistance program.

Date: 1987.

Type of publication: journal article.

Source: *Journal of Occupational Medicine*, 29(1): 32–37.

Aims of study: to examine the impact of EAP use on work performance.

Method: work performance data was collected on employees using an EAP, for the six months prior to the EAP consultation, and the six months following it. Data sources included: lost time (days off and absence episodes), health insurance claims, disciplinary proceedings, accidents and supervisor-rated work productivity.

Sample: all 97 clients seen during a six-month period were eligible for the study; 67 were included in the study population (others left employment, died, retired or their data was unusable for a variety of reasons).

Type of counselling: EAP – no details given.

Organisational context: large service industry; USA (Detroit Edison).

Results: following EAP use, there were reductions of 18% in lost time episodes; 29% in lost days; 26% in value of insurance claims; 13% fewer written warnings; 40% fewer suspensions; 41% fewer accidents. There were also significant improvements in supervisor-rated quality of work and relationship with supervisor.

Methodological issues: supervisors were aware that employees they were rating had used the EAP and it is possible that their work performance ratings could have been influenced by this knowledge.

Methodological quality rating: low.

Author: Park, D.A.

Title: Client satisfaction evaluation: University employee assistance program.

Date: 1992.

Type of publication: journal article.

Source: *Employee Assistance Quarterly*, 8(2): 15–34.

Aims of study: to evaluate faculty and staff satisfaction with the EAP at California State University, Chico.

Method: anonymous questionnaire distributed to all university staff and academic faculty members. Questionnaire included items relating to: EAP awareness and use, evaluation of EAP services, self-assessment of work performance before and after EAP use, respondent demographic information.

Sample: 35% response rate (out of total employee population of 1900).

Type of counselling: primarily brief crisis counselling leading to referral to external therapy provider, plus follow-up interview.

Organisational context: university. Mature EAP (in existence six years at time of survey).

Results: 17% of survey respondents were not aware of the existence of the EAP. Lack of awareness was greatest in men, older employees and the academic faculty. 64% self-referral; 17% referral by co-workers. 99% of users felt the service was confidential. High levels of satisfaction (90%) reported by those who had used the EAP. 73% of users reported that the EAP had helped or greatly helped their work performance. 74% of users said they had already referred a co-worker.

Methodological issues: the high levels of client satisfaction reported in this study reflect similar results in other satisfaction studies. It seems likely that, given a response rate of 35%, the data may be biased in the direction of the views of satisfied users eager to support the service.

Methodological quality rating: low.

Authors: Philips, S.B.

Title: Client satisfaction with university Employee Assistance Programs.

Date: 2004.

Type of publication: journal article.

Source: *Employee Assistance Quarterly*, 19: 59–70.

Aims of study: to assess levels of client satisfaction in university employees making use of EAP services; to estimate the cost savings to the universities of providing EAP cover.

Method: an 11-item client satisfaction questionnaire (developed for this study) was used in 19 university EAPs in the USA and Canada. Clients were mailed the questionnaire four months after their first contact with the EAP.

Sample: 1,780 questionnaires were received (response rate of around 33%); information not provided on age, gender and so on of clients.

Type of counselling: not specified.

Organisational context: higher education; Canada/USA.

Results: an average annual utilisation rate across these EAPs was 4%. Overall levels of satisfaction with EAP services were 94%. However, when clients were referred to other agencies or therapists for further treatment, satisfaction was lower: 74%. 63% of employees stated that their problems interfered with work performance or productivity at the point they first contacted the EAP; 61% stated that their work productivity was enhanced by the help they received from the EAP. Based on these figures, the authors estimated a cost-benefit ratio of around 4:1 for these university EAPs.

Methodological issues: there was a disappointing lack of detail concerning the presentation of data in this study. The economic analysis was based on a number of assumptions that were not based on actual economic information collected from the participating organisations.

Methodological quality rating: low.

Authors: Preece, M., Cayley, P.M., Scheuchl, U. and Lam, R.W.

Title: The relevance of an Employee Assistance Program to the treatment of workplace depression.

Date: 2005.

Type of publication: journal article.

Source: Journal of Workplace Behavioral Health, 21: 67–77.

Aims of study: what proportion of employees presenting to an EAP are identified as having depression? What are the characteristics of clients who are depressed? How effective is an EAP intervention in assisting these clients?

Method: ratings of work impairment, work absence and global functioning were made by the counsellor at intake and again at closing. The counsellor provided a classification of the presenting problem.

Sample: 463 males; 948 female. The average age was 42.

Type of counselling: brief, approach not specified. Counsellors all had Masters degrees in social work.

Organisational context: large EAP offering services to more than 350 companies; Canada.

Results: 27% of clients were categorised as depressed (anxiety 25%; alcohol dependence 4%; drug dependence 2%). Gender and age mix similar in depressed and non-depressed groups. Depressed clients were more likely to have a family history of mental health issues (4% of depressed clients) or addiction (5% of depressed clients) and to be taking antidepressants (22%). Depressed clients more likely to be on leave from work at time of EAP use (20%, compared with 7% of non-depressed clients), and to report impaired work and global functioning. Although EAP intervention produced a statistically significant improvement in work and global functioning for depressed clients, at the end of counselling their scores were still higher (ie lower levels of functioning) than the intake scores of non-depressed clients.

Methodological issues: the lack of detail provided over the counselling intervention (eg number of sessions) and the invalidated assessment tools used represented severe methodological limitations.

Methodological quality rating: low.

Authors: Reese, R.J., Conoley, C.W. and Brossart, D.F.

Title: Effectiveness of telephone counselling: a field-based investigation.

Date: 2002.

Type of publication: journal article.

Source: Journal of Counselling Psychology, 49: 233–242.

Aims of study: to evaluate the effectiveness of a telephone-based EAP counselling service.

Method: questionnaires (500) were sent out to those who had used the service, comprising items on satisfaction, the Bond sub-scale from the Working Alliance Inventory, and the Counsellor Rating Form – short version (CRF-S). Questionnaires were sent out by the intake worker, who scheduled appointments with the telephone counsellor. Participants who returned the questionnaire were eligible for a prize draw.

Sample: 186 clients (response rate 37%); 73% female; white 76%, African American 7.5%, Hispanic 5.4%, native American 3.2%. 62% were classified as low income; only 35% of respondents in the study had health coverage for mental health issues. Range of presenting problems: depression, anxiety, panic, marital. 79% were first-time callers.

Type of counselling: solution-focused counselling; median number of sessions was three (range one to 99 sessions). All counsellors had at least Masters-level qualifications and were regularly supervised. No limit to the number of sessions a client may have. An average session lasted 30 minutes. Callers with severe problems were advised on how to access local mental health services.

Organisational context: the service was open to employees and family members of three large corporations (area of activity not specified in the article). More than 15,000 people used the service in 1998.

Results: 80% reported that the specific problem that led them to counselling had improved. 68% were 'very satisfied' or ' completely satisfied' with telephone counselling. Those whose original problem was most severe were helped less than those whose original problems were less severe. Counsellors were perceived as expert and trustworthy. Client reported a strong bond with their counsellor. Clients who had been in counselling for one year or longer reported more improvement than those who had received less counselling. The authors concluded that (a) telephone-based employee assistance counselling is as effective as face-to-face counselling; (b) it may be most relevant for those who are unable to access face-to-face counselling (in this study, low income clients); (c) telephone counselling may not be appropriate for clients with the most severe problems.

Methodological issues: although this study did not include its own control/comparison group, the results of the questionnaire were compared to 'benchmarking' figures for best practice face-to-face counselling, thus allowing the authors to justify their claims regarding the comparative effectiveness of telephone counselling. This was an analytic strategy that might valuably be used by other EAP researchers.

Methodological quality rating: high.

Notes: a commentary by Kenny and McEacharn (2004) has highlighted the practical and ethical implication of the findings reported by Reese et al (2002). In a later paper, based on the same data, but published too late to be included as a main entry in the present review, Reese, Conoley and Brossart (2006) reported that, of the 186 participants who responded to the survey, 96% would be willing to seek telephone counselling again (compared to 63% being willing to seek face-to-face counselling again); of those who had received both telephone and face-to-face counselling, 58% preferred telephone counselling. The Reese et al (2006) study also included a factor analysis of clients' perceptions of the value of telephone counselling. Three main factors emerged: *control* (eg 'I felt I could hang up if I did not like it'; 'I liked that the counsellor could not see me'); *convenience* ('I liked that I could call when I wanted to'), and absence of *inhibiting* influences (eg 'I liked that telephone counselling was free').

Author: Reynolds, S.

Title: Psychological wellbeing at work: is prevention better than cure?

Date: 1997.

Type of publication: journal article.

Source: *Journal of Psychosomatic Research*, 43(1): 93–102.

Aims of study: to compare the implementation, impact and outcome of individual counselling with an organisation-level stress-management strategy.

Method: three offices of a City Council department were offered either counselling, an organisational intervention (action research project) or no intervention (control group). Outcomes were assessed through questionnaire measures of wellbeing (GHQ-12), depression (Beck Depression Inventory), somatisation (SCL-90R), mood and job satisfaction, collected prior to the intervention and at one-year and two-year follow-up. At the end of the study period, absenteeism data was collected for each employee. Client satisfaction data collected were through questionnaires at follow-up.

Sample: counselling condition: 27 employees in the office, of whom 15 accepted the offer of counselling; organisational intervention: 76 employees; control group: 43 employees. Mix of blue collar and managerial/professional staff. Details on age and gender were not given.

Type of counselling: three sessions (two weekly meetings with a final session three months later). Delivered by clinical psychologists in a university research clinic. Cognitive-behavioural model. Further information on the type of counselling used in this study, and a case study, can be found in Barkham (1989).

Organisational context: local authority/municipal housing department; UK. Newly initiated counselling, temporary service.

Results: high levels of satisfaction with counselling. Positive perceptions of counselling even in those who had not received it. Compared to other two groups, employees in the office that had been offered counselling (including those who had received counselling and those who had not) reported significant improvements in mental health and somatic symptoms. At least 80% of those who received counselling reported clinically significant change in depression. None of the interventions produced an effect on absenteeism or job satisfaction.

Methodological issues: there was a disappointing lack of detail in this paper around the reporting of findings. The circumstances of this study were that a university team was called in by management to a department perceived by them as being in crisis, it delivered a set of interventions and then withdrew. Given the lack of ongoing counselling (or any other) provision, it was not surprising that organisational impacts (eg job satisfaction, sickness absence) were not found.

Methodological quality rating: high.

Notes: in this study, the mental health and somatisation problems of employees in the comparison and control groups continued to deteriorate over the follow-up period. This is an important result – it addresses the criticism that is often made of naturalistic counselling outcome studies (ie studies that do not have control groups) that many or most clients would get better anyway without receiving counselling. In this study, those who were denied it got significantly worse. Another important feature of Reynolds (1997) is that, even though only 55% of the employees in the 'counselling intervention' office took up the offer of counselling, there was an improvement in mental health across the whole group.

Authors: Rogers, D., McLeod, J. and Sloboda, J.

Title: Counsellor and client perceptions of the effectiveness of time-limited counselling in an occupational counselling scheme.

Date: 1995.

Type of publication: journal article.

Source: *Counselling Psychology Quarterly*, 8(3): 221–231.

Aims of study: to examine counsellor and client views of the helpfulness of time-limited counselling.

Method: clients and counsellors completed questionnaires at the end of counselling. Scales included: number of sessions, demographic characteristics, satisfaction and presenting problems.

Sample: 429 clients who used the service over a two-year period. 223 clients (52%) completed questionnaires – 73% female; 27% male. The average age was 35 to 44.

Type of counselling: in-house. All counsellors had at least two years' post-diploma experience. Range of counselling models used. There was a maximum of six sessions.

Organisational context: social services; UK.

Results: clients reported more personal than work-related problems. Overall, there were high levels of client satisfaction (90% or higher). Problem type not consistently related to satisfaction or number of sessions. 17% of clients were dissatisfied with the number of sessions offered. Counsellors were dissatisfied with number of sessions in 38% of cases. 23% of clients were referred on to other agencies. There were highest levels of satisfaction in clients who had completed five sessions. On the basis of counsellor ratings, there was strong evidence that more satisfied clients were more likely to complete end-of-counselling questionnaires.

Methodological issues: the high proportion of missing data (clients not completing questionnaires) meant that these findings needed to be interpreted cautiously. The reported finding that clients who do not complete questionnaires are likely to be rated by their counsellors as poor outcome cases suggested that the client satisfaction levels found in this study (and other similar ones) may be over-estimating the benefits of counselling.

Methodological quality rating: low.

Notes: this paper reports analysis of further data derived from the Sloboda et al (1993) study.

Authors: Rost, K., Fortney, J. and Coyne, J.

Title: The relationship of depression treatment quality indicators to employee absenteeism.

Date: 2005.

Type of publication: journal article.

Source: *Mental Health Services Research*, 7: 161–168.

Aims of study: to examine the impact of treatment on employee users of a managed health plan, who were diagnosed with depression.

Method: participants were recruited to the study at the time of their first visit to their physician for depression, and were re-interviewed at six months and 12 months. On each occasion, data was collected about the treatment being received by the patient, and number of workdays missed.

Sample: 230 patients in five health plans (67% female; 39% ethnic minority). They were mainly office workers in managerial and clerical roles.

Type of counselling: information about the counselling approach was not specified (participants were able to access a wide range of therapists). Participants were considered as receiving psychotherapy if they had completed four or more sessions in a six-month period (the average number of sessions was 7.2). (Those in the medication group needed to have been taking antidepressants for at least 12 weeks.)

Organisational context: not specified; USA.

Results: those who had received psychotherapy alone reported a 26% drop in absenteeism. Those who had received medication, or combined medication and psychotherapy, showed a minimal decrease in absenteeism, which was not statistically significant.

Methodological quality rating: high.

Methodological issues: it is important to note that participants were only defined as having received psychotherapy if they had completed at least four sessions. The authors argue that less than four sessions would be insufficient to make an impact on behaviour. Other studies of workplace counselling have not adopted this criterion, and have included data from counselling clients who have only received one or two sessions. The significant finding of this study – that psychotherapy is more effective than drug therapy – may be due to the selection of only those clients who have meaningfully engaged in counselling.

Authors: Salmela-Aro, K., Naatanen, P. and Nurmi, J. E.

Title: The role of work-related personal projects during two burnout interventions: a longitudinal study.

Date: 2004.

Type of publication: journal article.

Source: *Work and Stress*, 18: 208–230.

Aims of study: to compare the effectiveness of experiential and analytic group therapy for work-related burnout.

Method: participants were recruited from professional and clerical staff who had contacted the Helsinki Occupational Health Service for burnout. Participants were randomly allocated into three conditions: experiential group therapy, analytic group therapy and a waiting list control group. Those in the waiting list control were offered treatment as usual (contact every two months with a doctor or psychotherapist). Questionnaire measures of burnout (Bergen Burnout Indicator) and involvement in personal projects were administered before therapy, at the halfway point and one month following the end of the group. There were 16 one-day fortnightly group therapy sessions (group size eight; two therapists) orientated toward work and burnout issues.

Sample: 62 participants received therapy; 28 in the control condition. 73% women; the average age was 49.

Type of counselling: long-term experiential or analytic group therapy, adapted to address work burnout issues.

Organisational context: public-sector white-collar workers, occupational health service; Finland.

Results: compared to those in the control condition, those who received therapy showed significantly more improvement in terms of both burnout symptoms and their attitude to projects in which they were engaged (eg they became more willing to ask for support, less negative emotions and less self-demanding). The experiential therapy was marginally more effective than the analytic therapy intervention.

Methodological issues: although this was an exceptionally well-conducted controlled study, there were two areas in which it would have been useful to have been provided with further information. First, it would be have been helpful to know how many of the therapy group members demonstrated clinical improvement in relation to burnout symptoms (ie moved into the 'normal' range of functioning). Second, it would have been useful to carry out a longer-term follow-up of these clients, to determine whether their gains persisted over time.

Methodological quality rating: high.

Notes: this is a particularly important study, because it demonstrates how basic theory and research into a work stress condition (burnout) can be used to design a therapeutic intervention tailored to the needs of a specific group of clients.

Authors: Saroja, K.I., Ramphal, K.G., Kasmini, K., Ainsah, O. and Bakar, O.C.

Title: Trends in absenteeism rates following psychological intervention – preliminary results.

Date: 1999.

Type of publication: journal article.

Source: *Singapore Medical Journal*, 40(5): 349–351.

Aims of study: to examine the effect of a psychotherapeutic intervention on absenteeism rates in an agency, which had reported high absenteeism rates.

Method: all 334 employees were screened using the GHQ (Malay translation) and measures of work stress. Employees identified as having mental health problems were interviewed by a psychiatrist. All were offered counselling, referral or medication during a six-month intervention period. Rates of absenteeism (days) and absence episodes were estimated for the whole workforce for the six-month period before the three six-month periods before the intervention (baseline) and the intervention period itself.

Sample: number and demographic profile of those receiving therapy not specified.

Type of counselling: not specified.

Organisational context: not specified.

Results: when compared with the equivalent six-month period in the previous year, there were significantly fewer days off, and fewer episodes of short-term absence (<seven days) but significantly more cases of long-term absence (>seven days).

Methodological issues: the absence of descriptive information made it difficult to interpret the results of this study.

Methodological quality rating: low.

Notes: highly significant seasonal patterns of sickness absence were found in this study, suggesting that it is important to control for seasonal effects (eg holiday periods) when comparing company-wide absence data. Psychological therapy also appeared to have a differential impact on short-term and long-term absence rates, indicating the importance of developing differentiated measures of absence. The level of voluntariness of the type of psychological intervention offered appears to have been somewhat different from that existing in North American and European EAPs, perhaps reflecting cultural differences.

Authors: Schmit, M.J. and Stanard, S.J.

Title: The utility of personality inventories in the employee assistance process: a study of EAP referred police officers.

Date: 1996.

Type of publication: journal article.

Source: *Employee Assistance Quarterly*, 11(4): 21–42.

Aims of study: to examine the utility of personality assessment scales (MMPI, CPI) in the employee assistance process.

Method: police department employees undergoing 'fitness for duty' evaluations on removal from duty because of psychological problems, or at the point of return to duty following counselling, completed the MMPI-2 and or the CPI and an intelligence test. MMPI-2 is a 567-item questionnaire, which provides a personality profile based on 10 clinical scales (eg depression, hysteria, paranoia, schizophrenia and so on). CPI is a 462-tier personality questionnaire with 20 subscales (eg dominance, sociability, empathy, flexibility and so on).

Sample: 376 police employees referred over a four-year period. Study is based on 171 employees who had completed an intervention and were reassessed for return to active duty (the remainder were still in treatment or had been initially assessed as fit for duty). Comparison group of 18 personnel who refused intervention. Gender: 82% male; 18% female.

Type of counselling: provided by a variety of external agencies, including psychotherapists, AA, in-patient care, usually over a three-to four-month period.

Organisational context: police; USA.

Results: significant, but moderate, improvement found on the majority of MMPI-2 and CPI scales, and on the intelligence test.

Methodological issues: although this was an important study, the lack of detailed information about how data was collected and analysed meant that the findings must be interpreted with caution.

Methodological quality rating: low.

Notes: the MMPI and CPI have been designed to measure enduring dimensions of personality, and are not particularly sensitive to change. The finding of moderately high shifts in MMPI and CPI scores, in the direction of increased mental health, is therefore of interest.

Authors: Selvik, R., Stephenson, D., Plaza, C. and Sugden, B.

Title: EAP impact on work, relationship and health outcomes.

Date: 2004.

Type of publication: journal article.

Source: *Journal of Employee Assistance*, 21, 18–22.

Aims of study: to evaluate the effectiveness of the US Federal occupational health EAP.

Method: at the beginning and end of counselling, clients completed a brief health outcome questionnaire (items on productivity and sickness absence) and counsellors carried out a global assessment of functioning (GAF) and noted presenting problems.

Sample: 59,685 federal or military employees who completed pre- and post-counselling questionnaires (51% of cases seen over a three-year period); the average age was 45 to 54; two-thirds white, 20% African-American, 10% Hispanic; 60% self-referral; information on gender was not provided.

Type of counselling: not specified, mainly face-to-face but some telephone counselling. Typical time span of counselling was eight weeks.

Organisational context: government agencies; USA.

Results: nearly 50% of clients reported that their problems had an impact on their work performance. 60% had mental health problems (anxiety and depression; 15% family/relationship issues; 15% job issues; 10% alcohol or drug problems. Pre-counselling, clients reported 2.37 days absent in previous 30 days; by end of counselling: 0.91 days. There were significant improvements in global functioning and self-estimate of productivity. At onset of counselling, 16% were in lowest health status category; at end of counselling, it was 11%.

Methodological issues: this was a short article, which provided only brief details on the research that was carried out. There was no follow-up data, so it was not possible to know whether the gains that were reported would remain over time.

Methodological quality rating: low.

Authors: Shakespeare-Finch, J. and Scully, P.

Title: A multi-method evaluation of an Australian emergency service employee assistance program.

Date: 2004.

Type of publication: journal article.

Source: *Employee Assistance Quarterly*, 19: 71–91.

Aims of study: to carry out an evaluation of an EAP for ambulance personnel.

Method: a multi-method approach was adopted, involving (i) analysis of records on utilisation of services over a two-year period; (ii) focus groups with different sub-groups of the staff population; (iii) survey of all ambulance service personnel. Rich qualitative data was collected and analysed in terms of themes.

Sample: survey: 661 personnel – 75% male; the average age was 41; focus groups: 51 participants.

Type of counselling: the EAP provided a range of services: 24-hour telephone counselling; critical incident debriefing/defusing sessions; network of Peer Support Officers (ambulance personnel trained in counselling skills); counselling service provided by external therapists.

Organisational context: emergency service (ambulance); Australia.

Results: high levels of satisfaction were expressed in survey responses. There were positive perceptions of the service in all areas of the organisation. There was a very high level of utilisation (precise figure not given, but 'more than half' of staff used the service during a 12-month period). The average number of sessions with external counsellors was 2.9. There were 30 debriefings per annum. Key issues raised were personnel's increasing workload; some concerns about confidentiality of peer support officers; more staff (eg in communications centres) wished to be able to attend critical incident debriefings; and a need for improving management awareness of the value of the service.

Methodological quality rating: high.

Sheffield Psychotherapy Project I

Key sources:

Shapiro, D.A. and Firth, J. (1987) Prescriptive vs. exploratory psychotherapy. Outcomes of the Sheffield psychotherapy project. *British Journal of Psychiatry*, 151: 790–799.

Firth, J. A. and Shapiro, D. A. (1986) An evaluation of psychotherapy for job related distress, *Journal of Occupational Psychology*, 59: 111–119.

Shapiro, D.A. and Firth-Cozens, J.A. (1990) Two-year follow-up of the Sheffield psychotherapy project. *British Journal of Psychiatry,* 157, 389–391.

Aims of study: the primary research questions underpinning this study were: (i) what types of job-related problems are found in a sample of distressed workers? (ii) does interest in the job rise proportionally to a fall in distress? (iii) can job-related distress be reduced to the normal range after 16 sessions of psychotherapy? (iv) does cognitive-behavioural or psychodynamic psychotherapy have the greater impact on job-related distress?

Method: clients with work-related problems received either eight sessions of cognitive-behavioural therapy followed by eight sessions of psychodynamic therapy, or psychodynamic followed by cognitive-behavioural. Clients remained with same therapist throughout treatment. Assessment conducted at intake, between therapies, at the end of therapy and at three-month follow-up. Outcome assessment measures included the Present State Examination (interview to determine psychiatric 'caseness'), Social Adjustment Scale (interview measure of depression in relation to work, encompassing factors such as time off, performance loss, lack of interest and feeling of inadequacy), Personal Questionnaire (client ratings of severity of self-defined problems, completed three times each week), Beck Depression Inventory, SCL-90 (a symptom checklist) and the Rosenberg self-esteem scale.

Sample: 40 clients (23 male, 17 female; the average age was 40), who were managerial/professional workers. All clients included in the study had high levels of psychological problems (psychiatric 'caseness') at the start of therapy. The clients seen in this study were similar to those who would make use of an EAP or in-house counselling service: '…

patients…made their initial contact with our clinic in response to publicity materials distributed in appropriate employment settings by welfare and personnel staff. Initial screening criteria excluded people not complaining that their work was affected by their problems' (Shapiro and Firth, 1987, p 792).

Type of counselling: psychodynamic and cognitive-behavioural, combined in sequence (see above).

Organisational context: therapy was carried out in a university research clinic. Clients were drawn from a variety of work settings: health, education, engineering and civil service.

Results: at intake, scores reflected 'a population with mean levels of symptomatology and distress well into the clinical range of severity' (Shapiro and Firth, 1987, p. 794). 28% of the problems identified by clients were work-related. Of these, 62% referred to difficulties in relationships at work. Psychodynamic and cognitive-behavioural therapies were equally effective overall, with some indications that CB might have more impact on psychological symptoms but not on work factors. 75% of clients had moved from psychiatric 'caseness' into the normal range at follow-up. Around 60% of clients improved significantly on work-related factors. Both psychological distress and interest in the job improved equally rapidly in the first phase of therapy, but then diverged, with some clients improving in distress but not interest in the second phase and vice-versa. Gains in relation to depressive symptoms were maintained at the two-year follow-up.

Methodological issues: as with the other studies conducted by the Sheffield group, the design of this piece of research was sufficiently robust to enable the results to be treated with confidence.

Methodological quality rating: high.

Notes: although clients reported high levels of psychological distress at the start of therapy, their scores on the work-related scales of 'time off' and 'performance deficit' were within the normal range: 'this means that, despite their high clinical levels of symptomatology, these clients may not be recognised as distressed by the usual criteria of absenteeism or poor work performance' (p. 117). Analyses of individual cases drawn from this study are available in Firth (1985) and Parry, Shapiro and Firth (1986).

Sheffield Psychotherapy Project II

Key sources:

Shapiro, D.A., Barkham, M., Hardy, G. and Morrison, L.A. (1990) The second Sheffield Psychotherapy Project: rationale, design and preliminary outcome data. British Journal of Medical Psychology, 63: 97–108.

Firth-Cozens, J. A. and Hardy, G. E. (1992) Occupational stress, clinical treatment and changes in job perceptions, *Journal of Occupational and Organisational Psychology*, 65: 81–86.

Shapiro, D.A., Barkham, M., Rees, A., Hardy, G. Reynolds, S. and Startup, M. (1994) Effects of treatment duration and severity of depression on the effectiveness of cognitive-behavioural and psychodynamic-interpersonal psychotherapy. Journal of Consulting and Clinical Psychology, 62 (3): 522–34.

Aims of study: to evaluate the effectiveness of eight and 16-session cognitive-behavioural (CB) and psychodynamic-interpersonal (PI) psychotherapy for clients with job-related stress.

Method: clients randomly allocated to four groups: eight sessions CB, eight sessions PI, 16 sessions CB, 16 sessions PI. Assessment of clients at intake, after eight sessions, after 16 sessions (or three-month follow-up for eight-session cases), three-month follow-up (16-session cases only) and one-year follow-up. Measures included: psychiatric status, Beck Depression Inventory, symptom checklist (SCL-90R), anxiety (STAI), self-esteem, interpersonal problems (IIP), job perceptions (Aspects of Work Inventory, encompassing perception of job environment and job satisfaction sub-scales) and client-defined ratings of problems.

Sample: 120 (30 in each condition; three dropped out of therapy); 'professional, managerial and white-collar workers suffering from depression and/ or anxiety ... (and) complaining that their work is affected by their problems' (Shapiro et al, 1990, p. 100)'; inclusion in study dependent on diagnosis of depression.

Type of counselling: eight or 16-session cognitive-behavioural or psychodynamic-interpersonal psychotherapy, delivered by experienced clinical psychologists in a University research clinic.

Organisational context: various (clients were recruited from a variety of work settings).

Results: both eight and 16-session versions of each therapy proved to be effective in terms of all measures used. No difference between effectiveness of cognitive-behavioural and psychodynamic-interpersonal models. Substantial levels of improvement (Effect Sizes of between 1.00 and 2.32, depending on measure used) between intake and follow-up. Effectiveness of cognitive-behavioural and psychodynamic-interpersonal approaches was 'broadly equivalent'. Only the most severely depressed clients gained from having 16 rather than eight sessions; for moderate and low severity depressed clients eight sessions were just as effective as 16. The authors suggest that 'therapist-client dyads adjust the pace of therapy to the time they have available' (p. 530). Significant improvements on most attitude to work factors: opportunity for control, skill use, job demand, clarity, feeling valued, interpersonal contact, competence, work spillover, adequacy of pay and job satisfaction. Only perceived job variety did not shift. Symptom changes were of higher magnitude than changes in job perceptions. Key finding: 'as symptom levels are reduced, perceptions of jobs become more positive' (Firth-Cozens and Hardy, 1992, p. 84).

Methodological issues: as with the other Sheffield studies, this study displayed a high degree of methodological rigour. Initially 540 people applied for treatment at this clinic. Those who had previous history of psychiatric disorder, BDI score below 16 or previous recent psychotherapy were excluded. The remaining 257 underwent a screening interview to establish suitability for the study, in terms of level of psychiatric disturbance. This procedure yielded a final group of 138 clients entering therapy, of whom 117 completed therapy and submitted sufficient usable questionnaire data. Compared to the typical EAP or workplace counselling service, therefore, this client group represented a highly selected, and possibly highly motivated, sample.

Methodological quality rating: high.

Notes: a description of a case drawn from this study can be found in Firth-Copzens, 1992). Several further analyses of the data collected in this study have been published, exploring various aspects of the process of therapy. However, these subsequent papers have not examined work-related factors.

Sheffield Psychotherapy Project III

Key source:

Barkham, M. Shapiro, D.A., Hardy, G.E. and Rees, A. (1999) Psychotherapy in two-plus-one sessions: outcomes of a randomised, controlled trial of cognitive-behavioural and psychodynamic-interpersonal therapy for subsyndromal depression. Journal of Consulting and Clinical Psychology, 67 (2): 201–211.

Aims of study: to compare the effectiveness of two methods of brief therapy in clients whose psychological problems affected their work.

Method: clients received two sessions of therapy one week apart, followed by another session three months later (the '2+1' model). Questionnaires were completed at pre-screening (assessment), before the first therapy session, two weeks before the second therapy session, two weeks before and then two weeks after the third session, and finally one year following entry into the study. Clients' psychiatric status was evaluated at the pre-treatment assessment interview only. Change measures administered throughout treatment were the Beck Depression Inventory (depression), SCL-90-R (psychological distress/symptoms) and the IIP-32 (interpersonal/relationship problems). Clients were randomly allocated to either cognitive-behavioural or psychodynamic-interpersonal versions of the 2+1 approach. Some clients were required to wait for four weeks to create a waiting list control group.

Sample: 116 clients, in professional/managerial jobs (67 men; 49 women). The average age was 45. Clients were recruited to reflect a mild-moderate level of symptom severity. For purposes of data analysis, clients were allocated to three groups on the basis of their BDI scores: (i) 'stressed' (mildly symptomatic, within the normal population range); (ii) 'subclinical depression'; (iii) low-level clinical depression.

Type of counselling: three sessions of brief cognitive-behavioural or psychodynamic-interpersonal delivered by clinical psychologists in a university research clinic.

Organisational context: various; UK.

Results: therapy was effective for all groups. At one-year follow-up, clinically significant levels of improvement were found in 67% of stressed clients, 72% of subclinical clients and 65% of low-level clinically depressed clients. Overall, the subclinical clients gained more than the other two groups on a range of outcome measures. The four-week delay for some clients did not compromise the effectiveness of the intervention. The cognitive-behavioural intervention was no more effective than psychodynamic-interpersonal during the course of treatment, but emerged as significantly more effective at the one-year follow-up. The more distressed (low level clinically depressed) clients were less able to make use of the three-month delay between sessions two and three.

Methodological issues: one of the reasons for the high Effect Sizes found in this study (compared with other research into workplace counselling) arose from the use of pre-treatment assessment as the comparison point from which therapeutic change is evaluated. It is known that clients improve between initial contact (assessment, screening) and the first actual therapy session: studies in which questionnaires are distributed just prior to the first session lose the opportunity to detect this early beneficial shift (which is usually attributed to the effect of instillation of hope).

Methodological quality rating: high.

Notes: additional reports of the findings of this study, including case vignettes, can be found in Barkham (1989) and Barkham and Shapiro (1990a,b).

Authors: Sloboda, J.A., Hopkins, J.S., Turner, A., Rogers, D.R. and McLeod, J.

Title: An evaluated staff counselling programme in a public sector organization.

Date: 1993.

Type of publication: journal article.

Source: Employee Counselling Today, 5(5): 10–16.

Aims of study: to evaluate the effectiveness of an in-house counselling service.

Method: questionnaires were completed by clients and counsellors following counselling, designed to collect data on client demographic characteristics, number of sessions, presenting problems and satisfaction.

Sample: 255 clients (154 completed questionnaires). 22% male; 78% female.

Type of counselling: not specified (range of approaches used); maximum six sessions. All counsellors were professionally qualified with at least two years' post-diploma experience.

Organisational context: social services; UK.

Results: male and younger employees were over-represented in client group. Presenting problems included personal and work issues. 92% of clients rated the service as good or very good. Differences were found between client and counsellor ratings of success (clients were consistently more positive).

Methodological issues: the substantial amount of missing data (101/255 clients did not complete questionnaires) meant that it was necessary to interpret satisfaction data with caution.

Methodological quality rating: low.

Notes: the paper includes a full account of the rationale and operation of the programme. Further analysis of data from this study can be found in Rogers et al (1995).

Author: Sprang, G.

Title: Utilising a brief EAP-based intervention as an agent for change in the treatment of depression.

Date: 1992.

Type of publication: journal article.

Source: *Employee Assistance Quarterly*, 8(2): 57–65.

Aims of study: to evaluate the impact of an EAP intervention on depression.

Method: the Beck Depression Inventory was administered pre-counselling and at the end of treatment.

Sample: 116 clients (including both employees and family members) who had approached the EAP for treatment of depression. The average age was 32; 34% male, 66% female. There was a comparison group of 83 individuals (similar age and gender distribution as client group) who had been assessed but did not return after the first session and did not seek treatment elsewhere. Clients who required medication for depression were excluded from the study.

Type of counselling: solution-focused brief therapy. All clients gave an extensive psychosocial history during a pre-therapy telephone screening interview. Information on the number of sessions or background of counsellor(s) was not given.

Organisational context: no information provided; USA.

Results: the BDI scores for the client and comparison groups were equivalent at intake (average score: 21, indicating low-level clinical depression). At the end of therapy the average client group score was 6.68 (within the normal range), while the comparison group score remained at 20. Analysis of specific BDI items relevant to work functioning revealed that the comparison group showed significant improvements in decision-making and ability to work, although the gains in the client group were more substantial.

Methodological issues: the use of a treatment 'drop out' group for comparison purposes was unusual, since it is difficult to interpret the meaning of refusal to take up the offer of treatment. For example, some members of the comparison group may have felt that the initial contact they received was sufficient to bring about change, while others may not have been ready to change at all. However, even if the comparison group is disregarded, the level of gain in the client group is highly significant in itself.

Methodological quality rating: high.

Authors: Stephenson, D., Bingaman, D., Plaza, C., Selvik, R., Sudgen, B. and Ross, C.

Title: Implementation and evaluation of a formal telephone counselling protocol in an Employee Assistance Program.

Date: 2003.

Type of publication: journal article.

Source: *Employee Assistance Quarterly*, 19: 19–33.

Aims of study: to evaluate the effectiveness of introducing a protocol for the use of telephone counselling in a large EAP.

Method: analysis of data collected during the first year of implementation of a new protocol, and in the previous year, for telephone counselling cases and face-to-face cases. Data included: client ratings of satisfaction; counsellor ratings of client functioning at the beginning and end of treatment; length of sessions; counsellor self-ratings of confidence and competence in telephone counselling; brief case reports submitted by counsellors.

Sample: 'over 21,000 face-to-face and telephone counselling cases'. Information not provided on gender, age, ethnicity and so on.

Type of counselling: approach not specified; combination of in-house counsellors and referral to external affiliates. All telephone counselling carried out by in-house staff.

Organisational context: federal government; USA.

Results: introduction of the protocol did not make any difference to the proportion of cases dealt with by telephone. Average length of telephone sessions in implementation period was 32 minutes (face-to-face sessions: 60 minutes). Clients were equally satisfied with telephone and face-to-face consultations. Counsellors rated telephone cases as improving more than face-to-face cases, and rated themselves as able to provide satisfactory counselling relationships by this method. Counsellor feedback suggested that the protocol enabled them to be more effective in their telephone work. Case reports indicated a range of categories for differentiating between cases where telephone assistance might be helpful, or where face-to-face counselling might be more effective.

Methodological issues: little detail was provided on the research data that was collected, which made it difficult to assess the validity of the analysis.

Methodological quality rating: low.

Notes: this paper includes a valuable discussion of the issues involved in implementing telephone counselling in an EAP setting.

Authors: Van Dierendonck, D., Schaufeli, W.B. and Buunk, B.P.

Title: The evaluation of an individual burnout program: the role of inequity and social support.

Date: 1998.

Type of publication: journal article.

Source: Journal of Applied Psychology, 83: 392–407.

Aims of study: to evaluate the effectiveness of a CBT-based group counselling intervention for employees suffering from occupational burnout.

Method: employees from a large care organisation in the Netherlands were offered an opportunity to take part in a group experience that allowed them to 'look at their present career situation'. Managers within the organisation encouraged attendance among staff who they believed might benefit from the programme. Two comparison groups were used: one from within the organisation and one from a similar organisation that was not providing any stress support for staff. All participants in the study completed a questionnaire package that incorporated scales measuring burnout, perceived equity of relationship with clients, perceived equity of relationship with the organisation, perceived social support and intention to leave the job. Questionnaires were completed before the start of the programme, and six months and one year after it ended. Levels of absenteeism (frequency and duration of absences) were analysed using organisational records, for the 12 months prior to the programme and 12 months after it.

Sample: health and social care professionals who worked with clients with learning disabilities. The average age of participants was 33, with an average of seven years of work experience. 72% were female. 352 participants completed pre-intervention questionnaires. Data was analysed for only the 149 participants who completed end of intervention measures (36 in the burnout counselling group and 113 in the comparison groups; the low completion rate for post-intervention questionnaires appeared to be because recipients were absent from work when they were distributed).

Type of counselling: structured small group (six to eight members; five half-day sessions), facilitated by a psychologist. The design of activities within the group was informed by CBT theory and by equity theory (the idea that burnout results from an imbalance between what the person gives to and gets from the recipients of their work and the organisation within which they are employed).

Organisational context: health and social care (residential); Netherlands.

Results: a complex pattern of results was obtained. Overall, the burnout intervention had a positive impact on participants, with a small Effect Size (ES) of 0.26. Compared with the comparison groups, the participants who engaged in group counselling reported lower levels of emotional exhaustion, higher levels of perceived equity/ balance in their relationship with their organisation, and lower levels of sickness absence. Participants who had higher levels of social support benefited more than those who had lower levels of support. However, no change was found on several variables that were assessed.

Methodological issues: this was a carefully conducted study, which received a high rating for methodological quality. Nevertheless, there are two methodological issues that need to be taken into account when interpreting the findings of this study. First, participants were not randomly allocated to intervention or no-intervention conditions. This could mean that the employees who received counselling were at a stage of active readiness to change (which could enhance the effectiveness of any intervention they received). Second, follow-up data could not be collected for a large proportion of those who entered the study. The authors carried out a careful comparison of the characteristics of those who provided follow-up data against those who did not. Although there was no difference in terms of demographic variables, the non-respondents did have higher sickness absence rates. This factor might have influenced the finding of the study. On the other hand, the use of a long follow-up period (one year) is a particularly strong aspect of the study.

Methodological quality rating: high.

Author: Van der Klink, J.J.L., Blonk, R.W.B., Schene, A.H. and van Djik, F.J.H.

Title: Reducing long-term sickness absence by an activating intervention in adjustment disorders: a cluster randomised, controlled design.

Date: 2003.

Type of publication: journal article.

Source: Occupational and Environmental Medicine, 60: 429–437.

Aims of study: to evaluate the effectiveness of a CBT-based intervention, delivered by occupational health doctors, on sickness absence in employees absent from work because of mental health difficulties that had arisen in response to recent stressful events (adjustment disorders).

Method: a method of cluster randomisation was used – half of the occupational health doctors delivered the research intervention, while the other half restricted themselves to treatment as usual. A range of factors were measured at baseline, three months and 12 months: work stress, coping, symptoms, sense of personal mastery/control and number of days absent from work.

Sample: 109 employees were allocated to the intervention, with 83 in the treatment as usual condition. 63% male; the average age was 41; mainly secondary school education. More than 60% had worked for the organisation for more than 10 years.

Type of counselling: a three-stage graded activity approach based on CBT principles, focusing on problem solving and structuring daily activity. Occupational physicians delivering the intervention received three days of training. Four or five sessions were during the first six weeks of sickness absence. Treatment as usual consisted of empathic listening and instruction about stress and lifestyle issues.

Organisational context: large telecommunications company; Holland.

Results: all employees (in both conditions) had returned to work within 12 months. The employees receiving the intervention returned to work significantly sooner and had fewer recurrences of sickness absence in the next 12 months. There were no differences between the intervention and treatment-as-usual groups in terms of psychological outcomes and symptoms – employees in both groups improved, but their symptom scores remained higher than those in healthy comparison groups.

Methodological issues: this study did not strictly meet the inclusion criteria for the present review, because those who received counselling did not volunteer for treatment. However, the study can be viewed as an investigation of the effect of enhancing counselling skills in occupational health staff within an organisation. The organisation required employees absent from work on health grounds to meet regularly with an occupational health doctor, so the 'counselling' sessions would have occurred in any case.

Methodological quality rating: high.

Appendix B. Studies of factors related to outcome

Author: Arthur, A.R.

Title: Mental health problems and British workers: a survey of mental health problems in employees who receive counselling from Employee Assistance Programmes.

Date: 2002.

Type of publication: journal article.

Source: Stress and Health, 18: 69–74.

Aims of study: to investigate the severity of mental health problems in employees who attend EAP counselling.

Method: new referrals for counselling were invited to complete the GHQ-12 (a mental health screening instrument) and a supplementary questionnaire (designed for the study) that elicited information on gender, age, ethnicity, chronicity and severity of problems, and disturbance of work performance.

Sample: 111 clients (69% male; the average age was 41). More than 400 questionnaire packs were distributed to counsellors, but it was not known how many of these were passed on to clients.

Type of counselling: approach not specified; external EAP.

Organisational context: 33 organisations; mix of public and private sector.

Results: using a conservative cut-off score to define psychiatric 'caseness', it was found that 87% of clients could be categorised as cases. 43% of clients recorded scores that were effectively at the ceiling of the scale. Most clients (86%) reported that their problems had affected them for six months or longer; 92% described their problem as 'moderate' or 'serious'; 77% believed that their problem had an impact on their work performance; 65% stated that they would have taken time off work if counselling had not been available; 71% categorised their problem as 'personal' and 29% as work-related.

Authors: Courtois, P. Hajek, M., Kennish, R., Paul, R., Seward, K., Stockert, T.J. and Thompson, C.

Title: Performance measures in the Employee Assistance Program.

Date: 2004.

Type of publication: journal article.

Source: Employee Assistance Quarterly, 19: 45–58.

Aims of study: to develop a consensus statement around performance measures that can be utilised in evaluating the quality of EAP service delivery.

Method: a working group convened by the lead US professional body for EAP providers met over a three-year period to formulate a set of criteria for EAP performance measurement. Surveys and other data were collected and analysed, and initial findings were distributed to members for comment and feedback.

Sample: sample details not specified – large pool of EAP professionals and stakeholders.

Type of counselling: various – not specified.

Organisational context: various/all sectors – not specified.

Results: a set of key performance measures was established, encompassing a series of domains: implementation, network development (eg ease of access to counselling); customer and member service; member satisfaction; reimbursement of providers; quality of customer service; other factors. Within these domains, benchmarks were specified regarding acceptable levels of performance. For example: 90% of employees working in urban locations should have access to an EAP counsellor within 10 miles/10 minutes; affiliates/counsellors should be reimbursed within 30 days; average speed of answer to telephone inquiries should be 30 seconds; 15–20% of referrals should be from supervisors; all counselling should be supervised; substance abuse assessments should comprise 30% of caseload.

Author: Denzin, N.K.

Title: Living and dying in an Employee Assistance program.

Date: 1995.

Type of publication: journal article.

Source: Journal of Drug Issues, 25(2): 363–378.

Aims of study: to analyse the effects of change in EAP provision in one organisation.

Method: ethnographic case study, using participant observation and official documents.

Sample: a major university in the USA.

Type of counselling: external EAP.

Organisational context: higher education; USA.

Results: the study describes the process by which 'Midwestern University', in an attempt to cut costs, changed from a state-run EAP providing access to local therapists to a private sector EAP provider. This shift resulted in reduced benefits to employees, specifically a reduction in access to therapists who had been highly valued by employees. Various forms of organised protest were mounted by both university staff and mental health professionals.

Methodological issues: the rich qualitative data presented in this study conveyed a convincing picture of the importance of this EAP for its users. However, there was no attempt to carry out a systematic evaluation.

Notes: this paper is unique in demonstrating the impact of a *reduction* in EAP provision, and the degree of employee resistance to such a move. The effectiveness of an EAP to employees can be gauged, in part, by the extent of employee resistance to its removal or reduction. The paper also illustrates the contribution that can be made by qualitative research in this instance in being able to offer a detailed and richly textured account of a single case.

Authors: Hiatt, D., Hargrave, G. and Palmertree, M.

Title: Effectiveness of job performance referrals.

Date: 1999.

Type of publication: journal article.

Source: *Employee Assistance Quarterly*, 14: 33–43.

Aims of study: to evaluate the effectiveness of an EAP intervention in terms of supervisor ratings; to compare characteristics of supervisor-referred and self-referred clients.

Method: ratings on five-point scales completed by supervisors and EAP therapists, before and after counselling.

Sample: 753 supervisor-referred cases over an eight-year period. Information on number of self-referred cases was not provided.

Type of counselling: 'broad-brush' external EAP that provided services to 'several hundred' companies.

Organisational context: not specified.

Results: compared to self-referral, supervisor referral cases were more likely to be male clients with substance abuse and job performance issues (self-referrals were more likely to be female with personal/family issues). The key issue for supervisors making referrals was attendance at work. Supervisors rated attendance, behaviour at work, interpersonal relations at work, and quality and quantity of work as significantly improved following counselling. Counsellors rated only marginal improvement in these clients and perceived 25% of supervisor-referred clients as difficult to engage in counselling. The overall utilisation rate for this EAP was 8%.

Note: this paper described a process of consultation between the supervisor making the referral and the EAP co-ordinator, which is unusual and innovative, and which may be a factor in the high levels of supervisor satisfaction with outcomes.

Methodological issues: the rating scales used in this study had not been validated or used previously. Although they had face validity, they may not have been reliable. In addition, details about research procedures were not described in sufficient detail.

Authors: Lambert, M.J., Hansen, N.B. and Finch, A.E.

Title: Patient-focused research: using patient outcome data to enhance treatment effects.

Date: 2001.

Type of publication: journal article.

Source: Journal of Consulting and Clinical Psychology, 69: 159–172.

Aims of study: to determine the number of sessions required for psychotherapy clients to report a significant level of improvement.

Method: clients in a large number of counselling and psychotherapy agencies completed the OQ-45 scale at the beginning of every session. An analysis was carried out of the number of sessions required for the client to achieve a normal range of functioning (recovery).

Sample: a total of 6,072 clients in a national database, of whom 3,269 were EAP users, predominantly diagnosed with adjustment/ stress disorders. Information about age, gender and ethnicity was not provided.

Type of counselling: not specified – the EAP clients were drawn from a large number of agencies from 30 states across the USA.

Organisational context: various.

Results: the analysis of this large data set demonstrated that at least seven sessions of therapy are required for reliable change (ie a sufficient shift to be measured with confidence) to occur in 50% of clients, while at least 14 sessions are required for clinically significant change (ie achievement of a normal level of functioning).

Comments: the importance of this study is that it suggests that the average number of sessions received by typical EAP clients (ie six or fewer) is not sufficient to bring about meaningful change. The apparently positive outcome figures reported by some studies of EAPs may be due to the fact that clients who did not improve dropped out of the study, with the result that the end-of-counselling data collected by the researchers were skewed in the direction of more satisfied clients – the approach taken by Lambert et al (2001) of requiring clients to complete a questionnaire at each session meant that data from those making less progress was captured more consistently. (A further section of this article examined the impact on psychotherapy of providing the therapist with session-by-session data on the progress of the client. However, EAP clients were not included in this part of the study.)

Authors: Masi, D.A., Jacobson, J.M. and Cooper, A.R.

Title: Quantifying quality: findings from clinical reviews.

Date: 2000.

Type of publication: journal article.

Source: Employee Assistance Quarterly, 15(4): 1–17.

Aims of study: to evaluate the quality of clinical services being provided by EAPs, using a clinic review process.

Method: an eight-step clinical review process, carried out by independent expert clinicians on a random selection of case files, using a standard protocol.

Sample: more than 4,000 cases drawn from 42 organisations in the USA, ranging in size from 300 to 500,000 employees. The counselling services were mainly delivered by external EAP providers.

Type of counselling: various.

Organisational context: various; USA.

Results: the demographic characteristics of cases reviewed were: 53% female; 27% ethnic minority; 64% self-referral, 18% referred by family or co-workers, 18% referred by management. The average number of sessions was 3.3. The level of overall documentation in files was generally poor. In comparison with research guidelines, counsellors were underdetecting or underrecording alcohol and drug problems, and psychiatric symptomatology.

Note: this paper incorporates a valuable brief review of the literature on clinical review procedures.

Authors: Rost, K., Smith, J.L. and Dickinson, M.

Title: The effect of improving primary care depression management on employee absenteeism and productivity: a randomised, trial.

Date: 2004.

Type of publication: journal article.

Source: *Medical Care*, 42: 1201–1210.

Aims of study: to compare the effect of an enhanced depression care intervention, and treatment as usual, on symptoms and work functioning.

Method: 12 primary care practices were randomly allocated to provide treatment as usual or an enhanced intervention for depressed patients. The enhanced intervention was based on additional training for doctors and care managers, and regular phone calls from the care manger to the patient, monitoring progress and encouraging them to engage with antidepressant drug treatment and counselling. The research team interviewed patients at six, 12, 18 and 24 months, and administered measures of depressive symptomatology, emotional functioning, work productivity and absence from work.

Sample: 158 patients completed the enhanced treatment package; 168 in the treatment as usual condition. 85% female; 13% ethnic minority; the average age was 39.

Type of counselling: not specified – patients received counselling from a wide range of agencies. The number of sessions was not specified.

Organisational context: patients worked in a range of occupations; USA.

Results: the enhanced depression management package increased the uptake of counselling from 23% to 42% of patients, and average time of antidepressant use from eight to nine months. The enhanced intervention had a marginal effect on depression symptoms, and no impact on emotional functioning, but significant impact on work productivity (6.1% increase) and absenteeism (22% decrease). The enhanced depression had a higher relative effect on patients who were full-time employed – those who were employed part-time were helped to a lesser extent.

Methodological issues: the main difference between treatment as usual and the enhanced intervention was the amount of counselling received by the latter group (from specialist therapists and from care managers). This study was unusual in being able to contrast the effect of counselling on symptoms and on work functioning. It was striking that the impact on work functioning was greater than that on symptoms.

Authors: Schneider, R.J., Casey, J. and Kohn, R.

Title: Motivational versus confrontational interviewing: a comparison of substance abuse assessment practices at employee assistance programs.

Date: 2000.

Type of publication: journal article.

Source: *Journal of Behavioral Health Services and Research*, 27: 60–74.

Aims of study: to compare the effectiveness of two contrasting approaches to assessing clients referred to an EAP for substance abuse problems.

Method: clients from 14 organisations were randomly allocated to different assessment conditions: confrontational interviewing (CI) or motivational interviewing (MI). A range of measures of drug and alcohol misuse and addiction severity were administered at the first meeting, and at three and nine-month follow-up telephone interviews.

Sample: 89 clients (80% male; the average age was 38).

Type of counselling: clients received two assessment sessions, based on either a CI or MI approach. The intervention was manualised and counsellors were supervised. There was a high level of adherence to the approach. 30 counsellors (60% female; average age was 39) were used, the majority with Masters levels qualifications; the average length of post-qualifying experience was nine years. Following the assessment, clients were referred to inpatient treatment (17%), outpatient counselling (16%), self-help-meetings (35%), additional EAP counselling (79%) or a mix of these interventions.

Organisational context: multiple, not specified; mix of internal and external EAPs.

Results: overall, clients in both groups showed substantial and equivalent improvement over the study period (20% abstaining from drug use at nine months). 63% of MI clients reported following the treatment plan agreed at assessment (54% of the CI group). The conclusion drawn by the authors is that MI methods are at least as effective as the more traditional confrontational approach that has generally been applied in work with substance abusing clients.

Methodological issues: this was a well-designed and carefully conducted trial; the paper included a wealth of detail about the interventions and change measures that were employed.

Notes: the paper incorporates a valuable discussion of how EAP counsellors might incorporate motivational interviewing techniques into their work with clients.

Authors: Shumway, S.T., Wampler, R.S., Dersch, C. and Arredondo, R.

Title: A place for marriage and family services in Employee Assistance Programs (EAPs): a survey of EAP client problems and needs.

Date: 2004.

Type of publication: journal article.

Source: *Journal of Marriage and Family Therapy*, 30: 71–79.

Aims of study: to explore the perceptions of EAP clients regarding their needs in relation to different kinds of presenting problems.

Method: all new users of an EAP, over a two-year period, were invited to complete a questionnaire that asked them to rate problem severity and need for services in six areas: family, psychological, medical, work/employment, alcohol/drugs and legal. Participants also completed a symptom checklist and a scale of marital satisfaction.

Sample: 800 clients (31% male; the average age was 38; married 61%; 73% Anglo-American, 19% Hispanic, 4.5% African-American; 97% self-referred).

Type of counselling: approach not specified; included individual, marital and family work.

Organisational context: the EAP served a range of commercial and public sector organisations; USA.

Results: 66% of clients rated their family problems as considerable or extreme; 65% rated psychological/emotional problems similarly. 49% reported significant individual psychological problems *and* marital problems. Other problem areas received significantly lower severity ratings. 54% of clients were in the caseness/clinical range on the symptom checklist, and 72% were on the marital satisfaction scale. Alcohol problems were reported by 5% of the sample and drug problems by 3%.

Methodological issues: a limitation of this study, acknowledged by the authors, was that it was conducted in an EAP that advertised itself as offering marital and family services. Compared to other EAPs that offered only individual counselling, this one may have attracted a higher proportion of clients with family/marital issues.

Note: similar findings are reported in Shumway, Wampler and Arredondo (2003), based on an analysis of a larger sample of clients from the same EAP.

Authors: Vermeersch, D.A., Lambert, M.J. and Burlingame, G.M.

Title: Outcome Questionnaire: item sensitivity to change.

Date: 2000.

Type of publication: journal article.

Source: *Journal of Personality Assessment*, 74(2): 242–261.

Aims of study: to analyse the validity of a new questionnaire measure of mental health (the Outcome Questionnaire) in psychotherapy settings.

Method: the questionnaire was completed by different groups of clients/patients (including EAP clients) and a non-clinical control group.

Sample: 559 EAP clients. 61% female; the average age was 35.

Type of counselling: not specified. EAP.

Organisational context: various.

Results: scores, and number of therapy sessions, were compared for EAP clients and: (a) student counselling clients, (b) patients using a university-based clinic; (c) clients receiving outpatient psychotherapy. Scores for a control group of students were also available. The EAP clients reported scores (mean pretreatment OQ score of 73.07) that were somewhat lower than psychotherapy clients (86.35) and clinic patients (77.49) but higher than student counselling service clients (70.32). All client groups reported much higher scores than the control group mean of 48.87. The mean number of counselling/psychotherapy sessions used for each client group was: EAP 4.8; psychotherapy 5.2; clinic 7.0 and student counselling 5.4.

Notes: this study is not primarily focused on EAP workplace counselling issues. However, it provides a useful comparison between EAP and other client groups around levels of dysfunction and use of therapy.

Appendix C. Studies of the economic costs and benefits of workplace counselling

Authors: Blaze-Temple, D. and Howat, P.

Title: Cost benefit of an Australian EAP.

Date: 1997.

Type of publication: journal article.

Source: *Employee Assistance Quarterly.*

Aims of study: to carry out a cost-benefit analysis of an EAP in a government organisation in relation to industry standard benchmarking (25% improvement in absenteeism, workers' compensation and turnover, and that the EAP should at least pay for itself).

Method: quasi-experimental time-series analysis in a 400 employee regional government organisation (Hospital Laundry and Linen Service). Comparisons carried out over a 2.5 year period between: (i) employees who used the EAP; (ii) employees who used self-arranged counselling; (iii) employees who had no counselling, on data collected from company records. Four employee surveys were carried out.

Sample: approximately 400 blue-collar employees.

Type of counselling: external EAP.

Organisational context: regional government service organisation; Australia. Newly introduced EAP.

Results: annual utilisation rates between 4–5%. EAP counselling produced significant cost savings in absenteeism and turnover. Cost:benefit ratio for counselling compared with no counselling was 1:1 (ie the EAP paid for itself). However, self-arranged counselling produced more cost-benefit for the company than EAP counselling. The company would have accrued financial benefits from the EAP if the utilisation rate had reached 6%.

Methodological issues: this paper represents a particularly good example of how to carry out a cost-benefit analysis.

Notes: the literature review cites benefit-cost ratios of EAPs reported in the previous studies as ranging from 7:1 to 1:2.

Authors: Bray, J.W., French, M.T., Bowland, B.J. and Dunlap, L.J.

Title: The cost of employee assistance programs (EAPs): findings from seven case studies.

Date: 1996.

Type of publication: journal article.

Source: *Employee Assistance Quarterly*, 11(4): 1–19.

Aims of study: to analyse the comparative costs of seven EAPs; to demonstrate the use of a methodology for analysing EAP costs.

Method: EAP directors and staff completed a structured, comprehensive cost interview guide.

Sample: EAPs providing services to seven contrasting worksites (manufacturing, health, municipal, financial, communications).

Type of counselling: internal and external EAPs; wide variation in services provided.

Organisational context: variety of contexts; USA.

Results: utilisation rates ranged between 4% and 20% of eligible employees per annum. Higher utilisation rates consistently associated with higher costs per employee. EAPs can have different cost mixes while arriving at the same overall cost (eg in one site, 70% of costs were spent on personnel; in another site, personnel accounted for 36% of costs). Internal EAPs are more costly than external provision (but have higher utilisation rates).

Notes: one of the important contributions made by this paper is to illustrate a comprehensive and highly informative, yet succinct, approach to analysing EAP costs and services. The authors of this paper are professional health economists.

Author: Bruhnsen, K.

Title: EAP evaluation and cost benefit savings: a case example.

Date: 1989.

Type of publication: journal article.

Source: *Health Values*, 13(1): 39–42.

Aims of study: to carry out a cost-benefit analysis of the University of Michigan EAP as a means of reducing employee sick-time use, during the first year of operation of an expanded service.

Method: analysis of sickness absence records of EAP cases; cost estimates of sickness absence; cost estimate for providing EAP service.

Sample: detailed case analysis was carried out on 122 cases (38% seen in one year).

Type of counselling: crisis intervention, diagnosis and referral for wide range of personal problems. Delivered through University Medical Centre.

Organisational context: large urban university; USA. 24,000 employees, dependents and retirees had access to the EAP.

Results: EAP used by 4% of employees. Comparing six months pre-EAP consultation and six months post-consultation, 60% of EAP users showed substantial reductions in sickness absence; 6% no change and 34% an increase in absence. The average absence pre-EAP use was 9.53 days/year; post-EAP use was 6.66 days/year. (Norm for university employees: 8.4 days/year.) The cost-benefit saving ratio was calculated at 1.5:1 (ie net savings for year of $87,000 set against cost of $35,000). Most dramatic changes were seen in alcoholism cases (21% drop in sickness absence) and drug abuse cases (50% drop).

Methodological issues: the use of only one cost indicator (sickness absence) was a weakness of this study. On the one hand, inclusion of other cost factors (accidents, disciplinary costs, supervisor time, cost of recruiting and training replacement staff, productivity and so on) would have resulted in a more favourable cost-benefit ratio. On the other hand, in many cases of short-term sickness absence, staff (eg academic staff) would not actually be replaced, so the cost saving was notional rather than real.

Authors: Dainas, C. and Marks, D.

Title: Evidence of an EAP cost offset.

Date: 2000.

Type of publication: journal article.

Source: *Behavioral Health Management*, July/August, pages 34–41.

Aims of study: to examine the healthcare costs associated with EAP use in employees of an organisation whose employees were members of a managed healthcare scheme funded by the company.

Method: review paper, summarising two studies carried out by the organisation in the 1990s, based on analysis of health costs.

Sample: 2,200 employees and family members working for Abbott Laboratories.

Type of counselling: assessment and referral to specialist services.

Organisational context: pharmaceutical; USA.

Results: the analysis looked at health costs associated with two categories of treatment: mental health/substance abuse (MHSA) and general medical care. A cost comparison was conducted between employees/family members who had used the EAP and those who had not. Those who had used the EAP were associated with higher MHSA costs, but lower general medical costs and lower overall healthcare costs. These findings suggest that, although EAP users cost the company more in relation to care for their mental health needs, this spending was more than offset by the lower use by EAP clients of general medical services. No explanation is given for this finding. An overall 2:1 cost saving was reported.

Methodological issues: this paper provided only a brief report of some complex economic analyses. No references were provided for further information on the studies that are described.

Authors: Hargrave, G.E. and Hiatt, D.

Title: The EAP treatment of depressed employees: implications for return on investment.

Date: 2004.

Type of publication: journal article.

Source: *Employee Assistance Quarterly*, 19: 39–49.

Aims of study: to estimate the cost savings to organisations arising from EAP interventions for depressed employees.

Method: routine evaluation data collected by a large EAP were analysed. Clients rated problems and symptoms at the first session of counselling, and then two months following the end of treatment. Although modelled on established questionnaires, the scales used were adapted for the specific purposes of the EAP. Some validation information on the scales is provided.

Sample: 11,756 EAP users (68% female; the average age was 40).

Type of counselling: not specified.

Organisational context: not specified; USA.

Results: following counselling, the number of employees reporting moderate to severe symptoms of depression had decreased by 48%. Using figures for the effect of depression on work performance, developed by other researchers, the authors estimated that the EAP represented a return on investment of 142%.

Methodological issues: there were several methodological weaknesses in this study. Insufficient detail was provided on the outcome data that was collected. In addition, a series of assumptions were made, when calculating cost-effectiveness, that were not based on actual economic evidence collected directly from organisations involved.

Author: Houts, L.M.

Title: Survey of the current status of cost-savings evaluations in employee assistance programs.

Date: 1991.

Type of publication: journal article.

Source: *Employee Assistance Quarterly*, 7(1): 57–72.

Aims of study: to describe the use of cost-savings evaluations in EAPs in the USA.

Method: questionnaire survey of directors of EAPs.

Sample: 82 EAPs, from a total of 95 surveys distributed (response rate 86%).

Type of counselling: all types of EAPs.

Organisational context: various – hospitals, municipal government, post offices, universities, companies, corporations (not specified in detail).

Results: all EAPs dealt with drug and alcohol abuse; 96% with emotional problems unrelated to substance abuse; 89% with financial problems. 21% of EAPs had been in existence three years or less, 41% between four and nine years, and 38% for 10 years or longer. 83% believed that cost saving represented an important criterion on which to evaluate EAP performance. 98% believed that the cost-savings potential of their EAP was 'moderate' or 'high'. Only 40% had collected cost-savings data, but 79% wished to do so in the future. A number of obstacles to cost-savings evaluation were identified. In the 33 organisations carrying out economic analyses, the most commonly collected data referred to absenteeism and accidents. Other data collected included costs of medical and insurance services, sick leave, disciplinary action, training costs, lost productivity and grievance costs. A few organisations attempted to quantify morale and productivity. Only eight organisations claimed to be able to calculate the dollar return on EAP investment. Directors also described ways in which they used cost-saving information.

Authors: Klarreich, S.H., DiGiuseppe, R. and DiMattia, D.J.

Title: Cost effectiveness of an employee assistance program with rational-emotive therapy.

Date: 1987.

Type of publication: journal article.

Source: *Professional Psychology: Research and Practice*, 18(2): 140–144.

Aims of study: to evaluate the cost-effectiveness of RET counselling provided with an in-house EAP.

Method: analysis of absenteeism data on 295 clients who had completed RET therapy over a two-year period and for whom adequate personnel records were available. There was also analysis of the cost of counselling and saved supervisor time. A satisfaction scale was completed by clients.

Sample: 295 employees who used an EAP. 431 employees contacted the EAP during a two-year period; 364 completed counselling.

Type of counselling: time-limited (average four sessions) rational-emotive therapy, focused on personal-emotional issues (54%), job problems (22%), marital-family issues (20%) and alcohol/drug issues (4%).

Organisational context: large North American oil company.

Results: absenteeism data for one year pre-EAP treatment: average 10.28 days; post-EAP treatment: 2.98 days. (Company norm: 13 days/year). 75% of EAP users rated their problems as having improved. Few clients needed to be referred to external services. Cost of supervisor time saved in dealing with these 'troubled employees' was calculated at four hours per employee (ie the average number of psychologist hours used by each employee). Cost-benefit ratio was calculated at 2.74:1.

Methodological issues: there appeared to be a number of contestable assumptions underlying this analysis. The use of sickness absence as a cost indicator was problematic: in many cases of short-term sickness absence, staff may not actually be replaced, so the cost saving was notional rather than real. It could also be that a post-therapy sickness absence rate of 2.98 days/year was too low, and reflected obsessive overwork, or lack of self-care, rather than real productivity. Estimating the saving in supervisor time was also problematic – in many cases supervisors would deal with these 'troubled employees' cases by avoiding them. These factors made the estimation of cost-effectiveness difficult in this study. Nevertheless, it did record a substantial fall in sickness absence, and lower referral rates to external agencies, which must generate real cost savings.

Author: McClellan, K.

Title: Cost-benefit analysis of the Ohio EAP.

Date: 1989.

Type of publication: journal article.

Source: *Employee Assistance Quarterly*, 5(2): 67–85.

Aims of study: to estimate the cost-benefit ratio of the Ohio EAP for the 1988 calendar year.

Method: estimation of direct and indirect expenses, and cost outcomes, associated with the EAP. Data mainly collected from official documents and records, plus client satisfaction questionnaires.

Sample: single case study. Large employer (60,000 employees) of whom 6% per annum use the EAP.

Type of counselling: EAP encompassing training, assessment and referral, telephone helpline, and some brief therapy. Delivered through community mental health centres, non-profit EAPs and private clinicians.

Organisational context: large public service organisation.

Results: the Ohio EAP is cost-effective as an *employee* benefit. In other words, therapeutic services are delivered that employees regard highly, at a reasonable cost; 'it has been a meaningful benefit to the vast majority of State employees who use the service' (p. 81). However, the EAP does not produce a financial benefit to the *employer*. No plausible cost offsets could be identified in such areas as health insurance costs, paid sick leave, productivity improvements or employee turnover.

Methodological issues: this study represented a particularly careful and balanced attempt to weigh costs and benefits in a comprehensive manner.

Appendix D. Attitude/utilisation studies

Authors: Asen, J. and Colon, I.

Title: Acceptance and use of Police Department Employee Assistance Programs.

Date: 1995.

Type of publication: journal article.

Source: Employee Assistance Quarterly, 11(1): 45–54.

Aims of study: identifying the factors that contribute to the acceptance and use of EAPs in the context of a police setting.

Method: brief (anonymous) questionnaire distributed to police officers during shift changes. Items: demographic (five items), awareness of EAP (six items; yes/no format), acceptance of EAP (12 items; five-point Likert scale).

Sample: 82 police officers (75 male, seven female; 58 patrol, 24 supervisory/administrative) from 4 municipalities in New Jersey (range of social class and urban/rural). 91% of all serving officer completed questionnaire. No-one refused to participate.

Type of counselling: external broad-brush EAP.

Organisational context: police departments.

Results: all respondents were aware of the EAP; 22% had used it; 16% had used it for a family member; 55% knew a colleague who had used it. There was a strong belief that the EAP must be confidential and not based on site. Female officers, and officers with more children, were more likely than males to use an EAP. Perceptions of the EAP were generally positive.

Notes:

This paper includes interesting literature review around the extent and nature of psychosocial problems reported by police officers. The rate of 22% use is an estimate of the proportion of employees who had *ever* used the service, not an estimate of the annual utilisation rate.

Author: Basso, R.

Title: A consumer's grapevine in an employee assistance program.

Date: 1989.

Type of publication: journal article.

Source: Employee Assistance Quarterly, 4(3): 1–10.

Aims of study: what are the sources of clients' perceptions and expectations of an EAP?

Method: Participant observation. Qualitative field notes.

Sample: 19 clients (predominantly women and manual workers) who used an EAP counselling service provided by a medium-sized industrial unit.

Type of counselling: individual, time-limited psychotherapy focusing on socio-personal or emotional concerns.

Organisational context: local site (350 employees) of a multi-national whisky distiller (Canada). EAP had been established for eight years.

Results: service users learn about the EAP through an informal grapevine, which reassures them about confidentiality, provides examples of how counselling helped other colleagues, and supports the client while undergoing counselling.

Methodological issues: there was a lack of detail on how the fieldwork was conducted.

Authors: Bennett, J.B. and Lehman, W.E.K.

Title: Workplace substance abuse prevention and help seeking: comparing team-oriented and informational training.

Date: 2001.

Type of publication: journal article.

Source: Journal of Occupational Health Psychology, 6: 243–254.

Aims of study: to compare the effectiveness of two contrasting forms of providing staff with information about EAP services: (i) information-giving meetings, (ii) team-based sessions including active role-play.

Method: groups of staff completed questionnaire measures of their knowledge and attitudes toward the EAP; utilisation rates were assessed. Measures were administered before the training, at the end of training and at six-month follow-up.

Sample: 380 members of staff took part in the training; 260 completed follow-up data.

Type of counselling: external EAP, mainly focusing on alcohol-abuse issues.

Organisational context: local authority; south-western USA.

Results: significant shifts in staff knowledge and attitudes, which were retained at six-month follow-up, and higher utilisation rates.

Authors: Brummett, P. O.

Title: A comparison of Employee Assistance Programs providing internal versus external treatment services: a research note.

Date: 2000.

Type of publication: journal article.

Source: *Employee Assistance Quarterly*, 15(4): 19–28.

Aims of study: to examine the differences between EAPs that provide treatment services themselves (internal) and those that limit their activity to assessment and referral (external).

Method: questionnaire survey, carried out in 1996, of EAP organisations, selected from the membership directory of the Employee Assistance Professional Association (EAPA).

Sample: 277 organisations (response rate 42%).

Type of counselling: various.

Organisational context: various; USA.

Results: internal EAPs were more likely to be based in larger organisations, and those with a higher proportion of female employees and younger employees. Internal EAPs were more likely to offer prevention services (eg stress management workshops). Internal EAPs were more likely to be based in organisations that were perceived by their employees as being more stressful.

Authors: Blum, T.C. and Roman, P.M.

Title: A description of clients using employee assistance programs.

Date: 1992.

Type of publication: journal article.

Source: *Alcohol Health and Research World*, 16(2): 120–128.

Aims of study: to identify patterns of EAP use, with particular focus on alcohol problems.

Method: EAP administrators completed a questionnaire for each client (on completion of the case) concerning information about demographics, referral categories, treatment history and assessment. EAP clients completed a questionnaire (on intake), which included items on job function and performance, satisfaction with relationships, influences on referral, alcohol use and depression (short form of the Beck Depression Inventory). Data was compared with a survey of 3,000 employees in similar workplaces.

Sample: 6,400 employees from 84 work sites in the USA. Data collected 1990–92. Family members using EAPs were not included in the study.

Type of counselling: a range of EAP provisions, including alcohol, drug, mental health and family issues.

Organisational context: a broad range of organisations.

Results: EAP users (compared with national sample of employees) were more likely to be: female, younger, black, unmarried, longer in post and depressed. EAPs were used by both manual and managerial/professional employees. Client problem categories were psychological/emotional problems (44%); family (30%); marital (28%); alcohol problems (16%) and drugs (4%). Referral routes were co-worker, supervisor and self. 14% only received EAP counselling, with 86% referred on to other professional or self-help services.

Methodological issues: information on response rate was not provided. Given that an average of 80 cases were collected from each site, it is likely that a substantial number of EAP clients at these sites were not included in the study.

Notes: this study is part of a wider programme of research into the epidemiology of workplace alcohol use in the USA, and includes useful references to other studies.

Authors: Braun, A.L. and Novak, D.E.

Title: A study of EAL non-utilisation.

Date: 1986.

Type of publication: journal article.

Source: *EAP Digest*, November/December, pp. 52–55.

Aims of study: to identify the characteristics of employees who do not use EAP services.

Method: questionnaire survey.

Sample: 145 EAP directors in USA and Canada (29% response rate; 498 questionnaires distributed).

Type of counselling: EAP.

Organisational context: various.

Results: non-users were believed to be more likely to belong in the following groups: management and professional; 50 years or older; men; victims of high job stress. Non-users were seen as denying their problems, being too self-reliant and with a belief that EAP use would devalue them.

Methodological issues: this study relied only on counsellor perceptions of non-users – the extent to which these views were based on reality, or are stereotypes, was not evaluated.

Authors: Brodzinsky, J.D. and Goyer, K.A.

Title: Employee Assistance Program utilisation and gender.

Date: 1987.

Type of publication: journal article.

Source: *Employee Assistance Quarterly*, 3: 1–13.

Aims of study: to examine gender differences in referral patterns and utilisation of an EAP.

Method: analysis of case records of EAP users over a three-year period.

Sample: 1,162 clients of an EAP linked to a government department – 53% female; 41% self-referred; a wide range of problem areas.

Type of counselling: not specified.

Organisational context: federal government; USA.

Results: compared to male users of the EAP, female clients were more likely to be self-referred, and had psychological and interpersonal problems (in contrast to men, who were more likely to report problems with alcohol or drug misuse). The higher levels of supervisor and court referrals in male clients were interpreted as evidence that male problems were more 'intrusive' of life and work.

Methodological issues: the absence of information or analysis concerning the gender mix of the wider workforce population made it difficult to interpret these findings.

Authors: Burke, R.J.

Title: Utilisation of Employees' Assistance Program in a public accounting firm: some preliminary data.

Date: 1994.

Type of publication: journal article.

Source: *Psychological Reports*, 75: 264–266.

Aims of study: to examine employee use of, and satisfaction with, a newly created EAP in a single company.

Method: anonymous survey questionnaire sent to all employees.

Sample: questionnaire was sent to 2,150 employees; replies were received from 1,595. There were approximately equal numbers of male and female respondents (reflecting the gender mix within the company).

Type of counselling: not specified.

Organisational context: accountancy firm; USA.

Results: 78% of employees were aware of the existence of the EAP. 60% indicated that they would use the service if they saw a need (women more likely to use than men). Annual utilisation rate: 6% (equal rates for men and women). Employees who had used the programme were generally satisfied with the service they had received.

Methodological issues: the questions that were used were invalidated and the questionnaire was very brief. No information was reported on ethnicity, roles within organisation and so on.

Methodological quality: low.

Author: Butterworth, I.E.

Title: The components and impact of stigma associated with EAP counselling.

Date: 2001.

Type of publication: journal article.

Source: *Employee Assistance Quarterly*, 16: 1–9.

Aims of study: to explore the level of stigma that employees associate with use of EAP counselling.

Method: survey questionnaire, developed for this study following focus group sessions with employees.

Sample: 513 questionnaires were distributed; 171 returned (33% response rate); 59% male.

Type of counselling: not specified.

Organisational context: two medium-sized manufacturing and distribution companies; Australia.

Results: 66% were supportive of the existence of the EAP. Stigma was more associated with male rather than female employees. Female participants who perceived stigma were less likely to be willing to attend the EAP; male participants less inclined to rule out EAP attendance on the basis of stigma. Key dimensions for men were: 'make me feel like a weak person', loss of respect from others', 'indicate that I was losing my independence'.

Methodological issues: this was very much an exploratory study; no reliability or validity data was offered in support of the use of the questionnaire.

Author: Csiernik, R.

Title: Internal versus external Employee Assistance Programs: what the Canadian data adds to the debate.

Date: 1999.

Type of publication: journal article.

Source: *Employee Assistance Quarterly*, 15: 1–12.

Aims of study: to compare characteristics of internal and external EAPs in Canada.

Method: a review of data on EAPs available in professional publications.

Sample: 21 case studies.

Type of counselling: various.

Organisational context: various – public and private sectors, from 750 to 37,000 employees.

Results: the mean utilisation rate for internal EAPS was 7% (range 2.5% to 29.3%); external EAPs mean 5.4% (range 2.5% to 9%). Internal EAPs saw more clients with drug-related and work-related problems. External EAPs tended to see more clients with family, marital and emotional problems. No data was found on costs.

Author: Csiernik, R.

Title: Employee Assistance program utilisation: developing a comprehensive scorecard.

Date: 2003.

Type of publication: journal article.

Source: *Employee Assistance Quarterly*, 18: 45–60.

Aims of study: to determine the factors associated with differences in utilisation rates for EAPs in Canada.

Method: a survey questionnaire (developed for the study) distributed to organisations with EAPs.

Sample: 154 organisations (39.7% response rate); all sectors of the economy were included.

Type of counselling: not specified – the survey covered many different forms of EAP provision.

Organisational context: various; Canada.

Results: the mean utilisation rate for the 102 companies providing this data was 9.2% (range 1% to 30%). Higher utilisation rates were found in organisations that were: private sector; unionised; no restriction on number of sessions; existence of a company EAP policy; annual promotion campaign was operated; where unions had been involved in setting up the service; where the service involved the use of volunteers from within the workforce in addition to paid counsellors; where the service was staffed by social workers rather than counsellors. Utilisation rates were also associated with regional differences, with higher rates in western provinces of Canada and lower in the east. Key conclusion: 'the greater the involvement of employees, the more the EAP is used' (p. 50).

Methodological issues: the survey included questions about not only the utilisation rate, but how the rate was calculated within each organisation. 19 different formulae for calculating EAP utilisation were reported: '…at the present time, for research purposes, the calculation and use of utilisation rates has restricted value and may even be a futile exercise; for when this statistic is examined, it appears as if we are comparing apples with kumquats' (p. 54). The main areas of divergence in estimations of utilisation concerned: (a) whether family members were counted as users, and then whether each family member was treated as an individual case or the family as a whole constituted a case; (b) the question of what counted as a recordable case – a referral, a new case, a face-to-face meeting, a telephone contact (of what lengths?), a return visit or only a situation where an actual treatment plan had been agreed. To overcome service caps, for example, one EAP would treat a client who returned within a year with two different problems as two cases; another EAP stated that after every 12 hours of counselling they considered the situation as a new case. These issues were discussed in detail within this paper, and the author made a carefully argued proposal for a standardised approach to assessing two key variables: utilisation rate and penetration rate. The concept of penetration rate was defined as 'the depth of EAP involvement in the organisation', and incorporated data on number of referrals, telephone inquiries, participants in educational workshops/seminars, mediation sessions, debriefing, group sessions, and family members, retirees and employees using counselling. A framework was provided for a standard 'EAP utilisation scorecard' that encompassed these factors.

Authors: Delaney, W., Grube, J.W. and Ames, G.M.

Title: Predicting likelihood of seeking help through the employee assistance program among salaried and union hourly employees.

Date: 1998.

Type of publication: journal article.

Source: Addiction, 93(3): 399–410.

Aims of study: to investigate the influence of EAP beliefs, social support and individual characteristics on seeking help through a workplace EAP.

Method: large-scale survey conducted through individual face-to-face interviews conducted in informants' homes. The interview schedule covered: demographic information, likelihood of using an EAP, perceived social support, expectations of efficacy of EAP, supervisor encouragement, negative consequences of using the EAP and drinking behaviour. Data was analysed by use of statistical modelling.

Sample: 984 randomly selected hourly and salaried employees (response rate: 75%) – male: 88%; female: 12%; white: 67%; black: 30%: Latino: 3%. The average age was 44.

Type of counselling: in-house EAP (three full-time staff) covering substance abuse, mental health, family and legal problems. Referrals made to external clinics and mental health practitioners.

Organisational context: manufacturing. Large unionised fabrication and assembly plant that was part of a multi-national company; mid-west USA.

Results: use of the EAP for a drinking problem was more likely by black and Hispanic, older, hourly paid employees, and those who drank less, with a positive belief in EAP efficacy and more supervisor support. There was no gender difference. The statistical model implied that the likelihood to use an EAP for a drinking problem largely depends on a belief in its efficacy combined with support from co-workers and supervisor encouragement (rather than supervisor confrontation).

Methodological issues: the study focused predominantly on the role of EAP in helping employees with alcohol problems. There was very limited discussion of wider mental health functions of the EAP and how these might interact with alcohol issues.

Authors: French, M.T., Dunlap, L.J., Roman, P.M. and Steele, P.D.

Title: Factors that influence the use and perceptions of employee assistance programs at six worksites.

Date: 1997.

Type of publication: journal article.

Source: Journal of Occupational Health Psychology, 2(4): 312–324.

Aims of study: to identify demographic and attitudinal factors that influence an employee's use of a company EAP.

Method: a lengthy (30-page) anonymous questionnaire completed by randomly selected employees at six work sites. Items included demographics, health, drug and alcohol use, and EAP utilisation. Careful attention given to confidentiality; employees completed questionnaires in work time.

Sample: 1,578 employees – the average age was 42; male: 58%; female: 42%. 38% were in managerial positions.

Type of counselling: study design specified EAPs with contrasting features (eg internal, external, mixed). All were 'mature' EAPs.

Organisational context: various, including public sector and manufacturing.

Results: there were large differences in employee perceptions and use of EAPs across the six sites. EAP use (lifetime) ranged from 7% to 22% of employees. Satisfaction ranged from 60% to 92%. The perception that a visit to an EAP had a negative effect on their job ranged from 0% to 21%. At three sites, employees in good or excellent health were more likely to use the EAP than those with health problems. Over all the sites, women were more likely than men to use it. A significant percentage of all employees lacked information about EAP practices and policies. Job dissatisfaction was not related to EAP use. On the whole, demographic variables and substance misuse variables were not strong predictors of EAP use: 'this suggests that all types of workers in each of the worksite samples were equally likely to use the company EAP if the need should arise' (p. 232).

Methodological issues: the use of self-report could have meant that some informants were misrepresenting their use of EAPs and/or illicit drug use (as compared with objective records). However, the careful attention that was given to confidentiality in this study should minimise this problem.

Notes: this is one of the few studies that used a standardised method of data-collection across a number of contrasting work sites. The discovery of major differences in attitudes and EAP use across these sites underscores the difficulty in generalising about EAP provision. In addition, the findings clearly suggest that EAP use cannot be satisfactorily predicted in terms of demographic categories.

Authors: Gammie, B.

Title: Employee Assistance Programmes in the UK oil industry: an examination of current operational practice.

Date: 1997.

Type of publication: journal article.

Source: Personnel Review, 26(1/2): 66–80.

Aims of study: to examine the role of EAPs in the North Sea oil and exploration industry.

Method: semi-structured interviews with managers responsible for monitoring company EAPs.

Sample: 12 companies were active in this sector at the time of the study. Five of these companies had EAPs (another two were actively considering introducing an EAP). All five companies with EAPs were included in the study.

Type of counselling: 'broad-brush' external EAPs.

Organisational context: oil industry; UK.

Results: utilisation rates ranged between 7% and 12% (average 8.6%). Annual cost per employee was very similar for all companies (around £33 per employee per annum). There was a lack of monitoring and evaluation carried out by companies.

Authors: Gerstein, L., Gaber, T., Dainas, C. and Duffey, K.

Title: Organisational hierarchy, employee status and use of employee assistance programs.

Date: 1993.

Type of publication: journal article.

Source: Journal of Employment Counselling, 30: 74–78.

Aims of study: to examine the link between employee status and EAP use.

Method: 18-item EAP survey questionnaire, which included items on demographic characteristics, likelihood to refer co-workers to the EAP and personal use of the EAP. The questionnaire was completed anonymously.

Sample: 359 randomly selected participants (157 supervisors; 232 employees). 21% in upper level of organisational hierarchy, 39% middle level, 39% lower level. 63% were male; 37% female. The average age was 39; 80% were white. On average, they had been employed by the company for 10 years.

Type of counselling: not specified.

Organisational context: health sector (laboratory).

Results: supervisors were more likely than non-supervisors to refer others to EAP. Upper-level staff described themselves as just as likely to suggest referral as other groups. Middle-level staff used the EAP more than did higher-status or lower-status staff. It is suggested that this is because they have more contact with it and therefore have more positive attitudes.

Methodological issues: a lack of detailed information about the EAP and its relationship with the company made it difficult to interpret the findings of this study. There was a possibility that senior managers might have over-represented their referral practices on a questionnaire, as compared to objective records/observations of their actual referral behaviour.

Authors: Gerstein, L., Moore, D.Y., Duffey, K. and Dainas, C.

Title: The effects of biological sex and ethnicity on EAP utilisation and referrals.

Date: 1993.

Type of publication: journal article.

Source: Consulting Psychology Journal, 45(4): 23–27.

Aims of study: to explore the impact of gender and ethnicity on the EAP referral process.

Method: EAP survey questionnaires were completed by employees of a healthcare company. Two main items analysed from the questionnaire were 'How many times have you received services for your own troubles from the EAP in the last year?' and 'To how many males and females have you made the suggestion (you need to receive services from the EAP) in the last year?' Demographic data was also collected from respondents.

Sample: 155 supervisors and employees (80 male; 75 female). Ethnicity: 19 Asian; 36 Hispanic; 50 Caucasian; 50 African-American.

Type of counselling: not specified.

Organisational context: healthcare.

Results: neither ethnicity nor gender related to EAP utilisation or to likelihood of making a referral. The only significant pattern was that women were more likely to refer other women to the EAP (men were equally likely to refer male or female co-workers).

Authors: Grosch, J.W., Duffy, K.G. and Hessink, T.K.

Title: Employee assistance programs in higher education: factors associated with program usage and effectiveness.

Date: 1996.

Type of publication: journal article.

Source: *Employee Assistance Quarterly*, 11(4): 43–57.

Aims of study: to gain a better understanding of how EAPs operate in higher education.

Method: survey questionnaires mailed to representatives of universities. Included questions on characteristics of the institution and its workforce, and its EAP. Respondents were asked to base their replies on actual institutional data collected in the previous year.

Sample: questionnaires were mailed to 275 colleges and universities in the USA known to have EAPs or to be interested in having an EAP. 115 questionnaires were returned from institutions, of which 38 did not have an EAP. The responding institutions were representative of higher education in the USA.

Type of counselling: EAP, not specified.

Organisational context: higher education; USA.

Results: most (95%) institutions described 'broad-brush' EAPs, with a wide range of services. Only 3% had solely substance-abuse orientated EAPs. 22% reported joint union-management sponsored EAPs. Types of EAP: external (7%), internal (35%) and mixed internal/external (56%). Internal provision associated with higher rates of utilisation. 70% of clients were self-referred, with 19% supervisor-referred. Most frequent presenting problems were marital/family (25%), psychological (21%) and alcohol (19%). The average utilisation rate per annum was 7%. The academic faculty was less likely to use the EAP than other staff groups. Women used EAPs proportionally more than men. 42% of institutions had conducted a formal evaluation of their EAP. The success of the EAP was associated with higher levels of peer referral and faculty use of service.

Authors: Gyllensten, K., Palmer, S. and Farrants, J.

Title: Perceptions of stress and stress interventions in finance organisations: overcoming resistance towards counselling.

Date: 2005.

Type of publication: journal article.

Source: *Counselling Psychology Quarterly*, 18: 19–30.

Aims of study: to explore the attitudes toward counselling of managers in finance companies.

Method: individual semi-structured interviews; data analysed using Interpretative Phenomenological Analysis (IPA).

Sample: seven managers (two male, five female), drawn from different finance organisations.

Type of counselling: not specified.

Organisational context: finance sector, mix of medium and large companies; UK.

Results: the key theme identified was 'resistance to counselling', comprising negative stereotyped attitudes ('there is a stigma in going to a counsellor'), concerns around confidentiality, doubts over the effectiveness of counselling and a belief that executive coaching might be more appropriate for some employees.

Methodological issues: the absence of information about procedures for recruiting and selecting informants, and the organisational contexts within which they worked, made it difficult to assess the findings of this study.

Authors: Hall, L., Vacc, N.A. and Kissling, G.

Title: Likelihood to use employee assistance programs: the effects of socio-demographic, social-psychological, socio-cultural and community factors.

Date: 1991.

Type of publication: journal article.

Source: *Journal of Employment Counselling*, 28: 63–73.

Aims of study: to examine the factors influencing the likelihood of an employee to use an EAP.

Method: research participants completed a questionnaire, which asked them to rate (on a five-point scale) their likelihood of using the EAP if referred for particular problems by a supervisor or by a co-worker.

Sample: 200 randomly selected employees were contacted; 62 volunteered to participate in the study (48 white, 14 African-American; 38 women, 24 men). The majority were between 30 and 50 years old. 59% had completed college education.

Type of counselling: not specified.

Organisational context: telecommunications company (1,400 employees); USA.

Results: 7% reported that they had used the EAP in the past. 62% were likely to self-refer if necessary. 97% would use the EAP if referred by their supervisor; 72% if referred by a co-worker. Women and individuals with high income and education levels reported themselves as being more likely to use the EAP. Employees were more likely to use the service if they perceived that: (i) it was confidential (ii) it would help them keep their job and (iii) their supervisor viewed the EAP as helpful.

Methodological issues: there were a number of issues with this study. Asking participants about a hypothetical situation ('how likely would you be to use the EAP if…') was not the same as measuring or observing actual behaviour. Also, the relatively small number of employees who participated suggested possible sampling biases: did those who took part do so because they were 'supporters' of the EAP?

Author: Harlow, K.C.

Title: A comparison of internal and external employee assistance programs.

Date: 1987.

Type of publication: journal article.

Source: *New England Journal of Human Services*.

Aims of study: to compare the patterns of utilisation of an internal and external EAP operating in the same organisation.

Method: an analysis of case records in an organisation that changed from in-house to external EAP provision.

Sample: 100 randomly selected cases per year (around 30% of the annual utilisation of the EAP).

Type of counselling: brief (two sessions) leading to referral. The service was available to family members as well as employees.

Organisational context: large public utility company (12,000 employees); USA.

Results: senior management and Hispanic employees were relatively unlikely to use either internal or external services. Comparison of the demographic pattern of employees using the services revealed that external ones were more likely to be used by older employees with more children. External services were used more often for marital and family problems, while internal services had more clients reporting substance abuse issues. More people referred themselves to the external EAP, while there was more supervisor referral in the internal one. The conclusion was that 'internal and external EAPs serve somewhat different groups' (p. 19).

Methodological issues:

1. It was necessary to be cautious in generalising from a case study based in one organisation.
2. The external EAP provider in this case was a 'well-known non-profit family counselling organisation' – this factor may explain the shift in patterns of use.

Author: Harlow, K.C.

Title: Employee attitudes toward an internal employee assistance program.

Date: 1998.

Type of publication: journal article.

Source: *Journal of Employment Counselling*, 35: 141–150.

Aims of study: to examine the attitudes of adult employees and their dependents toward an internal EAP in a large, multi-national company.

Method: short (13-item) anonymous client satisfaction survey questionnaire (typical items were 'how easy was it to make contact with the EAP?' and 'the EAP protects confidentiality').

Sample: four groups: employees who had not used the EAP (response rate 19%); employees who had used the EAP (response rate 48%); adult dependents who had not used the EAP (response rate 9%) and adult dependents who had used the EAP (response rate 19%). 3,768 questionnaires were returned.

Type of counselling: in-house EAP covering 65,000 employees and their dependents. 45 counsellors. Services included assessment, referral and telephone helpline.

Organisational context: large multi-national company. Information about the sector of operation was not provided.

Results: employees and dependents who had used the EAP were highly positive about it; non-users were neutral. The likelihood to use it was predicted by past use, belief in confidentiality, belief that it would not have a negative career effect, belief that other colleagues were supportive of the EAP and perception that EAP would authorise access to external services. Women were more likely than men to believe that it was effective.

Methodological issues: the low response rate to the questionnaire among employees who had not used the EAP (19%) opened up the possibility that a representative sample of non-users may not have been achieved. Similarly, it was possible that the more positive users (rather than dissatisfied users) may have responded. These sampling biases was not sufficiently analysed or discussed. The lack of detailed information about the actual EAP service made it difficult to interpret the results.

Author: Keaton, B.C.

Title: The effect of voluntarism on treatment attitude in relationship to previous counselling experience in an employee assistance program.

Date: 1990.

Type of publication: journal article.

Source: *Employee Assistance Quarterly*, 6(1): 57–66.

Aims of study: to examine the relationship between voluntarism (vs. mandatory referral) in choice of counselling and attitude toward treatment.

Method: short attitude scale completed by clients prior to their scheduled counselling session.

Sample: 67 (out of 70) employees or family members who requested assistance during March 1989; 48% were male, 52% female. 55% were skilled/unskilled workers; 45% salaried employees. (Demographic pattern similar to employees as a whole.) 31% were family members. The average length of service was 16 years.

Type of counselling: internal EAP, which focused on work and emotional problems, with referrals made as appropriate. The EAP had been in existence for 11 years.

Organisational context: industrial. Large steel company; West Virginia, USA.

Results: 77% of respondents used the EAP on a voluntary basis. 73% reported previous use. Voluntary clients had a significantly more positive attitude towards it. Some clients, who were mandatory referrals on 'last chance' letters, nevertheless defined themselves as voluntary.

Notes: the high level of 'previous' use clients in this study makes generalisation to other EAPs problematic. The paper includes a valuable discussion of the nature of voluntarism and details of a useful one-item voluntarism scale.

Authors: Leong, D.M. and Every, D.K.

Title: Internal and external EAPs: is one better than the other?

Date: 1997.

Type of publication: journal article.

Source: *Employee Assistance Quarterly*, 12(3): 47–62.

Aims of study: to compare utilisation and cost-effectiveness of internal and external EAP services offered within the same company.

Method: EAP utilisation and cost data were collected over a three-year period. In year one, the company provided external EAP services; in years two and three, an internal service was offered. Questionnaires were completed by clients.

Sample: case study of a nuclear power plant, of around 2,300 employees (58% male, 42% female).

Type of counselling: internal and external EAPs, 'broad-brush' service.

Organisational context: power industry; USA.

Results: utilisation rates were 2.1% in year one (external), 6.8% in year two and 7.5% in year three (both internal). Referral to the internal EAP was more likely to be made on the basis of co-worker recommendation, indicating a 'grapevine' effect.

Methodological issues: cost data was not collected or analysed in detail. The information provided suggested that the internal EAP was somewhat more costly. As a single case study, any generalisation must be carried out with caution. For example, it could have been that the success of the internal EAP was accountable in terms of the skills/qualities of the one full-time counsellor who was employed.

Notes: the design of this study is a noteworthy feature. Comparing change in EAP provision within one organisation enables control of employee factors, which may vary considerably when different organisational sites are contrasted.

Author: Maddocks, M.

Title: Working wounded.

Date: 2000.

Type of publication: journal article.

Source: *Health Service Journal*, 110: 26–27.

Aims of study: brief report on utilisation rates and client presenting problems.

Method: analysis of case files.

Sample: 306 health service staff (further details not provided).

Type of counselling: counselling approach was not specified; counselling integrated with training and consultation services.

Organisational context: National Health Service (community services); UK.

Results: annual utilisation rate: 4%. Presenting issues: workplace and personal 43%; personal 39%; workplace 19%.

Methodological issues: this was a short paper, which lacked detailed analysis of data.

Author: May, K.M.

Title: Referrals to employee assistance programs: a pilot analogue study of expectations about counselling.

Date: 1992.

Type of publication: journal article.

Source: *Journal of Mental Health Counselling*, 14(2): 208–24.

Aims of study: to investigate whether expectations for counselling differ on the basis of referral type (self-referred or supervisor-referred) and employee gender.

Method: an analogue study in which participants were invited to imagine that they had a personal problem that was affecting their job performance, and were entering workplace counselling either on the basis of their own choice or through referral by their supervisor. They were then asked to complete a standardised Expectations About Counselling questionnaire (EAC; Tinsley et al, 1980) as if in this role and taking part in an initial counselling interview. The EAC included sub-scales of client attitudes and behaviour, counsellor attitudes and behaviour, and counselling process and outcome.

Sample: 103 employees from a wide range of occupational settings, drawn from classes on a management-training course in a college. The average age was 32. Most participants were white; male: 58; female: 45.

Type of counselling: short-term, confidential EAP counselling.

Organisational context: not applicable.

Results: more than 90% of participants reported that they were able to enter the roles prescribed in the study. The referral condition (self vs. supervisory referral) had no effect on attitudes to counselling. There were some significant differences associated with gender – women reported more positive expectations for counselling than men and, compared to male participants, expected their counsellor to be more confrontational, less directive, trustworthy and to use more immediacy. There were no gender differences in expectations around counsellor acceptance, empathy, warmth, genuineness, tolerance and self-disclosure.

Methodological issues: as acknowledged by the researcher, it was difficult to generalise from analogue studies to real-life situations. For example, an employee being referred to an EAP by their supervisor may have job security worries that would be difficult capture in an analogue/role-play study of this kind.

Authors: Milne, S.H., Blum, T.C. and Roman, P.M.

Title: Factors influencing employees' propensity to use an employee assistance program.

Date: 1994.

Type of publication: journal article.

Source: *Personnel Psychology*, 47: 123–145.

Aims of study: to investigate the influence of confidence, familiarity, accessibility and management support on employee willingness to use an EAP.

Method: a mailed survey questionnaire. Demographic questions were followed by 91 items, using a five-point scale that was designed to measure perceptions of the EAP. No questions were included on actual EAP use in order to reinforce confidentiality.

Sample: 1,987 employees (response rate 65%); 54% male. The average age was 42. The average length of time in the company was 19 years. There was a representative sample of all the occupational groups in the organisation.

Type of counselling: little detail was given. It was an internal EAP, which had been in existence for several years.

Organisational context: large communications company; USA.

Results: the data was analysed using a sophisticated form of regression analysis, which yielded a structural model of propensity to use the EAP. Management level (occupational role), gender and length of employment with the company did not predict propensity to use the service. The only factor that was clearly linked to this was the employees' level of confidence in the EAP (ie perceived trust and confidentiality). Previous familiarity with the EAP, and a belief that management supported it, contributed to confidence, but this was not independently associated with the inclination to use the service.

Note: the authors suggest that, because the EAP had been established for several years, it had become accepted throughout the organisation. This resulted in the fact that gender and organisational status had ceased to be factors influencing employee propensity to use the service. They suggest that these factors may be more significant in more recently established services.

Authors: Muscroft, J. and Hicks, C.

Title: A comparison of psychiatric nurses' and general nurses' reported stress and counselling needs: a case study approach.

Date: 1998.

Type of publication: journal article.

Source: *Journal of Advanced Nursing*, 27: 1317–1325.

Aims of study: to investigate occupational stress levels in two groups of nurses and to evaluate their preparedness to use workplace counselling to manage their problems.

Method: 21-item questionnaire circulated to a random stratified sample of nurses in two hospitals. Questionnaire items covered: visual analogue scale of occupational and personal stress, coping strategies (five-point scale), views about counselling (five-point scale; 12 items).

Sample: nurses from general hospital and psychiatric hospital settings. Questionnaires sent to 100 nurses. 52 returned. Female: 80%. The age range was from 22 to 58. Time spent in jobs ranged from zero to 30 years.

Type of counselling: not relevant (no counselling provided to either group of nurses).

Organisational context: National Health Service; UK.

Results: general nurses reported higher levels of stress; higher-grade nurses reported more stress than junior nurses; general nurses were more likely than psychiatric nurses to talk about their problems to a friend, colleague or counsellor. Psychiatric nurses were significantly more negative about the value of a workplace counselling service. Psychiatric nurses perceived seeking counselling as an admission of weakness and professional incompetence.

Notes: the psychiatric nurses in this study were drawn from a unit that was under threat of closure and experiencing high levels of absenteeism and low morale. The authors suggest that a process of denial may have contributed to an under-reporting of problems by informants from this group.

Authors: Mushet, G. and Donaldson, L.

Title: A psychotherapist in the house: a service for distressed hospital doctors.

Date: 2000.

Type of publication: journal article.

Source: British Journal of Medical Psychology, 73: 377–380.

Aims of study: to describe a psychotherapy service for distressed junior doctors, provided within a health region.

Method: analysis of clinical case records.

Sample: 66 referrals over a three-and-a-half-year period; 64% were female.

Type of counselling: psychodynamic: assessment followed by up to 12 sessions of individual therapy; telephone support was also available.

Organisational context: National Health Service; UK.

Results: a relatively small number of doctors made use of the service. 60% of clients reported problems related to their job, including relationships with senior colleagues, emotional responses to the health issues of patients and workload pressure. The authors emphasise the difficulties that doctors have in seeking help for psychological problems, the importance of confidentiality and the pressures on the therapist in this situation.

Authors: Muto, T., Fujimori, Y. and Suzuki, K.

Title: Characteristics of an external employee assistance programme in Japan.

Date: 2004.

Type of publication: journal article.

Source: Occupational Medicine, 54: 570–575.

Aims of study: to describe the characteristics of an external EAP in Japan.

Method: analysis of information collected on users of the service by counsellors.

Sample: 10,260 counselling sessions over a five-year period.

Type of counselling: confidential telephone or face-to-face counselling, or assessment, conducted by a clinical psychologist.

Organisational context: a major external EAP (HKD-EAP), which offered a service to 133 organisations from all sectors of the economy.

Results: utilisation of the EAP had doubled over the five-year period of the study, from 0.13% in 1996 to 0.27% in 2000. Some of the organisations contracted reported a 0% utilisation rate; the highest rate was 2.2%. There were consistent differences in the problems reported by men (mainly career and anxiety about diseases) and women (job dissatisfaction and childcare). Rates of alcohol problems were low (1%). Main mental health issues were depression and fatigue. The key finding in this study was a utilisation rate that was dramatically lower than in North American and UK studies (five to 10%). The authors attribute this difference to (a) the relative novelty of EAPs in Japan and (b) the availability of other healthcare services.

Methodological issues: the utilisation rate reported in this study was an overestimate, compared to the rates found in other studies, because each separate employee contact with the EAP was counted as one case (there was no facility for tracking an employee's continued visits to the service).

Author: Oher, J.M.

Title: Survey research to measure EAP customer satisfaction: a quality improvement tool.

Date: 1999.

Type of publication: book chapter.

Source: Oher, J.M. (ed.) The employee assistance handbook. (New York: Wiley) (pp. 117–138).

Aims of study: to evaluate the attitudes and satisfaction levels of human resources (personnel) staff in relation to the EAP provider contracted by their organisation.

Method: a survey questionnaire was distributed to human resource managers. It included sections on: demographic information, service satisfaction, decision to use services, recommended service changes, types of problem referred to service and effectiveness of service.

Sample: questionnaires were sent to 205 human resource managers; replies received from 55 (80% female).

Type of counselling: external broad-brush EAPs.

Organisational context: various; USA.

Results: more than half (55%) had never referred an employee to their EAP. Of those who did refer, reasons were: productivity/performance problem with employee (46%), employee emergency (46%), aggressive behaviour (29%), employee attitude problem (25%), alcohol/drug use (25%) and absenteeism (17%). Respondents were largely satisfied with the timeliness, professionalism and effectiveness of the EAP response, but only 25% were satisfied with its 'level of understanding of business realities'. 21% were uncertain over the confidentiality of the EAP. 100% agreed that it should be continued.

Methodological issues: the low response rate meant that these findings needed to be interpreted with caution.

Notes:

1. One of the interesting findings, in relation to other research into managers' referral patterns to EAP/counselling, is that while around half of these managers had never made a referral, the other half used the EAP a great deal.
2. The report includes a copy of the questionnaire used in the survey.

Authors: Poverny, L.M. and Dodd, S.J.

Title: Differential patterns of EAP service utilisation: a nine-year follow-up study of faculty and staff.

Date: 2000.

Type of publication: journal article.

Source: *Employee Assistance Quarterly*, 15(4): 29–42.

Aims of study: to compare differences between 1987 and 1996 in utilisation of a university EAP.

Method: analysis of client intake case records.

Sample: 267 clients who used the service in 1996 (number of clients reviewed in 1987 – 302).

Type of counselling: not specified.

Organisational context: urban university; USA.

Results: the key characteristics of those who used the service remained stable over a nine-year period: young, female, ethnic minority, on temporary work contracts, seeking help for work-related and family concerns; 'those who appear to be vulnerable in the workplace'. Main changes were increases in the proportion of non-academic staff using the service and in those with mental health problems.

Authors: Reynolds, G.S. and Lehman, H.E.K.

Title: Levels of substance abuse and willingness to use an Employee Assistance Programme.

Date: 2003.

Type of publication: journal article.

Source: *Journal of Behavioral Health Services Research*, 20: 238–248.

Aims of study: to examine the factors associated with employee decisions to use an EAP.

Method: employees completed a questionnaire (designed for the study) that included items on the likelihood to use the EAP, levels of drug and alcohol use, attitudes toward the organisation and tolerance of co-worker substance abuse.

Sample: 909 employees (97% response rate – researchers visited units within the organisation to invite staff to complete questionnaires); 67% male; 55% white; 24% African-American; 17% Hispanic.

Type of counselling: external provider – further information about the service was not supplied in the report.

Organisational context: local authority (municipal); USA.

Results: employees with drug and alcohol misuse problems were significantly less likely to use the EAP: 'those who might benefit most from the EAP are those most reluctant to use it'. However, this result could be attributable to a lack of awareness of the service: drug and alcohol abusers who knew about it reported similar rates of potential use as other workers. Overall, the likelihood to use the EAP was associated with positive attitudes toward the organisation and its policies. Age, gender and ethnicity had no relationship with perceptions of the service.

Methodological note: this study showed that it was possible to achieve a high response rate when using a survey questionnaire, as long as personal contact was made with respondents.

Author: Straussner, S.L.A.

Title: A comparative analysis of in-house and contractual Employee Assistance Programs.

Date: 1988.

Type of publication: journal article.

Source: *Employee Assistance Quarterly*, 3: 43–56.

Aims of study: to provide an overview of the scope and services offered by in-house and external (contractual) EAPs in the New York Metropolitan area in 1983.

Method: identification of EAPs through analysis of professional association membership lists, detailed (200-item) interviews with managers.

Sample: 23 private sector EAPs (15 internal; eight external), chosen to reflect a representative sample of all private sector New York EAPs.

Type of counselling: internal and external EAP – range of services offered.

Organisational context: private sector (finance/insurance, manufacturing, service).

Results: of all 125 EAPs identified in the initial trawl, 82% were in-house and 18% external (contracted). From a study sample of 23 EAPs, the main differences found between internal and external were: external ones were more recently established, more likely to be offering 'broad-brush' services, to offer telephone helpline and emergency cover, to have mainly self-referrals and to deal with mental health and legal issues'; internal EAPs were more likely to deal with alcohol problems, depend on employer referrals and receive union support. Annual utilisation rates: external 5.7%; internal 3.8%. External programmes reported to higher-level managers than did internal services and cost three times as much. More external services were used by women; no differential gender usage was found in internal EAPs. High-status workers were more likely to use external EAPs. Ethnic minority employees were more likely to use in-house services.

Author: Weiss, R.M.

Title: Effects of program characteristics on EAP utilisation.

Date: 2003.

Type of publication: journal article.

Source: *Employee Assistance Quarterly*, 18: 61–70.

Aims of study: to analyse the factors associated with different levels of EAP utilisation.

Method: a survey questionnaire designed for this study was mailed to senior human resource executives of all US corporations with more than 1,000 employees, and half of US companies with 500 to 1,000 employees.

Sample: 1,347 companies (38% response rate) – only 133 supplied usable information on their EAP. Reasons for not supplying information were: the company did not collect the information, information was not available and there were concerns over confidentiality of information.

Type of counselling: various.

Organisational context: various; USA.

Results: information about actual utilisation rates was not provided. A number of factors were found to be associated with higher utilisation: written procedures, training of first-line supervisors, dissemination information to employees and higher staffing levels. The following factors were not associated with variations in utilisation: confidentiality of service, training of middle managers or HR staff.

Methodological issues: one of the interesting aspects of this study was the high proportion of organisations that declined to supply relevant information and the decision of the author not to publish utilisation rate data. These factors may reflect the degree of commercial sensitivity that surrounds research into EAPs in the commercial sector.

Authors: West, M.A. and Reynolds, S.

Title: Employee attitudes to work-based counselling services.

Date: 1995.

Type of publication: journal article.

Source: *Work and Stress*, 9(1): 31–44.

Aims of study: to develop a scale for measuring attitudes to work-based counselling services; to examine employee attitudes to those who seek counselling; to identify factors that determine attitudes to counselling.

Method: 94-item questionnaire, in six sections: biographical information, knowledge of the counselling service, attitudes to the service, mental health (GHQ12), coping styles and attitudes to those seeking counselling.

Sample: 213 randomly selected staff in a district health authority in the UK (nurses, ancillary, professions allied to medicine). 490 questionnaires were distributed; response rate was 44%; female: 86%; male: 14%. The sample was representative of the overall workforce.

Type of counselling: in-house staff care service; counselling was delivered by clinical psychologists employed by the Health Authority.

Organisational context: healthcare. Large organisation; UK.

Results: development of the questionnaire identified three dimensions/factors: attitudes to workplace counselling, attitudes to counselling in general and perceptions of managerial attitudes to counselling. Attitudes to counselling were generally positive (an average of 4.3 on five-point scale); attitudes to workplace counselling were less positive (the average was 3.44). Attitudes to those seeking counselling were neutral or negative. Counsellors were perceived as trustworthy but low in competence. There were low levels of awareness of the counselling service and concerns about its confidentiality. Knowledge of the service was associated with a pro-active coping style. No gender or age differences were found. The attitude to counselling was predicted primarily by the perception of those who were after it and the perceived confidentiality of the service.

Authors: Whelan, L., Robson, M. and Cook, P.

Title: Health at work in the British National Health Service: a counselling response.

Date: 2002.

Type of publication: journal article.

Source: Counselling Psychology Quarterly, 15: 257–267.

Aims of study: to describe the first two years of operation of an external staff counselling service within the UK National Health Service.

Method: case study.

Sample: analysis of demographic and counselling utilisation data from 121 clients seen over a two-year period.

Type of counselling: person-centred and Gestalt, offering a maximum of eight sessions. It was organised through a local university counselling training centre.

Organisational context: NHS Health Trust in north-east England; a wide range of health professionals had access to the counselling service.

Results: 6% utilisation rate. The average number of sessions was 4.2. There were high levels of non-attending clients and unplanned endings. Clients presented with a wide range of personal problems. Some issues were identified around the gender mix of clients (proportionally more female staff used the service). Satisfaction ratings were consistently very positive.

Methodological issues: a limitation of this study was that it did not include any outcome information about the impact of the service on client problems.

Authors: Willbanks, K.D.

Title: The role of supervisory referral in employee assistance programs.

Date: 1999.

Type of publication: journal article.

Source: Employee Assistance Quarterly, 15: 13–28.

Aims of study: to review the literature on research into factors that influence supervisors to refer employees to an EAP.

Method: thematic literature review.

Sample: 18 studies published between 1980 and 1997.

Type of counselling: not specified.

Organisational context: not specified.

Results: some evidence was found for a positive association between the likelihood to refer and the following factors: familiarity with the EAP; positive attitude towards the EAP; social distance between the supervisor and employee (never worked as a peer with the subordinate); existence of a supervisor network; have personally been in previous receipt of help; training in making referrals.

Methodological issues: the authors point out a number of methodological weaknesses in existing research and make suggestions for improving the quality of this in this area.

Note: the paper includes a valuable discussion of theoretical models that can be used in making sense of supervisor behaviour.

Authors: Zarkin, G.A., Bray, J.W., Karuntzos, G.T. and Demiralp, B.

Title: The effect of an enhanced Employee Assistance Program (EAP) intervention on EAP utilisation.

Date: 2001.

Type of publication: journal article.

Source: *Journal of Studies on Alcohol*, 62: 351–358.

Aims of study: to develop an enhanced EAP package that was more relevant to the needs of ethnic minority and female users, and evaluate the effect of the enhanced programme on employee utilisation rates.

Method: initial evaluation of existing EAP provision, followed by identification of areas for enhancement. An improved programme was then designed and implemented within 18 organisations. Assessment of utilisation was over a seven-year period. Utilisation rates in 107 other organisations using the EAP, that had not received the enhanced implementation, were analysed for comparative purposes.

Sample: 6,500 employees in two organisations.

Type of counselling: EAP package including assessment, brief counselling, training, referral to outside agencies.

Organisational context: large organisations, nature of business not specified; USA.

Results: the enhanced intervention generated higher utilisation rates not only for the target populations (women and ethnic minority employees) but also for white male employees, compared to rates in control organisations. An analysis of costs associated with the enhancement was provided. The implications of this study are that it is possible to increase EAP utilisation with a relatively inexpensive outreach project, but that (in this case, at least) it is not possible to effectively target specific employee groups.

Methodological issues: the study made use of advanced statistical techniques to control the possible confounding effects on utilisation rates of other factors within the participating organisations.

Appendix E. Studies of organisational factors

Author: Csiernik, R.

Title: An overview of employee and family assistance programming in Canada.

Date: 2002.

Type of publication: journal article.

Source: Employee Assistance Quarterly, 18: 17–33.

Aims of study: to describe the characteristics of EAP provision in Canada.

Method: a questionnaire, developed in collaboration with key EAP sector stakeholders, was distributed to EAP co-coordinators.

Sample: responses were received from 154 organisations (size ranged from seven to 60,000 employees; mean size 3,144 employees).

Type of counselling: not specified.

Organisational context: cross-sector; Canada.

Results: detailed information was reported on service delivery, qualifications of counsellors, access to services, programme management and evaluation, and range of services. Key findings included: highly qualified workforce (80% of organisations had at least one counsellor with a Masters degree); increasing use of a hybrid model that involved the use of internal volunteers (32% of organisations); family members were allowed to use services in 94% of organisations. Half of the organisations capped EAP provision (five to 12 sessions) and half supported uncapped services. The average number of sessions used by clients (five) was the same in capped and uncapped services.

Authors: Csiernik, R., Macdonald, S., Durand, P., Wild, T.C. and Rylett, M.

Title: Who do we serve? Worksite characteristics, workforce attributes and occupational assistance programming in Canada.

Date: 2005.

Type of publication: journal article.

Source: Journal of Workplace Behavioral Health, 21: 15–29.

Aims of study: to examine the characteristics of organisations that supported EAPs and other forms of employee wellbeing services, in Canada. The underlying goal of the study was to determine the extent to which EAPs could be regarded as a form of social/managerial control, or as a further benefit for those workers who were already economically and socially privileged.

Method: survey questionnaire (developed for this study but based on previous survey tools used by the authors) distributed to a stratified sample of worksites in Canada with more than 100 employees. The questionnaire included items on the characteristics of EAPs and other health promotion activities, management attitudes, extent of unionisation of the workforce and other workforce attributes. Follow-up calls were used to ensure maximum response rate to the survey.

Sample: 639 organisations (77.9% response rate); all sectors of the economy (manufacturing 26%; transportation/utilities 17%; services 16%; health and education 14%; other 27%).

Type of counselling: information about types of EAP provision (ie external vs. internal) in these organisations was not provided.

Organisational context: various.

Results: 67% of worksites reported that their employees had access to an EAP; 49% also provided other health/wellbeing services. EAPs were more likely to be found in organisations that were low in management authority and social control, high in levels of employee involvement in decision-making, had high levels of union membership, and a low proportion of ethnic minority employees. The authors suggest that these findings support a hypothesis that EAPs are largely a benefit enjoyed by more privileged employees and denied to socially marginalised worker groups in insecure jobs.

Authors: Dick, P.

Title: The social construction of the meaning of acute stressors: a qualitative study of the personal accounts of police officers using a stress counselling service.

Date: 2000.

Type of publication: journal article.

Source: *Work and Stress*, 14: 226–244.

Aims of study: to describe the therapy process in relation to police officers using an occupational stress counselling service.

Method: systematic analysis of case notes made by the counsellor following sessions.

Sample: 355 police officers (11 female); the average age was 31 (male), 27 (female).

Type of counselling: rational-emotive behavioural therapy (REBT); an average of six sessions.

Organisational context: police force; UK.

Results: the findings were presented in terms of key themes, and a series of case vignettes, which provided detailed descriptive accounts of the emotional and cognitive processes in different types of cases. The main conclusion of the study was that the psychological effects of work stress for police officers are complex, and that their work culture and environment plays a major role in determining how stressful events are understood.

Methodological issues: no information was provided about whether participants gave permission for their case material to be used for research purposes, and there was no mention of whether case vignette information had been altered to preserve anonymity.

Note: this paper provides a valuable account of how stress issues can be analysed from an REBT perspective.

Authors: Lawrence, J.A., Boxer, P. and Tarakeshwar, N.

Title: Determining demand for EAP services.

Date: 2002.

Type of publication: journal article.

Source: *Employee Assistance Quarterly*, 18: 1–15.

Aims of study: to find out about additional services that would be of interest to employees enrolled in a well-established EAP.

Method: questionnaire survey.

Sample: the survey questionnaire was circulated to all 264 employees; 92 returns (response rate 35%).

Type of counselling: assessment, counselling and referral conducted by clinical psychology trainees at a local university.

Organisational context: city employees in a small city (28,000 inhabitants); USA.

Results: 86% of those who responded indicated that they were aware of the EAP. 23% had used it at least once and were highly satisfied with the service they had received. Participants identified a wide range of additional services in which they would be interested, including career planning workshops, anger management, stress management and family counselling.

Author: Flannery, R.B.

Title: The Assaulted Staff Action Program (ASAP): ten year empirical support for Critical Incident Stress Management.

Date: 2001.

Type of publication: journal article.

Source: *International Journal of Emergency Mental Health*, 3: 5–10.

Aims of study: to review research into the operation and effectiveness of a programme designed to train and support healthcare staff who have been assaulted by patients.

Method: thematic literature review.

Sample: 14 research articles.

Type of counselling: brief counselling was embedded within a wider programme that included preventative training and critical incident de-briefing.

Organisational context: healthcare settings; USA.

Results: organisations that had implemented this programme reported a 25% to 62% reduction in staff assaults and improvements in staff retention.

Authors: Highley-Marchington, J.C. and Cooper, C.L.

Title: An assessment of employee assistance and workplace counselling programmes in British organisations.

Date: 1998.

Type of publication: government report (UK Health and Safety Executive).

Source: Her Majesty's Stationery Office (HMSO), Norwich.

Aims of study: to identify the characteristics of EAP/counselling provision in the UK in 1995.

Method: in-depth case studies of major EAP/counselling providers (interview-based) and a questionnaire survey of other providers. Questions covered in interviews and the questionnaire included: nature of provision, number of client organisations, counsellor qualifications, training and experience.

Sample: 14 case studies. Questionnaires were sent out to 25 other providers (16 replied).

Type of counselling: various.

Organisational context: various.

Results: the EAP/counselling organisations (providers) studied covered a total of 1.28 million employees in 599 client organisations. The top three providers held 29% of all contracts and covered 20% of all employees. 56% of providers operated nationally; 44% were locally based; 90% offered face-to-face counselling; 70% offered advice to managers; 40% offered telephone access. Around 75% offered services to dependents as well as employees. Around half of providers used performance objectives and audit. The majority (90%) of counsellors were sessionally paid 'affiliates'. Most counsellors (70%) used the professional term 'counsellor', with 17% clinical psychologists, 8% debt advisors and 5% psychotherapists. The training and experience levels demanded by providers varied widely. Employee annual utilisation rates ranged from between 1% and 25% (average eight to 10%), with 91% of clients being employees and 9% dependents. 75% of clients were self-referred. Presenting problems were emotional, work-related, family and legal, with a small proportion of alcohol (4%) and drug (1%) problems. The average number of sessions was four (majority of providers had a session limit of around six sessions). Fee structure was usually on a per capita system, at an average of around £25 per employee per year.

Notes: information on other aspects of this study can be found in separate entries.

Authors: Highley-Marchington, J.C. and Cooper, C.L.

Title: An assessment of employee assistance and workplace counselling programmes in British organisations.

Date: 1998.

Type of publication: Government report (UK Health and Safety Executive).

Source: Her Majesty's Stationery Office (HMSO), Norwich.

Aims of study: to identify the characteristics of EAP/counselling purchasers in the UK in 1995.

Method: questionnaire survey of UK organisations making use of EAP/counselling provision, supplemented by a series of in-depth case studies.

Sample: 234 questionnaires were distributed; 168 were returned (72% response rate). 11 case studies.

Type of counselling: various.

Organisational context: various.

Results: 63% of companies used an EAP; 15% had an internal counselling service; 13% external counselling service; the remainder had a combination of types of provision. In-house services were more likely to be located in larger companies. 87% of external services were open to family members; 28% of internal services were available to family and dependents. 50% of services had been in existence for less than two years; 19% for more than five years. The initial impetus for adopting a counselling service was personnel/human resources (48%), management (29%), managing director (11%) and occupational health (4%). A wide range of factors were cited as reasons for introducing counselling: EAPs were more likely to have been introduced for PR reasons and in-house services were associated with a desire to support staff and deal with organisational difficulties. Half of the companies felt there was a lack of independent advice about introducing counselling. 45% of organisations had carried out an audit of the counselling service (10% planned to do so in the future). 14% of organisations believed that absence rates had reduced since the introduction of counselling; 21% had perceived an improvement in substance abuse problems.

Note: information on other aspects of this study can be found in separate entries.

Author: Martin, P.

Title: Counselling skills training for managers in the public sector.

Date: 1997.

Type of publication: book chapter.

Source: Carroll, M. and Walton, M. (eds) *Handbook of counselling in organisations*. London: Sage. (pp. 240–259).

Aims of study: to evaluate the effect of counselling skills training on managers in a public sector organisation.

Method: open-ended questionnaires were distributed to participants on a counselling skills training course; data was analysed using grounded theory approach. A summary of findings was sent to respondents to collect their comments on accuracy.

Sample: 74 course participants; 57 completed questionnaires (77% response rate).

Type of counselling: skills training based on Egan model.

Organisational context: local authority; UK.

Results: key findings: counselling skills training brought about a heightened awareness of the framework, structure and focus of counselling skills; managers transferred these skills to other management situations; the training had an impact on the organisation through its effect on organisational culture and on the personal development of managers.

Authors: Rodriguez, J. and Borgen, W.A.

Title: Needs assessment: Western Canada's program administrators' perspectives on the role of EAPs in the workplace.

Date: 1998.

Type of publication: journal article.

Source: *Employee Assistance Quarterly*, 14: 11–29.

Aims of study: to explore the views of the people within an organisation who manage the contract with the EAP supplying counselling to that company.

Method: a survey questionnaire was mailed to administrators.

Sample: 62 administrators from 54 organisations (69% response rate; some organisations employed more than one administrator).

Type of counselling: various.

Organisational context: a variety of public and private sector organizations (a total of 400,000 employees); Canada.

Results: administrators believed that employees in their organisations often experienced stress, but tended not to regard the problem as serious enough to merit use of the EAP. A number of barriers to EAP utilisation were identified, with a lack of information about the EAP services being the most significant: only 22% of administrators believed that employees were well-informed about counselling; 82% said that having an EAP in place benefited their organisation as a whole.

Authors: Silvester, A.

Title: Counselling provision for staff in the National Health Service in England: a survey.

Date: 2003.

Type of publication: journal article.

Source: *Counselling and Psychotherapy Research*, 3: 61–64.

Aims of study: to analyse the role of counsellors providing services for staff in the National Health Service in England.

Method: a questionnaire survey (designed for this study; distributed by mail) with a combination of quantitative and open-ended items, to be completed by counsellors or occupational health managers.

Sample: 189 National Health Service Trusts (82% response rate).

Type of counselling: various.

Organisational context: healthcare; UK.

Results: 89% of Health Trusts participating in the survey offered a face-to-face counselling service for staff; 39% also provided telephone counselling; 71% provided critical incident debriefing. In 46% of Health Trusts, counselling services were perceived as being effectively integrated into general organisational policy-making. Only 6% of Trusts reported staffing levels of one full-time counsellor per 2,000 staff (a recommended service level at the time of the survey). A range of models of service provision were utilised: in-house (51%); EAP (16%); other types of external provision, eg independent counsellors (22%) – 9% of Trusts did not provide information on the model of service. The majority (64%) limited the number of sessions available to clients – six sessions was the modal number. Out of working hours, services were provided in 26% of Trusts. Formal evaluation was carried out by 75% of respondents. Other services offered included: group work (43%); couple counselling (41%); training (41%); conciliation/mediation (22%). The majority of counsellors described themselves as operating within an integrative theoretical orientation; 47% were fully professionally accredited; 37% had other roles within the organisation.

Note: utilisation rates were not reported. This survey was carried out in 2001.

Authors: Trubshaw, E.A. and Dollard, M.F.

Title: Representation of work stress in an Australian public hospital.

Date: 2001.

Type of publication: journal article.

Source: AAOHN Journal, 49: 437–444.

Aims of study: to examine the way in which occupational stress and counselling were represented within an organisation.

Method: content and thematic analysis of all annual reports produced by the management board of an Australian hospital over a 15-year period.

Sample: official documents.

Type of counselling: not specified.

Organisational context: healthcare; Australia.

Results: contradictions were identified between the espoused aims of the organisation, in relation to staff care, and the implementation of policies in the areas of sickness absence and compensation claims. Stress was generally presented as an individual issue rather than being linked to organisational factors. The use of the staff counselling service increased ten-fold during this period.

Authors: Young, G. and Spencer, J.

Title: General Practitioners' views about the need for a stress support service.

Date: 1996.

Type of publication: journal article.

Source: Family Practice, 13(6): 517–521.

Aims of study: to examine the views of GPs regarding the need for a stress support service.

Method: postal questionnaire to all GPs in a specific district.

Sample: 274 GPs completed questionnaires (80% response rate). 60% male; 40% female. The majority were under 45 years old.

Type of counselling: not specified – needs survey only.

Organisational context: National Health Service; UK.

Results: the preferences for sources of help in dealing with work stress were: family or close friend (72%); locally organised counselling service (60%); own GP (40%); partner in practice (35%) and a nationally organised counselling service (15%). Overall, 79% thought that there was a need for a formal, organisationally provided stress counselling service for GPs.

Authors: Williams, N., Sobti, A. and Aw, T.C.

Title: Comparison of perceived occupational health needs among managers, employee representatives and occupational physicians.

Date: 1994.

Type of publication: journal article.

Source: Occupational Medicine.

Aims of study: to compare how occupational health providers and their customers view the relative importance of different occupational health services.

Method: a questionnaire that asked respondents to rate (on a five-point scale) the importance of various occupational health functions.

Sample: 88 occupational health physicians; 37 union representatives; 150 managers of large and medium-sized companies.

Type of counselling: not specified.

Organisational context: various; UK.

Results: managers of medium-sized companies rated counselling as the most important of a list of 13 occupational health functions (eg health checks, first aid, advice on environmental issues and so on). Managers of large companies, union representatives and physicians all rated counselling significantly lower on the list (rankings between six and nine). There were high levels of consensus between groups on most other occupational health issues.

Appendix F. Process research in workplace counselling

Authors: Anderson, M.A.

Title: A case study of occupationally focused brief dynamic therapy using Mann's model of central conflict.

Date: 2003.

Type of publication: journal article.

Source: *Clinical Case Studies,* 2: 91–103.

Aims of study: to examine the use of brief psychodynamic psychotherapy in a case of occupational stress.

Method: analysis of case notes.

Sample: the client was a 47-year-old woman, with a diagnosis of bipolar disorder, who was experiencing difficulties in coping with stressful situations in her job as a sales assistant, to the extent that her job had been in jeopardy.

Type of counselling: psychodynamic time-limited therapy (12 sessions plus one follow-up meeting).

Organisational context: the client worked in a retail organisation; information on the context for therapy was not provided.

Results: the therapeutic work focused on the self-image of the client, specifically her acceptance of herself as a person with a mental health disability, and her relationships with co-workers. The case had a good outcome – the client was able to return to work successfully. The author observes that this client had initially been reluctant to enter therapy, but 'perhaps the threshold of seeking therapy is lowered when job security is threatened' (p.100).

Methodological issues: there was little information provided in this case study about the therapy process; no independent outcome measures were used.

Author: Bayer, D.L.

Title: Brief anger-management therapy.

Date: 1998.

Type of publication: journal article.

Source: *Employee Assistance Quarterly,* 14(2): 67–74.

Aims of study: to evaluate the effectiveness of cognitive-behavioural anger management interventions in an EAP context.

Method: clinical case studies; some use of test data; three-year follow-up.

Sample: two cases (male, 33 years, five sessions; couple: male 48 years, female 36 years, five sessions).

Type of counselling: brief anger-management therapy, mainly cognitive-behavioural in orientation.

Organisational context: not specified.

Results: both good outcome cases. Gains maintained at three-year follow-up.

Methodological issues: an absence of independent evidence (eg client self-report, standardised assessment data) meant that the case analysis was over-reliant on the therapist's perception of outcome.

Notes: this was a valuable example of the use of a case study approach to document an innovative approach to workplace counselling, and to establish the plausibility of an intervention in a form that may lead to further evaluation through a large-scale study.

Authors: Bayer, G.A. and Barkin, A.C.

Title: Employee assistance program utilisation: comparison of referral sources and problems.

Date: 1990.

Type of publication: journal article.

Source: *Employee Assistance Quarterly*, 5(4): 63–70.

Aims of study: to identify referral patterns (self-referral vs. institutional referral) associated with different types of problems presented by EAP users.

Method: EAP counsellors collected information, in initial treatment interviews, from clients concerning the problems, which prompted them to seek assistance and the source of their referral.

Sample: 747 federal employees (mainly white collar). Male: 40%; female: 60%. A proportion of minority clients reflected the distribution in the workforce.

Type of counselling: little information was provided. It covered both substance abuse and mental health issues.

Organisational context: federal government agency; USA.

Results: self-referral occurred in 68% of all cases. Referrals were fairly evenly divided between job problems, alcohol and drugs, psychological-emotional and supervisor consultations. In all categories, the majority were self-referral. The authors suggest that their results question the widely held assumption that supervisor 'confrontation' and referral is not particularly important, even in drug/alcohol cases or other psychological problems characterised by denial.

Methodological issues: the distinctive professional, white-collar organisational culture of this agency needed to be taken into account when interpreting these findings. It may be that this culture results in an under-use of supervisory referrals: the study did not present any evidence that overall EAP utilisation levels were optimal.

Authors: Blum, T.C., Roman, P.M. and Harwood, E.M.

Title: Employed women with alcohol problems who seek help from Employee Assistance Programs: description and comparisons.

Date: 1995.

Type of publication: book chapter.

Source: *Recent Developments in Alcoholism, Volume 12: Women and Alcoholism*, Galanter, M. (ed) New York: Plenum Press (pp. 125–156).

Aims of study: to examine the use and effectiveness of EAP interventions for women with alcohol problems.

Method: data on EAP clients was collected through: (i) a questionnaire on treatment history and demographic information completed by an EAP administrator (ii) a questionnaire completed by clients at the start of intervention, including items on work role, referral to the EAP, work relationships, alcohol use and depression (Beck Depression Inventory) and (iii) follow-up information collected from an EAP administrator 18 to 24 months after the initial session, concerning employment status of the client.

Sample: data was collected from 6,400 employees at 84 work sites. 238 women in this sample reported problems with alcohol and were included in the present study. 79% were white; the average age was 37 (with nine years in current job); average one child; the majority had some college education. All levels of employment were represented, from managerial to blue collar.

Type of counselling: EAP.

Organisational context: various; USA.

Results: the majority had multiple work problems around performance, attendance, warnings and so on. There were relatively low levels of family and spousal support. 34% self-referral; 34% supervisor referral; 16% co-worker referral. 51% also had psychological problems; 29% had family problems; 21% had other drug problems; 15% had legal problems. Referrals made by the EAP administrator included: outpatient treatment (43%), 12-step programme (18%), inpatient treatment (14%), a combination of self-help and counselling (8%), and EAP counselling only (5%). The EAP appeared to be effective as a form of early intervention. At follow-up, 69% were still employed, 9% had quit and 7% had been laid off. Women entered the EAP through referral routes similar to men. Higher-status women employees appeared to receive better treatment than manual/clerical female employees.

Notes: this was a lengthy and detailed report, which included a substantial list of references on women, EAPs and alcohol use.

Authors: Butterfield, L.D. and Borgen, W.A.

Title: Outplacement counselling from the client's perspective.

Date: 2005.

Type of publication: journal article.

Source: *Career Development Quarterly*, 53: 306–316.

Aims of study: to explore the experience of outplacement counselling from the point of view of the client.

Method: open-ended qualitative interviews in which participants were asked to describe critical incidents relating to their satisfaction with outplacement counselling they had received, and their 'wish list' for how the service might have been improved. Categories derived from these data were analysed using a systematic method of qualitative analysis.

Sample: 15 people (eight women, seven men; an average age of 47) who had received outplacement counselling. Previous jobs had been managerial and technical. The average length of unemployment was five months.

Type of counselling: structured, individual and group counselling oriented around job search strategies.

Organisational context: a variety of work settings; Canada.

Results: the experiences of participants were analysed in relation to 16 core themes/categories. The most important themes emerging from participants' accounts were: the quality of their relationship with their outplacement counsellor; the need for counselling to be more tailored to their individual needs and space to deal with emotion/ transition issues; the clinical skills of their counsellor. Informants made a large number of suggestions about ways in which the service they had received might have been improved.

Methodological issues: this was an exemplary study in terms of criteria for evaluating the quality of qualitative research.

Author: Carroll, C.

Title: Building bridges: a study of employee counsellors in the private sector.

Date: 1997.

Type of publication: book chapter.

Source: Carroll, M. and Walton, M. (eds) *Handbook of counselling in organisations*. London: Sage (pp. 222–239).

Aims of study: to explore the experiences of employee counsellors in the private sector.

Method: qualitative interviews.

Sample: 12 counsellors (six male, six female) from 12 companies.

Type of counselling: in-house/internal workplace counselling. The theoretical approach was mainly 'humanistic-eclectic, with one cognitive-behavioural.

Organisational context: private sector companies; UK.

Results: counsellors were engaged in a wide variety of roles, encompassing counselling staff, advising managers and health education. None had training in workplace counselling. All counsellors saw themselves as agents of change within their organisations. Perceived key attributes were being flexible, a pioneering spirit and assertiveness. Support networks and supervision were viewed as essential coping mechanisms. The organisational culture had a significant impact on counselling. Confidentiality was essential. A professional background in social work or nursing and effective assessment skills were seen as positive. The underlying theme in interviews was coping with competing roles and demands.

Authors: Burwell, R. and Chen, C.P.

Title: Applying REBT to workaholic clients.

Date: 2002.

Type of publication: journal article.

Source: *Counselling Psychology Quarterly*, 15: 219–228.

Aims of study: to explore the use of rational-emotive behavioural therapy (REBT) for a person who experiences a compulsion to overwork.

Method: descriptive case study.

Sample: female client, community worker.

Type of counselling: REBT.

Organisational context: not specified.

Results: the case study described a range of REBT designed to address various aspects of over-work.

Methodological issues: there was an absence of contextual information about the client, and the therapy setting within which the client received counselling. The study did not report data from independent measures of outcome. These limitations meant that it was difficult to determine the validity of this case study.

Authors: Conti, D.J. and Burton, W.N.

Title: Behavioural health disability management.

Date: 1999.

Type of publication: book chapter.

Source: J.M. Oher (ed.) *The employee assistance handbook*. New York: Wiley (pp. 319–336).

Aims of study: to analyse the costs of employee psychological problems in a large financial services organisation.

Method: analysis of data collected through medical insurance claims.

Sample: 38,000 employees.

Type of counselling: external EAP, which operated as a referral to other psychotherapy and psychiatric services partially reimbursed through company health insurance provision. The EAP 'manages psychiatric short-term disability' including follow-up counselling support.

Organisational context: large (38,000 employee) financial services organisation; USA.

Results: in 1996 there were 10 'short-term psychiatric events' per 1,000 employees. The average duration was 40 days per event (not counting the first five days leading up to the formal diagnosis). Depression was responsible for 65% of total short-term psychiatric days lost (anxiety 12%, substance abuse 11%). Illness was also associated with more sickness absence than any medical-surgical factor, including heart disease and low-back pain. There was a 20% likelihood of depression recurring within 12 months. There was a major increase in absence from work due to psychiatric problems during the 1990s. There were also many 'complex' cases, involving a combination of medical-surgical and psychological problems.

Notes: this study includes a valuable discussion of the relationship between EAP provision, the client organisation and medical services.

Authors: Cunningham, G.

Title: The EAP counsellor: attitudes, knowledge and beliefs.

Date: 1992.

Type of publication: journal article.

Source: *Employee Assistance Quarterly*, 8(1): 13–26.

Aims of study: to explore counsellors' attitudes towards working for an EAP.

Method: semi-structured, in-depth interviews (average 90 minutes).

Sample: 42 counsellors representing 35 EAPs (34 counsellors with social work backgrounds; eight with other professional experience). 30 women; 12 men. The average experience in EAP work was four-and-a-half years.

Type of counselling: various.

Organisational context: various; USA.

Results: the main theoretical orientations were psychodynamic (50%), systemic (31%) and brief therapy models (29%). Theoretical orientation viewed as most relevant for assessment purposes, but not for planning interventions. 71% were satisfied with EAP work, whereas 26% were ambivalent.

Authors: Firth-Cozens, J.

Title: Why me? A case study of the process of perceived occupational stress.

Date: 1992.

Type of publication: journal article.

Source: *Human Relations*, 45(2): 131–140.

Aims of study: to explore the personal meanings of job stress, and process of change, in a good outcome case of psychodynamic-interpersonal psychotherapy.

Method: standard measures of psychiatric symptoms, stress, social adjustment and client ratings of problems administered at intake, mid-therapy, end of therapy and at a three-month follow-up. All sessions were tape-recorded.

Sample: male, 36 years old, hospital manager suffering from work stress, anxiety, depression, alcohol abuse and gambling.

Type of counselling: 16-session psychodynamic-interpersonal psychotherapy provided at a university research clinic.

Organisational context: healthcare.

Results: a good outcome case. Change in job perceptions followed shifts in personal insight. The discussion provided a valuable analysis of the relationships between therapy process, personal change and organisational factors.

Author: Fisher, H.

Title: Plastering over the cracks? A study of employee counselling in the NHS.

Date: 1997.

Type of publication: book chapter.

Source: Carroll, M. and Walton, M. (eds) *Handbook of counselling in organisations*. London: Sage (pp. 288–308).

Aims of study: to explore the experiences of service managers of in-house staff counselling services in the NHS.

Method: qualitative interviews.

Sample: four service managers (demographic details not given).

Type of counselling: not specified – various.

Organisational context: National Health Service; UK.

Results: key characteristics of effective counsellors were viewed as: realism, awareness of limitations, knowledge of brief therapy and problem-solving techniques, previous experience of working in the NHS, flexibility and awareness of boundaries. It was seen as important to 'fit in' and understand the organisational culture. Networking and forming appropriate relationships with management was essential.

Authors: Highley-Marchington, J.C. and Cooper, C.L.

Title: An assessment of employee assistance and workplace counselling programmes in British organisations.

Date: 1998.

Type of publication: government report (UK Health and Safety Executive).

Source: Her Majesty's Stationery Office (HMSO), Norwich.

Aims of study: to identify the views of counsellors engaged in EAP/counselling provision in the UK in 1995.

Method: questionnaire survey of counsellors employed by EAPs. It included items relating to recruitment and selection, qualifications and experience, and levels of satisfaction with their work.

Sample: questionnaires were distributed to 52 counsellors. 22 replied (response rate of 42%). Information on age, gender and ethnicity was not given.

Type of counselling: various.

Organisational context: various.

Results: 62% of counsellors worked for at least two providers and 65% did less than 10 hours EAP counselling each week. Previous employment was highly varied; 72% saw clients in their own home. 76% held qualifications at professional accreditation level, but 11% had only a Certificate in Counselling and 11% held no formally recognised qualification in counselling. The majority used brief therapy approaches. 63% of recruitment was carried out by interview, but 18% were selected without any form of interview. All had more than four years of counselling experience, with 23% having more than 20 years' experience. 36% reported that they were often asked to counsel clients with specific problems, reflecting their areas of professional expertise. There were wide variations in client assessment procedures, supervision arrangements, case management systems and provision of feedback to companies. Counsellors were generally satisfied with carrying out EAP work, but 45% were dissatisfied with the level of ongoing training available to them. They were satisfied with arrangements around confidentiality. Some EAP providers were perceived by counsellors as providing a poor service for the client and the client organisation.

Notes: information on other aspects of this study can be found in separate entries.

Authors: Jenkins, D. and Palmer, S.

Title: A multimodal assessment and rational emotive behavioural approach to stress counselling: a case study.

Date: 2003.

Type of publication: journal article.

Source: *Counselling Psychology Quarterly*, 16: 265–287.

Aims of study: to describe and discuss the use of multimodal and REBT approaches in a case of work stress.

Method: at the beginning and end of counselling, the client completed the Maslach Burnout scale, Beck Depression Inventory, GHQ-28, Job Stress Survey and the Brief Symptom Inventory (BSI). The counsellor kept notes of each session.

Sample: female, 47 years old, senior nurse.

Type of counselling: multimodal assessment interview, followed by 19 sessions of REBT.

Organisational context: health; UK.

Results: at the initial interview, the client's scores on all scales were in the 'case' range; at the end of counselling, her scores had moved into the normal range. A detailed account was offered of the initial assessment, therapeutic plan and session-by-session development of treatment. The case analysis provided a valuable portrayal of the complex interaction between work and personal issues, and the use of an integrative REBT approach to work through a range of problem areas.

Authors: Kirk-Brown, A. and Wallace, D.

Title: Predicting burnout and job satisfaction in workplace counsellors: the influence of role stressors, job challenge and organisational knowledge.

Date: 2004.

Type of publication: journal article.

Source: *Journal of Employment Counselling*, 41: 29–37.

Aims of study: to examine the relative importance of various factors associated with burnout and job satisfaction in workplace counsellors.

Method: a survey questionnaire was mailed to workplace counsellors who were members of the Employee Assistance Professionals Association of Australia. The package included the emotional exhaustion subscale of the Maslach Burnout Inventory, and scales measuring intrinsic job satisfaction, role stress, perceived challenge of the job and organisational knowledge.

Sample: 82 practising workplace counsellors (response rate 74%; 67% male; the average age was 44; the average amount of experience was six years; qualifications included psychology, counselling, social work and nursing).

Type of counselling: not specified.

Organisational context: various; Australia.

Results: levels of emotional exhaustion were similar to those reported in other professions, such as social work and medicine. High role ambiguity was associated with elevated levels of emotional exhaustion; role conflict was not linked to emotional exhaustion. Counsellors who experienced their work as challenging, and who reported confidence in their knowledge of organisational procedures, had higher levels of job satisfaction. The factors that were assessed accounted for a reasonable proportion of the variance in satisfaction (41%) but only a small proportion of the variance in burnout (8%), suggesting that other factors (not measured in this study) might be contributing to burnout (eg workload; type of client; adequacy of supervision). Factors predicting burnout and job satisfaction in workplace counsellors included: the influence of role stressors, job challenge and organisational knowledge.

Methodological issues: the analysis did not differentiate between counsellors employed in in-house services and those who provided external/EAP services – it might be reasonable to expect that different organisational factors could be significant for each of these groups.

Authors: Kurioka, S., Muto, T. and Tarumi, K.

Title: Characteristics of health counselling in the workplace via e-mail.

Date: 2001.

Type of publication: journal article.

Source: *Occupational Medicine*, 51: 427–432.

Aims of study: to analyse the acceptability and use of email counselling for employees in a Japanese manufacturing company.

Method: employees were offered health counselling by email, telephone, ordinary mail or face-to-face contact. Information about the characteristics of each separate counselling session was recorded.

Sample: 700 head office employees (74% male).

Type of counselling: counselling approach not specified; delivered by two occupational health nurses.

Organisational context: head office of large manufacturing company; Japan.

Results: data was collected for 2,119 counselling sessions over two years. The most popular methods were face-to-face (70% of episodes) and telephone (15%); 13% of sessions were conducted through email. However, email counselling was the second most popular method for younger employees (20 to 39 years). While 11% of all sessions related to mental health issues, a significantly higher proportion (26%) of email sessions dealt with these issues. Email consultations were proportionally more likely to relate to prevention issues compared to other methods, and were more likely to refer to third parties (eg family members). The conclusion was that email counselling could have an important role to play within workplace counselling services.

Note: this paper includes a valuable discussion of broader issues around the provision of email counselling in organisational settings.

Author: Meier, A.

Title: An online stress management support group for social workers.

Date: 2002.

Type of publication: journal article.

Source: Journal of Technology in Human Services, 20: 107–132.

Aims of study: to evaluate the effectiveness of an online support group provided through an email *listserv.*

Method: participants completed the Occupational Stress Inventory on three occasions; there was qualitative analysis of themes in group and individual email postings.

Sample: 23 qualified and experienced social workers, working full-time.

Type of counselling: online group counselling, facilitated by a group leader, supplemented by individual email contact.

Organisational context: social work; USA.

Results: participants reported that the online support group had been helpful to them, although no significant changes were found on OSI data.

Methodological issues: this was an exploratory study, which provided a wealth of examples of the group process and the types of issues that were explored within it.

Note: the findings of a pilot study conducted by the same author are available in Meier (2000).

Authors: Parry, G., Shapiro, D.A. and Firth, J.

Title: The case of the anxious executive: a study from the research clinic.

Date: 1986.

Type of publication: journal article.

Source: British Journal of Medical Psychology, 59: 221–233.

Aims of study: to examine the process and outcome of psychotherapy for work-related problems through the use of a structured case study.

Method: process and outcome data from a good outcome case taken from the 'Sheffield I' research study were analysed. The client completed a range of measures of psychiatric symptoms, depression, self-esteem and self-rating of problems, before and in the middle of therapy, and at a three-month follow-up. Process data was collected through Helpful Aspects of Therapy questionnaires completed at the end of each session.

Sample: male, 42-year-old senior manager in a State-owned industry.

Type of counselling: eight sessions of psychodynamic therapy, followed by eight sessions of cognitive-behavioural therapy, delivered by an experienced clinical psychologist. Therapy took place in a university research clinic.

Organisational context: not relevant to this study.

Results: good outcome case. Most change occurred in the first eight sessions. Process analysis showed how personal and work issues were inter-related, and how different therapeutic interventions could have an impact on work attitudes and behaviour.

Methodological issues: this was a single case study, so generalisation was not possible.

Authors: Potter, P.T.

Title: An integrative approach to industrial trauma within emergency service occupations.

Date: 2002.

Type of publication: journal article.

Source: *Clinical Case Studies*, 1: 133–147.

Aims of study: to examine the use of a combination of cognitive-behavioural and narrative constructivist methods in a case of occupational stress.

Method: clinical case study, based on therapist notes, and standard measures.

Sample: the client was a 36-year-old man, employed in the military police, who reported PTSD symptoms and relationship difficulties following involvement as 'first responder' in a fatality incident several months previously.

Type of counselling: cognitive-behavioural and narrative constructivist; assessment, then seven sessions and a four-month follow-up.

Organisational context: military; USA.

Results: the client made a complete recovery. Key features of this case were the use of dream analysis to facilitate broader narrative interpretation, in addition to standard CBT stress-management techniques.

Methodological issues: the OQ45, a standard symptom assessment scale, was employed in the assessment interview, and yielded a score within the normal range, which was in contradiction to the level of client distress observed by the therapist. The author argues that the OQ45 score was skewed because it reflected the organisational culture in which the client worked, which required a stoical approach to distressing situations and failed to capture the true level of symptomatology of the client.

Authors: Sperry, L.

Title: Work-focused psychotherapy with executives.

Date: 1996.

Type of publication: journal article.

Source: *Individual Psychology*, 52: 193–199.

Aims of study: to describe and discuss the use of a brief therapy intervention in a case of a depressed executive.

Method: clinical case study.

Sample: single case; 43-year-old male manager.

Type of counselling: brief integrative approach.

Organisational context: finance sector; USA.

Results: described a behaviourally oriented therapeutic approach, with a successful outcome.

Methodological issues: there was a lack of specific detail or use of independent measures of change.

Note: this paper provides a valuable discussion of the issues faced by therapists in working in a time-limited fashion around work-related issues.

Authors: Sprang, G. and Secret, M.

Title: Employee crisis and occupational functioning.

Date: 1999.

Type of publication: journal article.

Source: *Employee Assistance Quarterly*, 15: 29–43.

Aims of study: to explore the ways in which employees respond to acute life events that threaten their performance at work.

Method: in-depth telephone interviews.

Sample: 527 interviews were conducted with a random sample of employees drawn from 83 organisations that adhered to worker-friendly policies and practices.

Type of counselling: not specified.

Organisational context: range of profit and not-for-profit organisations; USA.

Results: 388 (61%) of participants reported at least one personal crisis during their tenure with their current employer. More than 30% reported that the crisis had resulted in significant job disruption. More than 80% of participants worked for organisations in which EAP services were available; however, only 7.5% utilised these. Shortcomings in the organisational response to crisis were identified: taking time off without using sick or vacation time, and lack of emotional support from supervisor. The greatest difficulties in dealing with crisis were found in employees of non-profit health and social care organisations.

Note: the paper includes a useful case study of how an EAP can work with an organisation to deliver support to an employee in crisis.

Authors: Sweeney, A.P., Hohenshil, T.H. and Fortune, J.C.

Title: Job satisfaction among employee assistance professionals: a national survey.

Date: 2002.

Type of publication: journal article.

Source: *Journal of Employment Counselling*, 39: 50–60.

Aims of study: to examine levels of job satisfaction in EAP counsellors.

Method: survey questionnaire, delivered by mail to 354 members of the Employee Assistance Professionals Association (EAPA). The package included an extensive standardised job satisfaction scale, and an individual information form, designed for the study, that collected data on participant demographic characteristics, training and work role.

Sample: 211 EAP counsellors (response rate 60%). 52% female; the average age was 48; 74% with Masters degrees; 96% ethnic white. 35% had a social work qualification and 18% had specialist EAP qualifications. 63% held professional licences as social workers, counsellors, substance abuse professionals or psychologists. Mean years of experience in EAP work was 13 years. 72% worked for external EAPs. There was a mix of urban, suburban and rural settings.

Type of counselling: various, not specified.

Organisational context: cross-sector; USA.

Results: overall job satisfaction scores were similar to those reported in other studies of psychologists and counsellors. 24% reported that they planned to leave their post within the next 12 months. 90% were either satisfied or very satisfied with their present job. Only one respondent was clearly dissatisfied. Respondents who worked for external EAPs were significantly more satisfied than those who worked for in-house services. Counsellors in external EAPs had a more positive outlook regarding potential career advancement and perceived a higher degree of fairness concerning promotion.

References

Ablon, J. S. and Jones, E. E. (2002) Validity of controlled trials of psychotherapy: findings from the NIMH treatment of depression collaborative research program. *American Journal of Psychiatry,* 159: 775–783.

Ahn, K. K. and Karris, P. M. (1987) Number versus severity: the truth in measuring EAP cost benefits. *Employee Assistance Quarterly,* 4 (4): 1–14.

Akers, R. (1995) Supervisor referrals to EAP programmes: a social learning perspective. *Journal of Drug Issues,* 25(2): 341–361.

Allen, J. (1999) Responding to unemployment and inequalities in income and health. *European Journal of Psychotherapy, Counselling and Health,* 2: 143–152.

Allison, T., Cooper C. L., and Reynolds, S. (1989) Stress counselling in the workplace. The Post Office experience. *The Psychologist,* 2: 384–388.

Amaral, T. M. (1999) Benchmarks and performance measures for Employee Assistance Programs. In J.M. Oher (ed.) *The Employee Assistance Handbook.* New York: Wiley.

Anderson, M. A. (2003) A case study of occupationally focused brief dynamic therapy using Mann's model of central conflict. *Clinical Case Studies,* 2: 91–103.

Arthur, A.R. (2000) Employee Assistance Programmes: the emperor's new clothes of stress management? *British Journal of Guidance and Counselling,* 28: 549–559.

Arthur, A. R. (2002) Mental health problems and British workers: a survey of mental health problems in employees who receive counselling from Employee Assistance Programmes. *Stress and Health,* 18: 69–74.

Asen, J. and Colon, I. (1995) Acceptance and use of Police Department Employee Assistance Programmes. *Employee Assistance Quarterly,* 11: 45–54.

Atkins, D. C., Bedics, J. D., McGlinchey, J. B. and Beauchaine, T. B. (2005) Assessing clinical significance: does it matter which method we use? *Journal of Consulting and Clinical Psychology,* 73: 982–989.

Attridge, M. (2004) The business case for the integration of employee assistance, work–life and wellness services: a literature review. *Journal of Workplace Behavioral Health,* 20: 31–55.

Barkham, M. (1989) Brief prescriptive therapy in two–plus–one sessions: initial cases from the clinic. *Behavioural Psychotherapy,* 17: 161–175.

Barkham, M., Mellor–Clark, J., Connell, J. and Cahill, J. (2006) A CORE approach to practice–based evidence: a brief history of the origins and applications of the CORE-OM and CORE System. *Counselling and Psychotherapy Research,* 6: 3–15.

Barkham, M. and Shapiro, D. A. (1990a) Brief psychotherapeutic interventions for job related distress: a pilot study of prescriptive and exploratory therapy. *Counselling Psychology Quarterly,* 3(2): 133–147.

Barkham, M. and Shapiro, D. A. (1990b) Exploratory therapy in two-plus-one sessions: a research model for studying the process of change. In G. Lietaer, J. Rombauts and R. van Balen (eds) *Client-centered and experiential psychotherapy in the nineties.* Leuven, Belgium: Leuven University Press.

Barkham, M., Shapiro, D. A., Hardy, G. and Rees, A. (1999) Psychotherapy in two–plus–one sessions: outcomes of a randomised, controlled trial of cognitive-behavioral and psychodynamic-interpersonal therapy for subsyndromal depression. *Journal of Consulting and Clinical Psychology,* 67(2): 201–211.

Basso, R. (1989) A consumer's grapevine in an Employee Assistance Program. *Employee Assistance Quarterly,* 4(3): 1–10.

Bauman, Z. (2004) *Wasted Lives: modernity and its outcasts.* Cambridge: Polity Press.

Bayer, D. L. (1998) Brief anger-management therapy. *Employer Assistance Quarterly,* 14(2): 67–74.

Bayer, G. A. and Barkin, A. C. (1990) Employee Assistance Program utilisation: comparison of referral sources and problems. *Employee Assistance Quarterly,* 5: 63–70.

Bennett, J. B. and Lehman, W. E. K. (2001) Workplace substance abuse prevention and help seeking: comparing team-oriented and informational training. *Journal of Occupational Health Psychology,* 6: 243–254.

Black, N. (1996) Why we need observational studies to evaluate the effectiveness of health care. *British Medical Journal,* 312: 1215–1218.

Blaze–Temple, D. and Howat, P. (1997) Cost benefit of an Australian EAP. *Employee Assistance Quarterly,* 12(3): 1–24.

Blum, T. C. and Roman, P. M. (1992) A description of clients using Employee Assistance Programs. *Alcohol Health Research,* 16(2): 120–128.

Blum, T. C., Roman, P. M. and Martin, J. K. (1992) A research note on EAP prevalence, components and utilisation. *Journal of Employee Assistance Research,* 1: 209–229.

Blum, T. C., Roman, P. M. and Harwood E. M. (1995) Employed women with alcohol problems who seek help from Employee Assistance Programs. Descriptions and comparisons. In M. Galanter (ed.), *Recent Developments in Alcoholism. Women and Alcoholism. Volume 12.* New York: Plenum Press.

BOHRF (2005) *Workplace interventions for people with common mental health problems: evidence review and recommendations.* London: British Occupational Health Research Foundation.

Bond, F. W. and Bunce, D. (2000) Mediators of change in emotion-focused and problem-focused worksite stress management interventions. *Journal of Occupational Health Psychology,* 5: 156–163.

Bowling, A. (2001) *Measuring disease.* 2nd edn. Buckingham: Open University Press.

Bowling, A. (2004) *Measuring health.* 3rd edn. Buckingham: Open University Press.

Braun, A. L. and Novak, D. E. (1986) A study of EAP non-utilisation. *EAP Digest,* 7(1): 52–55.

Bray, J. W., French, M. T., Bowland, B. J. and Dunlap, L. J. (1996) The cost of Employee Assistance Programs (EAPs). Findings from seven case studies. *Employee Assistance Quarterly,* 11(4): 1–19.

Brodzinsky, J. D. and Goyer, K. A. (1987) Employee Assistance Program utilisation and gender. *Employee Assistance Quarterly,* 3: 1–13.

Bruhnsen, K. (1989) EAP evaluation and cost benefit savings: a case example. *Health Values,* 13(1): 39–42.

Brummett, P. O. (2000) A comparison of Employee Assistance P rograms providing internal versus external treatment services: a research note. *Employee Assistance Quarterly,* 15(4): 19–28.

Bunting, M. (2004) *Willing Slaves: how the overwork culture is ruling our lives.* London: HarperCollins.

Burke, R. J. (1994) Utilisation of Employees' Assistance Program in a public accounting firm: some preliminary data. *Psychological Reports*, 75: 264–266.

Burwell, R. and Chen, C.P. (2002) Applying REBT to workaholic clients. *Counselling Psychology Quarterly*, 15: 219–228.

Butterfield, L. D. and Borgen, W. A. (2005) Outplacement counselling from the client's perspective. *Career Development Quarterly*, 53: 306–316.

Butterworth, I. E. (2001) The components and impact of stigma associated with EAP counselling. *Employee Assistance Quarterly*, 16: 1–9.

Campbell, J. E. (1985) A role for nurse psychotherapists: primary prevention counselling for general hospital staff. *Perspectives in Psychiatric Care*, 23: 85–90.

Cairo, P. C. (1983) Counselling in industry: a selective review of the literature. *Personnel Psychology*, 36: 1–18.

Carroll, C. (1997) Building Bridges: a study of employee counsellors in the private sector. In M. Carroll, M. and Walton, M. (eds.) *Handbook of counselling in organisations.* London: Sage.

Carroll, M. (1996) *Workplace counselling: a systematic approach to employee care.* London: Sage.

Carroll, M. and Walton, M. (eds) (1997) *Handbook of counselling in organisations.* London: Sage.

Chadwick–Jones, J. K., Nicholson, N. and Brown, C. (1982) *Social psychology of absenteeism.* New York: Praeger.

Chandler, R. G., Kroeker, B. J., Fynn, M. and MacDonald, D. A. (1988) Establishing and evaluating an industrial social work programme: the Seagram, Amherstburg experience. *Employee Assistance Quarterly*, 3(3/4): 243–251.

Cheeseman, M. J. (1996) *Is staff counselling an effective intervention into employee distress? An investigation of two employee counselling services in the NHS.* Unpublished PhD thesis, Social and Applied Psychology Unit, University of Sheffield.

Christensen, A. and Jacobson, N. S. (1994) Who (or what) can do psychotherapy: the status and challenge of nonprofessional therapies. *Psychological Science*, 5: 8–14.

Cole, G. E., Tucker, L. A. and Friedman, G. M. (1982) Absenteeism, data as a measure of cost effectiveness of SRNs management programs. *American Journal of Health Promotion*, Spring 12–15.

Coles, A. (2003) *Counselling in the workplace.* Buckingham: Open University Press.

Concato, J., Shah, N. and Horwitz, R. I. (2000) Randomized, controlled trials, observational studies, and the hierarchy of research designs. *New England Journal of Medicine*, 342: 1887–1892.

Connell, J., Cahill, J., Barkham, M., Gilbody, S. and Madill, A. (2006) *A systematic scoping search of the research on counselling in Higher and Further Education.* Rugby: British Association for Counselling and Psychotherapy.

Conti, D. J. and Burton, W. N. (1999) Behavioural health disability management. In J.M. Oher (ed.) *The employee assistance handbook.* New York: Wiley.

Cooper, C. L. and Sadri, G. (1991) The impact of stress counselling at work. *Journal of Behavior and Personality*, 6(7): 411–423.

Cooper, C. L., Sadri, G., Allison, T. and Reynolds, P. (1990) Counselling in the Post Office. *Counselling Psychologist Quarterly*, 3(1): 3–11.

Cooper, C. L., Sloan, S. L. and William, S. (1988). *Occupational Stress Indicator: Management Guide.* Oxford: NFER-Nelson.

Corneil, W. (1995) Traumatic stress and organisational strain in the fire service. In L. R. Murphy, J. J. Hurrell, S. L. Sauter and G. P. Keita, (eds) *Job Stress Interventions.* Washington, DC: American Psychological Association.

Courtois, P., Hajek, M. et al (2004) Performance measures in the Employee Assistance Program. *Employee Assistance Quarterly*, 19: 45–58.

Csiernik, R. (1999) Internal versus external Employee Assistance programs: what the Canadian data adds to the debate. *Employee Assistance Quarterly*, 15: 1–12.

Csiernik, R. (2002) An overview of employee and family assistance programming in Canada. *Employee Assistance Quarterly*, 18: 17–33.

Csiernik, R. (2003) Employee Assistance Program utilisation: developing a comprehensive scorecard. *Employee Assistance Quarterly*, 18: 45–60.

Csiernik, R. (2004) A review of EAP evaluation in the 1990s. *Employee Assistance Quarterly*, 19: 21–37.

Csiernik, R. (2005a) Wellness and the workplace. In R. Csiernik (ed.) *Wellness and work: Employee Assistance Programming in Canada.* Toronto: Canadian Scholars Press.

Csiernik, R. (2005b) The evolution of occupational assistance: from social control to health promotion. In R. Csiernik (ed.) *Wellness and work: Employee Assistance Programming in Canada.* Toronto: Canadian Scholars Press.

Csiernik, R. (Ed.) (2005c). *Wellness and work: Employee Assistance Programming in Canada.* Toronto: Canadian Scholars Press.

Csiernik, R., Atkison, B., Cooper, R., Devereux, J. and Young, M. (2001) An examination of a combined internal-external Employee Assistance Program: the St Joseph's Health Centre employee counselling service. *Employee Assistance Quarterly*, 16: 37–48.

Csiernik, R., Macdonald, S., Durand, P., Wild, T. C. and Rylett, M. (2005) Who do we serve? Worksite characteristics, workforce attributes and occupational assistance programming in Canada. *Journal of Workplace Behavioral Health*, 21: 15–29.

Cunningham, G. (1992) The EAP counsellor: attitudes, knowledge and beliefs. *Employee Assistance Quarterly*, 8(1): 13–25.

Dainas, C. and Marks, D. (2000) Evidence of an EAP cost offset. *Behavioral Health Management*, July/August, pages 34–41.

Decker, J. T., Starrett, R. and Redhouse, J. (1986) Evaluating the cost-effectiveness of Employee Assistance Programs. *Social Worker*, 31: 391–393.

Deeks, J. J., Dinnes, J., D'Amico, R., Sowden, A. J. et al. (2003) Evaluating non-randomised, intervention studies. Health Technology Assessment, 7(27). Available at: www.hta.nhsweb.nhs.uk/fullmono/mon727.pdf.

DeGroot, T. and Kiker, D. S. (2003) A meta–analysis of the non-monetary effects of employee health management programs. *Human Resource Management*, 42: 53–69.

Deane, F. P., Spicer, J. and Todd, D. M. (1997) Validity of a simplified target complaints measure. *Assessment*, 4: 119–130.

Delaney, W., Grube, J. W. and Arnes, G. M. (1998) Predicting likelihood of seeking help through the Employee Assistance Program among salaried and union hourly employees. *Addiction* 93(3): 399–410.

Delaney, W., Grube, J. W. and Ames, G.M. (1998) Predicting likelihood of seeking employee assistance. *Addiction*, 93: 399–410.

Denzin, N. K. (1995) Living and dying in an Employee Assistance Program. *The Journal of Drug Issues*, 25(2): 363–378.

Dersch, C. A., Shumway, S. T., Harris, S. M. and Arredondo, R. (2002) A new comprehensive measure of EAP satisfaction: a factor analysis. *Employee Assistance Quarterly*, 17: 55–60.

Dewe, P. and Cooper, C. L. (2004) *Stress: a brief history*. Oxford: Blackwell.

Dick, P. (2000) The social construction of the meaning of acute stressors: a qualitative study of the personal accounts of police officers using a stress counselling service. *Work and Stress*, 14: 226–244.

Dickson, W. (1945) The Hawthorne Plan. *American Journal of Orthopsychiatry*, 15: 343–347.

Dickson, W. and Roethlisberger, F. J. (1966) *Counselling in an Organisation*. Cambridge, MA: Harvard University Press.

Doctor, R. S., Curtis, D. and Isaacs, G. (1994) Psychiatric morbidity in policemen and the effect of brief psychotherapeutic intervention – a pilot study. *Stress Medicine*, 10: 151–157.

Donohue, T. L., Johnson, J. T., Stevens, J. and Taquino, M. A. (1998) Self-disclosure as a predictor of EAP supervisory utilisation. *Employee Assistance Quarterly*, 14: 1–9.

Downs, S. H. and Black, N. (1998) The feasibility of creating a checklist for the assessment of the methodological quality both of randomised, and non–randomised, studies of health care interventions. *Journal of Epidemiology and Community Health*, 52: 377–384.

Edwards, S. J. L., Lilford, R. J., Braunholtz, D. A., Jackson, J. C., Hewison, J. and Thornton, J. (1998) Ethical issues in the design and conduct of randomised, controlled trials. *Health Technology Assessment*, vol. 2, no. 15.

Elliott, M. S. and Williams, D. I. (2002) A qualitative evaluation of an employee counselling service from the perspective of client, counsellor and organisation. *Counselling Psychology Quarterly*, 15: 201–208.

Elliott, R., Fischer, C. T. and Rennie, D. L. (1999) Evolving guidelines for the publication of qualitative research studies in psychology and related fields. *British Journal of Clinical Psychology*, 38: 215–229.

Employee Assistance Professionals Association (EAPA) (2006) Market research. Downloaded on 30 August 2006 from: http://www.eapa.org.uk/EAPA_MarketInfo.htm.

Evans, C., Mellor–Clark, J., Margison, F., Barkham, M., Audin, K., Connell, J. and McGrath, G. (2000) CORE: clinical outcomes in routine evaluation. *Journal of Mental Health*, 9: 247–255.

Every, D. K. and Leong, D. M. (1994) Understanding EAP cost effectiveness: profile of a nuclear power plant EAP. *Employee Assistance Quarterly*, 10(1): 1–14.

Falk, D. R., Shepard, M. F. and Elliott, B. A. (2002) Evaluation of a domestic violence assessment protocol used by employee assistance counsellors. *Employee Assistance Quarterly*, 17: 1–15.

Feldman, D. C. and Lankau, M. J. (2005) Executive coaching: a review and agenda for future research. *Journal of Management*, 31: 829–848.

Fidler, F., Cumming, G. et al (2005) Toward improved statistical reporting. *Journal of Consulting and Clinical Psychology*, 73: 136–143.

Finkle, L., Williams, J. and Stanley R. (1996) Nurses referred to a peer assistance program for alcohol and drug problems. *Archives of Psychiatric Nursing*, 10(5): 319–3240.

Firth, J. (1985) Personal meanings of occupational stress: cases from the clinic. *Journal of Occupational Psychology*, 58: 139–48.

Firth, J. A. and Shapiro, D. A. (1986) An evaluation of psychotherapy for job related distress. *Journal of Occupational Psychology*, 59: 111–119.

Firth–Cozens, J. (1992) Why me? A case study of the process of perceived occupational stress. *Human Relations*, 45: 131–142.

Firth–Cozens, J. A. and Hardy, G. E. (1992) Occupational stress, clinical treatment and changes in job perceptions. *Journal of Occupational and Organisational Psychology*, 65: 81–86.

Fisher, H. (1997) Plastering over the cracks? A study of employee counselling in the NHS. In M. Carroll and M. Walton (eds) *Handbook of Counselling in Organisations*. London. Sage.

Flannery, R. B. (2001) The Assaulted Staff Action Program (ASAP): ten year empirical support for Critical Incident Stress Management. *International Journal of Emergency Mental Health*, 3: 5–10.

French, M. T. (1995) Cost of Employee Assistance Programs. *Medical Benefits*, 12(12): 5.

French, M. T., Dunlap, L. J., Roman, P. M. and Steele, P. D. (1997) Factors that influence the use and perceptions of Employee Assistance Programs at six worksites. *Journal of Occupational Health Psychology*, 2(4): 312–324.

French, M. T., Dunlap, L. J., Zarkin, G. A. and Karuntzos, G.T. (1998) The costs of an enhanced Employee Assistance Program (EAP) intervention. *Evaluation and Program Planning*, 21(2): 227–236.

French, M. T., Zarkin, G. A., Bray, J. W. and Hartwell, T. D. (1997) Costs of Employee Assistance Programs: findings from a national study. *American Journal of Health Promotion*, 11(3): 219–222.

French, M. T., Zarkin, G. A., Bray, J. W. and Hartwell, T. D. (1999) Cost of Employee Assistance Programs: comparison of national estimates from 1993 and 1995. *Journal of Behavioural Health Services and* Research, 26(1): 95–103.

Frost, A. K. (1990) Assessing employees' awareness: a first step to utilisation. *Employee Assistance Quarterly*, 6(1): 45–55.

Fryer, D. and Fagan, R. (2003) Toward a critical community psychological perspective on unemployment and mental health research. *American Journal of Community Psychology*. 32: 89–96.

Gam, J., Sauser, W. I., Evans, K. L. and Lair, C. V. (1983) The evaluation of an Employee Assistance Program. *Journal of Employment Counselling*, 20: 99–106.

Gammie, B. (1997) Employee Assistance Programs in the UK oil industry: an examination of current operational practice. *Personnel Review*, 26(1/2): 66–80.

Gardner, B., Rose, J., Mason, O., Tyler, P. and Cushway, D. (2005) Cognitive therapy and behavioural coping in the management of work–related stress: an intervention study. *Work and Stress*, 19: 137–152.

Gersons, B. P. R., Carlier, I. V. E., Lamberts, R. D. and van der Kolk, B. A. (2000) Randomized clinic trial of brief eclectic psychotherapy for police officers with post–traumatic stress disorder. *Journal of Traumatic Stress*, 13: 333–347.

Gerstein, L. H. and Bayer, G. A. (1988) Employee Assistance Programs: a systematic investigation of their use. *Journal of Counseling and Development*, 66: 294–297.

Gerstein, L. H. Gaber, T. Dainas, C. and Duffey, K. (1993) Organisational hierarchy, employee status and use of Employee Assistance Programs. *Journal of Employment Counseling*, 30: 74–78.

Gerstein, L., Moore, D., Duffey, K. and Dainas, C. (1995) The effects of biological sex and ethnicity on EAP utilisation and referrals. *Consulting Psychology Journal*, 45: 23–27.

Giga, S. I., Noblet, A. J., Faragher, B. and Cooper, C. L. (2003) The UK perspective: a review of research on organisational stress management interventions. *Australian Psychologist*, 38: 158–164.

Goldberg, D. and Williams, P. (1988) *A user's guide to the General Health Questionnaire*. Windsor: NFER-Nelson.

Goodspeed, R. B. and Delucia, A. G. (1990) Stress reduction at the worksite: an evaluation of two methods. *American Journal of Health Promotion Psychology*, 4: 333–337.

Goss, S. and Mearns, D. (1997) Applied pluralism in the evaluation of employee counselling. *British Journal of Guidance and Counselling*, 25(3): 327–344.

Gray-Toft, P. (1980) Effectiveness of a counselling support program for hospice nurses. *Journal of Counseling Psychology*, 27: 346–354.

Grime, P. R. (2004) Computerized cognitive behavioural therapy at work: a randomized controlled trial in employees with recent stress-related absenteeism. *Occupational Medicine*, 54: 353–359.

Grosch, J. W., Duffy, K. G. and Hessink, T. K. (1996) Employee Assistance Programs in higher education: factors associated with program usage and effectiveness. *Employee Assistance Quarterly*, 11(4): 43–57.

Guppy, A. and Marsden, J. (1997) Assisting employees with drinking problems: changes in mental health, job perceptions and work performance. *Work and Stress*, 11(4): 341–50.

Gyllensten, K., Palmer, S. and Farrants, J. (2005) Perceptions of stress and stress interventions in finance organisations: overcoming resistance towards counselling. *Counselling Psychology Quarterly*, 18: 19–30.

Haines, V. Y., Petit, A. and Lefrancois, S. (1999) Explaining client satisfaction with an Employee Assistance Program. *Employee Assistance Quarterly*, 14: 65–78.

Hall, L., Vacc, N. A. and Kissling, G. (1991) Likelihood to use Employee Assistance Programs: the effects of sociodemographic, social-psychological, social cultural, organisational and community factors. *Journal of Employment Counseling*, 28: 63–73.

Hansen, S. (2004) From 'common observation' to behavioural risk management – workplace surveillance and employee risk management 1914–2003. *International Sociology*, 19: 151–171.

Hargrave, G. E. and Hiatt, D. (2004) The EAP treatment of depressed employees: implications for return on investment. *Employee Assistance Quarterly*, 19: 39–49.

Harlow, K. (1987) A comparison of internal and external Employee Assistance Programs. *New England Journal of Human Services*, 7(2): 6–21.

Harlow, K. C. (1998) Employee attitude toward an internal Employee Assistance Program. *Journal of Employment Counseling*, 35: 141–150.

Harris, M. M. and Ferrell, M. L. (1988) Perceptions of an Employee Assistance Programme and employees' willingness to participate. *Journal of Applied Behavioral Science*, 24: 423–438.

Harris, S. M., Adams, A., Hill, L., Morgan, M. and Solz, C. (2002) Beyond customer satisfaction: a randomised, EAP outcome study. *Employee Assistance Quarterly*, 17: 53–61.

Hartwell, T. D., Steele, P., French, M. T., Potter, F. J., Rodman, N. F. and Zarkin, G. A. (1996) Aiding troubled employees: the prevalence, cost and characteristics of Employee Assistance Programs in the United States. *American Journal of Public Health*, 86: 804–808.

Hayes, S. C., Luoma, J. B., Bond, F. W., Masuda, A. and Lillis, J. (2006) Acceptance and Commitment Therapy: model, processes and outcomes. *Behaviour Research and Therapy*, 44: 1–25.

Hiatt, D., Hargrave, G. and Palmertree, M. (1999) Effectiveness of job performance referrals. *Employee Assistance Quarterly*, 14: 33–43.

Highley–Marchington, J. C. and Cooper, C. L. (1998) An assessment of employee assistance and workplace counselling programmes in British organisations. *Report for the Health and Safety Executive*. HSE Books.

Houts, L. M. (1991) Survey of the current status of cost-savings evaluations in Employee Assistance Programs. *Employee Assistance Quarterly*, 7(1): 57–73.

Iwi, D. J., Watson, P., Barber, N., Kimber and Sharman, G. (1998) The self–reported wellbeing of employees facing organisational change: effects of an intervention. *Occupational Medicine* 48(6): 361–369.

Jacobson, N. S., Follette, W. C. and Revenstorf, D. (1984) Psychotherapy outcome research: methods for reporting variability and evaluating clinical significance. *Behavior Therapy*, 15: 336–352.

Jacobson, N. S. and Revenstorf, D. (1988) Statistics for assessing the clinical significance of psychotherapy techniques: issues, problems and new developments. *Behavioral Assessment*, 10: 133–145.

Jenkins, D. and Palmer, S. (2003) A multimodal assessment and rational emotive behavioural approach to stress counselling: a case study. *Counselling Psychology Quarterly*, 16: 265–287.

Keaton, B. C. (1990) The effect of voluntarism on treatment attitude in relationship to previous counselling experience in an Employee Assistance Program. *Employee Assistance Quarterly*, 6: 57–66.

Kenny, M. C. and McEachern, A. G. (2004) Telephone counselling: are offices becoming obsolete? *Journal of Counseling and Development*, 82: 199–202.

Kimball, T. G., Shumway, S. T., Korinek, A. and Arredondo, R. (2002) Using the Satisfaction with Organisation Scale (SOS): two samples compared. *Employee Assistance Quarterly*, 18: 47–65.

Kirk, A. K. and Brown, D. F. (2003) Employee Assistance Programs: a review of the management of stress and wellbeing through workplace counselling and consulting. *Australian Psychologist*, 38: 138–143.

Kirk-Brown, A. and Wallace, D. (2004) Predicting burnout and job satisfaction in workplace counsellors: the influence of role stressors, job challenge and organisational knowledge. *Journal of Employment Counseling*, 41: 29–37.

Klarreich, S. H., DiGiuseppe, R. and DiMattia, D. J. (1987) Cost effectiveness of an Employee Assistance Program with rational emotive therapy. *Professional Psychology: Research and Practice*, 18: 140–4.

Kuntz, R. and Oxman, A. D. (1998) The unpredictability paradox: review of empiricial comparisons of randomised, and non–randomised, clinical trials. *British Medical Journal,* 317: 1185–1190.

Kurioka, S., Muto, T. and Tarumi, K. (2001) Characteristics of health counselling in the workplace via email. *Occupational Medicine*, 51: 427–432.

Lambert, M. J. (2005) Emerging methods in providing clinicians with timely feedback on treatment effectiveness. *Journal of Clinical Psychology*, 61: 141–144.

Lambert, M. J. and Bergin, A. E. (1994) The effectiveness of psychotherapy. In A.E. Bergin and S.L. Garfield (eds) *Handbook of psychotherapy and behavior change*. New York: Wiley.

Lambert, M. J., Burlingame, G. L. et al (1996) The reliability and validity of the Outcome Questionnaire. *Clinical Psychology and Psychotherapy*, 3: 106–116.

Lambert, M. J. and Finch, A. E. (1999) The Outcome Questionnaire. In M.E. Maruish (ed.) *The use of psychological testing for treatment planning and outcome assessment*. 2nd edn. Mahwah, NJ: Erlbaum.

Lambert, M. J. (ed.) (2004) *Bergin and Garfield's handbook of psychotherapy and behavior change*. New York: Wiley.

Lambert, M. J. and Ogles, B. M. (2004) The efficacy and effectiveness of psychotherapy. In M. J. Lambert (ed.) *Bergin and Garfield's handbook of psychotherapy and behavior change*. New York: Wiley.

Lambert, M. J., Hansen, N. B. and Finch, A. E. (2001) Patient-focused research: using patient outcome data to enhance treatment effects. *Journal of Consulting and Clinical Psychology*, 69: 159–172.

Lawrence, J. A., Boxer, P. and Tarakeshwar, N. (2002) Determining demand for EAP services. *Employee Assistance Quarterly*, 18: 1–15.

Leong, D. M. and Every, D. K. (1997) Internal and external EAPs. Is one better than the other? *Employee Assistance Quarterly*, 12(3): 47–62.

Levinson, H. (1956) Employee counselling in industry: observations on three programs. *Employee Counselling in Industry*, 20: 76–84.

Lindquist, T. L. and Cooper, C. L. (1999) Using lifestyle and coping to reduce job stress and improve health in 'at risk' office workers. *Stress Medicine*, 15: 143–152.

Loo, R. (1996) Managing workplace stress: a Canadian Delphi study among human resource managers. *Work and Stress*, 10: 183–189.

Lubin, B., Shanklin, H. D. and Sailors, J. R. (1992) The EAP literature: articles and dissertations 1970–1990. *Employee Assistance Quarterly*, 8: 47–85.

Luborsky, L., Diguer, L. et al (1999) The researcher's own therapy allegiances: a "wild card" in comparisons of treatment efficacy. *Clinical Psychology: Science and Practice,* 6: 95–106.

Macdonald, S., Lothian, S. and Wells, S. (1997) Evaluation of an Employee Assistance Program at a transportation company. *Evaluation and Program Planning*, 20(4): 495–505.

Macdonald, S. and MacIntyre, P. (1997) The generic job satisfaction scale: scale development and its correlates. *Employee Assistance Quarterly*, 13: 1–15.

Macdonald, S., Wells, S., Lothian, S. and Shain, M. (2000) Absenteeism and other workplace indicators of Employee Assistance Program clients and matched controls. *Employee Assistance Quarterly*, 15: 41–57.

Maddocks, M. (2000) Working wounded. *Health Service Journal*, 110: 26–27.

Marlin, P. (1997) Counselling skills training for managers in the public sector. In M. Carroll and M. Walton (eds) *Handbook of counselling in organisations*. London: Sage.

Marmot, M. (2004) *Status Syndrome: how your social standing directly affects your health*. London: Bloomsbury.

Masi, D. A., Jacobson, J. M. and Cooper, A. R. (2000) Quantifying quality: findings from clinical reviews. *Employee Assistance Quarterly*, 15(4): 1–17.

Masi, D. A. and Jacobson, J. M. (2003) Outcome measurements of an integrated employee assistance and work-life program. *Research on Social Work Practice*, 13: 451–467.

May, K. M. (1992) Referrals to Employee Assistance Programs: a pilot analogue study of expectations about counselling. *Journal of Mental Health Counselling*, 14: 208–224.

McAllister, P. O. (1993) An evaluation of counselling for employer–referred problem drinkers. *Health Bulletin*, 51(5): 285–294.

McClellan, K. (1989) Cost–benefit analysis of the Ohio EAP. *Employee Assistance Quarterly*, 5(2): 67–85.

McGuire, J. M., Toal, P. and Blau, B. (1985) The adult client's concept of confidentiality in the therapeutic relationship. *Professional Psychology: Research and Practice*, 16: 375–384.

McLeod, J. (1999) *Practitioner research in counselling*. London: Sage.

McLeod, J. (2001) *Counselling in the workplace: the facts*. Rugby: BACP.

McLeod, J. (2003) *Doing counselling research*. 2nd edn. London: Sage.

Meier, A. (2000) Offering social support via the internet: a case study of an online support group for social workers. *Journal of Technology in Human Services*, 17: 237–266.

Meier, A. (2002) An online stress management support group for social workers. *Journal of Technology in Human Services*, 20: 107–132.

Mellor–Clark, J., Curtis Jenkins, A., Evans, R., Mothersole, G. and McInnes, B. (2006) Resourcing a CORE Network to develop a National Research Database to help enhance psychological therapy and counselling service provision. *Counselling and Psychotherapy Research,* 6: 16–22.

Mental Health Policy Group (2006) *The Depression Report: a new deal for depression and anxiety disorders.* Centre for Economic Performance: London School of Economics and Political Sciences. http://cep.lse.ac.uk/textonly/research/mentalhealth/depression report layard.pdf.

Michie, S, (1996) Reducing absenteeism by stress management. Valuation of a stress counselling service. *Work and Stress*, 10(4): 367–372.

Millar, A. (2002) Beyond resolution of presenting issues: experiences of an in–house police counselling service. *Counselling and Psychotherapy Research*, 2: 159–166.

Miller, N. E. and Magruder, K. M. (eds) (1999) *Cost–effectiveness of psychotherapy: a guide for practitioners, researchers and policy–makers.* New York: Oxford University Press.

Miller, S. D., Duncan, B. J., Brown, J., Sparks, J.A. and Claud, D. A. (2003) The Outcome Rating Scale: a preliminary study of the reliability, validity and feasibility of a brief visual analog measure. *Journal of Brief Therapy*, 2: 91–100.

Milne, S. H., Blum, T. C. and Roman, P. M. (1994) Factors influencing employees propensity to use an Employee Assistance Program. *Personnel Psychology* 47(1): 123–145.

Mintz, J., Mintz, L. I., Arrunda, M. J. and Hwang, S. S. (1992) Treatment of depression and the functional capacity to work. *Archives of General Psychiatry*, 49: 761–768.

MRC (2001) *A framework for development and evaluation of RCTs for complex interventions to improve health.* London: Medical Research Council.

Mueller, R. M., Lambert, M. J. and Burlingame, G. M. (1998) Construct validity of the Outcome Questionnaire. A confirmatory factor analysis. *Journal of Personality Assessment*, 70(2): 248–262.

Murphy, G. C. and Athanasou, J. A. (1999) The effect of unemployment on mental health. *Journal of Occupational and Organisational Psychology*, 72: 83–99.

Murphy, L. (1996) Stress management in work settings: a critical review of the health effects. *American Journal of Health Promotion*, 11: 112–135.

Muscroft, J. and Hicks, C. (1998) A comparison of psychiatric nurses and general nurses reported stress and counselling needs: a case study approach. *Journal of Advanced Nursing*, 27 (6): 1317–1325.

Mushet, G. and Donaldson, L. (2000) A psychotherapist in the house: a service for distressed hospital doctors. *British Journal of Medical Psychology*, 73: 377–380.

Muto, T., Fujimori, Y. and Suzuki, K. (2004) Characteristics of an external Employee Assistance Programme in Japan. *Occupational Medicine*, 54: 570–575.

Nadolski, J. N. and Sandonato, C. E. (1987) Evaluation of an Employee Assistance Programme. *Journal of Occupational Medicine*, 29 (1): 32–37.

Oher, J. M. (1993) Survey research to measure EAP customer satisfaction: a quality improvement tool. *Employee Assistance Quarterly*, 8: 41–75.

Oher, J. M. (1999) Survey research to measure EAP customer satisfaction: a quality improvement tool. In J. M. Oher (ed.) *The employee assistance handbook.* New York: Wiley.

Park, D. A. (1992) Client satisfaction evaluation: university Employee Assistance Program. *Employee Assistance Quarterly*, 8: 15–34.

Parry, G., Shapiro, D. A. and Firth, J. (1986) The case of the anxious executive: a study from the research clinic. *British Journal of Medical Psychology*, 59: 221–233.

Philips, S. B. (2004) Client satisfaction with university Employee Assistance Programs. *Employee Assistance Quarterly*, 19: 59–70.

Phillips, J. P. N. (1986) Shapiro Personal Questionnaire and generalized personal questionnaire techniques: a repeated measures individualized outcome measurement. In L.S. Greenberg and W. M. Pinsof (eds) *The psychotherapeutic process: a research handbook.* New York: Guilford Press.

Potter, P. T. (2002) An integrative approach to industrial trauma within emergency service occupations. *Clinical Case Studies*, 1: 133–147.

Poverny, L. M. and Dodd, S. J. (2000) Differential patterns of EAP service utilisation: a nine year follow-up study of faculty and staff. *Employee Assistance Quarterly*, 15(4): 29–42.

Preece, M., Cayley, P. M., Scheuchl, U. and Lam, R. W. (2005) The relevance of an Employee Assistance Program to the treatment of workplace depression. *Journal of Workplace Behavioral Health*, 21: 67–77.

Reese, R. J., Conoley, C. W. and Brossart, D. F. (2002) Effectiveness of telephone counseling: a field-based investigation. *Journal of Counseling Psychology*, 49: 233–242.

Reese, R. J., Conoley, C. W. and Brossart, D. F. (2006) The attractiveness of telephone counseling: an empirical investigation of client perceptions. *Journal of Counseling and Development*, 84: 54–60.

Reynolds, G. S. and Lehman, H. E. K. (2003) Levels of substance abuse and willingness to use an Employee Assistance Programme. *Journal of Behavioral Health Services Research*, 20: 238–248.

Reynolds, S. (1997) Psychological wellbeing at work: is prevention better than cure? *Journal for Psychosomatic Research*, 43(1): 93–102.

Reynolds, S. (2000) Interventions: what works, what doesn't? *Occupational Medicine*, 50: 315–319.

Rodriguez, J. and Borgen, W. A. (1998) Needs assessment: Western Canada's program administrators' perspectives on the role of EAPs in the workplace. *Employee Assistance Quarterly*, 14: 11–29.

Rogers, D., McLeod, J. and Sloboda, J. (1995) Counsellor and client perceptions of the effectiveness of time-limited counselling in an occupational counselling. *Counselling Psychology Quarterly*, 8(3): 221–231.

Roman, P. M. and Blum, T. C. (1996) A review of the impact of worksite interventions on health and behavioural outcomes. *The American Journal of Health Promotion*, 2(2): 136–149.

Roo, S. M. and Ross, L. E. (1995) Professional pilots' views of alcohol use in aviation and the effectiveness of Employee Assistance Programs. *The International Journal of Aviation Psychology*, 5(2): 199–214.

Rost, K., Fortney, J. and Coyne, J. (2005) The relationship of depression treatment quality indicators to employee absenteeism. *Mental Health Services Research*, 7: 161–168.

Rost, K., Smith, J. L. and Dickinson, M. (2004) The effect of improving primary care depression management on employee absenteeism and productivity: a randomized trial. *Medical Care*, 42: 1201–1210.

Rowland, N. (2007) BACP and NICE. *Therapy Today*, 18(5): 27–30.

Rowland, N. and Goss, S. (2000) *Evidence–based counselling and psychological therapies: research and applications.* London: Routledge.

Sadu, G., Cooper, C. and Allison, T. (1989) A Post Office initiative to stamp out stress. *Personnel Management,* August 40–45.

Safer, M. A. and Keuler, D. J. (2002) Individual differences in misremembering pre–psychotherapy distress: personality and memory distortion. *Emotion*, 2: 162–178.

Salmela–Aro, K., Naatanen, P. and Nurmi, J. E. (2004) The role of work–related personal projects during two burnout interventions: a longitudinal study. *Work and Stress*, 18: 208–230.

Saroja, K. I., Ramphal, K. G., Kasmini, K., Ainsah, O. and Baker, O. C. (1999) Trends in absenteeism rates following psychological intervention – preliminary results. *Singapore Medical Journal*, 40(5): 349–351.

Schmit, M. J. and Stanard, S. J. (1996) The utility of personality inventories in the employee assistance process. A study of EAP referred police officers. *Employee Assistance Quarterly*, 11(4): 21–42.

Schneider, R. J., Casey, J. and Kohn, R. (2000) Motivational versus confrontational interviewing: a comparison of substance abuse assessment practices at Employee Assistance Programs. *Journal of Behavioral Health Services and Research*, 27: 60–74.

Schulz, K. F., Chalmers, I., Hayes, R. J. and Altman, D. G. (1995) Empirical evidence of bias. Dimensions of methodological quality associated with estimates of treatment effects in controlled trials. *Journal of the American Medical Association*, 273: 408–412.

Sennett, R. (1998) *The Corrosion of Character: the personal consequences of work in the new capitalism*. New York: W.W. Norton.

Sennett, R. (2003) *Respect in a World of Inequality*. New York: W.W. Norton.

Shadish, W. R., Navarro, A. M., Matt, G. E. and Phillips, G. (2000) The effects of psychological therapies under clinically representative conditions: a meta-analysis. *Psychological Bulletin,* 126: 512–529.

Shakespeare-Finch, J. and Scully, P. (2004) A multi–method evaluation of an Australian emergency service Employee Assistance Program. *Employee Assistance Quarterly*, 19: 71–91.

Shapiro, D. A. and Firth, J. (1987) Prescriptive vs. exploratory psychotherapy. Outcomes of the Sheffield psychotherapy project. *British Journal of Psychiatry*, 151: 790–799.

Shapiro, D. A. and Firth-Cozens, J. A. (1990) Two-year follow-up of the Sheffield psychotherapy project. *British Journal of Psychiatry,* 157: 389–391.

Shapiro, D. A., Barkham, M., Rees, A., Hardy, G. E., Reynolds, S. and Startup, M. (1994) Effects of treatment duration and severity of depression on the effectiveness of cognitive-behavioral and psychodynamic-interpersonal psychotherapy. *Journal of Consulting and Clinical Psychology*, 62(3): 522–534.

Shapiro, D. A., Barkham, M., Hardy, G. E. and Morrison, L. A. (1990) The second Sheffield psychotherapy project: rationale, design and preliminary outcome data. *British Journal of Medical Psychology,* 63: 97–108.

Sharar, D. and Hertenstein, E. (2004) Perspectives on the integration of employee assistance and work-life programs: a survey of key informants in the EAP field. *Journal of Workplace Behavioral Health*, 20: 95–104.

Shumway, S. T., Dersch, C., Harris, S. M. and Arredondo, R. (2004) Two outcome measures of EAP satisfaction: a factor analysis. *Employee Assistance Quarterly*, 16: 71–79.

Shumway, S. T., Wampler, R. S. and Arredondo, R. (2003) A need for marriage and family services: a survey of Employee Assistance Program client problems and needs. *Employee Assistance Quarterly*, 19: 61–71.

Shumway, S. T., Wampler, R. S., Dersch, C. and Arredondo, R. (2004) A place for marriage and family services in Employee Assistance Programs (EAPs): a survey of EAP client problems and needs. *Journal of Marriage and Family Therapy,* 30: 71–79.

Silvester, A. (2003) Counselling provision for staff in the National Health Service in England: a survey. *Counselling and Psychotherapy Research*, 3: 61–64.

Slade, M. and Priebe, S. (2001) Are randomised, controlled trials the only gold that glitters? *British Journal of Psychiatry,* 179: 284–287.

Sloboda, J. A., Hopkins, J. S., Turner, A., Rogers, D. R. and McLeod, J. (1993) An evaluated staff counselling programme in a public sector organisation. *Employee Counselling Today*, 5: 10–16.

Sperry, L. (1996) Work–focused psychotherapy with executives. *Individual Psychology*, 52: 193–199.

Sprang, G. (1992) Utilizing a brief EAP-based intervention as an agent for change in the treatment of depression. *Employee Assistance Quarterly*, 8: 57–65.

Sprang, G. and Secret, M. (1999) Employee crisis and occupational functioning. *Employee Assistance Quarterly*, 15: 29–43.

Steele, P. D. and Hubbard, R. L. (1985) Management styles, perceptions of substance abuse and Employee Assistance Programs in organisations. *Journal of Applied Behavioral Science*, 21: 271–286.

Stephenson, D., Bingaman, D., Plaza, C., Selvik, R., Sudgen, B. and Ross, C. (2003) Implementation and evaluation of a formal telephone counselling protocol in an Employee Assistance Program. *Employee Assistance Quarterly*, 19: 19–33.

Straussner, S. L. A. (1988) Comparison of in-house and contracted-out Employee Assistance Programs. *Social Work*, 33: 53–55.

Sugarman, L. (1992) Ethical issues in counselling at work. *British Journal of Guidance and Counselling,* 20: 64–74.

Sullivan, R. and Poverny, L. (1992) Differential patterns of EAP service utilisation among university faculty and staff. *Employee Assistance Quarterly*, 8: 1–12.

Sweeney, A. P., Hohenshil, T. H. and Fortune, J. C. (2002) Job satisfaction among employee assistance professionals: a national survey. *Journal of Employment Counseling*, 39: 50–60.

Tehrani, N., Cox, S. J. and Cox, T. (2002) Assessing the impact of stressful incidents in organisations: the development of an extended impact of events scale. *Counselling Psychology Quarterly*, 15: 191–200.

Terluin, B., van Rhenen, W., Schaufeli, W. B. and de Haan, M. (2004) The four-dimensional symptom questionnaire (4DSQ): measuring stress and other mental health problems in a working population. *Work and Stress,* 18: 187–207.

Tolley, K. and Rowland, N. (1995) *Evaluating the cost-effectiveness of counselling in health care*. London: Routledge.

Trubshaw, E. A. and Dollard, M. F. (2001) Representation of work stress in an Australian public hospital. *AAOHN Journal*, 49: 437–444.

Van Dierendonck, D., Schaufeli, W. B. and Buunk, B. P. (1998) The evaluation of an individual burnout program: the role of inequity and social support. *Journal of Applied Psychology*, 83: 392–407.

Van der Hek, H. and Plomp, H. N. (1997) Occupational stress management programmes: a practical overview of published effect studies. *Occupational Medicine*, 47: 133–47.

Van der Klink, J. J. L., Blonk, R. W. B., Schene, A. H. and van Djik, F. J. H. (2001) The benefits of interventions for work-related stress. *American Journal of Public Health*, 91: 270–276.

Van der Klink, J. J. L., Blonk, R. W. B., Schene, A. H. and van Djik, F. J. H. (2003) Reducing long-term sickness absence by an activating intervention in adjustment disorders: a cluster randomised, controlled design. *Occupational and Environmental Medicine*, 60: 429–437.

Vermeersch, D. A., Lambert, M. J. and Burlingame, G. M. (2000) Outcome questionnaire: item sensitivity to change. *Journal of Personality Assessment*, 74(2): 242–261.

Vonachen, H. A., Mason, J. M. and Kronenberg, M. H. (1954) Study of five years of employee counselling in an industrial medical program. *Archives of Industrial Hygiene and Occupational Medicine*, 10(2): 91–123.

Wainwright, D. and Calnan, M. (2002) *Work Stress: the making of a modern epidemic*. Buckingham: Open University Press.

Weiss, R. M. (2003) Effects of program characteristics on EAL utilisation. *Employee Assistance Quarterly*, 18: 61–70.

Weiss, R. M. (2005) Overcoming resistance to surveillance: a genealogy of the EAP discourse. *Organisation Studies*, 26: 973–997.

Wessely, S. (2006) Randomised, controlled trials. In M. Slade and S. Priebe (Eds) *Choosing methods in mental health research*. London: Routledge.

West, M. A. and Reynolds, S. (1995) Employee attitudes to work–based counselling services. *Work and Stress*, 9: 31–44.

Westen, D. and Morrison, K. (2001) A multi-dimensional meta-analysis of treatments for depression, panic and generalised anxiety disorder: an empirical examination of the status of empirically supported therapies. *Journal of Consulting and Clinical Psychology*, 69: 875–899.

Westen, D., Novotny, C. M. and Thompson-Brenner, H. (2004) The empirical status of empirically supported psychotherapies: assumptions, findings and reporting in controlled clinical trials. *Psychological Bulletin*, 130: 631–663.

Whelan, L., Robson, M. and Cook, P. (2002) Health at work in the British National Health Service: a counselling response. *Counselling Psychology Quarterly*, 15: 257–267.

Wilensky, J. L. and Wilensky, H. L. (1951) The Hawthorne case. *American Journal of Sociology*, 25: 269–80.

Willbanks, K. D. (1999) The role of supervisory referral in Employee Assistance Programs. *Employee Assistance Quarterly*, 15: 13–28.

Williams, N., Sobti, A. and Aw, T. C. (1994) Comparison of perceived occupational health needs among managers, employee representatives and occupational physicians. *Occupational Medicine*, 44 (4): 205–208.

Wise, E. A. (2004) Methods for analysing psychotherapy outcomes: a review of clinical significance, reliable change and recommendations for future directions. *Journal of Personality Assessment*, 82: 50–59.

Worrall, L. (1999) *Evaluation of the effectiveness of an employee counselling programme*. Unpublished PhD thesis, Dept. of Psychology, Keele University.

Wright, D. A. (1888) A brief overview of research techniques used to evaluate three Employee Assistance Programs through the family service association of metropolitan Toronto experience. *Employee Assistance Quarterly*, 3: 205–208.

Young, G. and Spencer, J (1996) General Practitioners' views about the need for a stress support service. *Family Practitioner*, 13: 517–521.

Zarkin, G. A., Bray, J. W., Karuntzos, G. T. and Demiralp, B. (2001) The effect of an enhanced Employee Assistance Program (EAP) intervention on EAP utilisation. *Journal of Studies on Alcohol*, 62: 351–358.

Notes